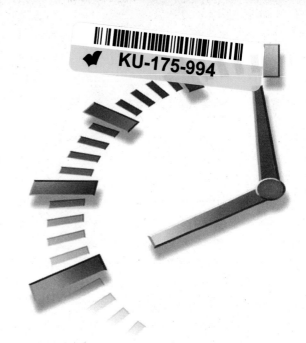

SAMS
Teach Yourself

Microsoft® Office 97

in 24 Hours

Second Edition

Greg Perry

SAMS
Teach Yourself
Microsoft® Office 97
in 24 Hours
Second Edition

SAMS

A Division of Macmillan Computer Publishing
201 West 103rd Street, Indianapolis, Indiana, 46290 USA

For Mr. Ben Stein, a man who knows life, love, and what's right. Meeting you only verified that you are indeed gracious and kind.

Copyright © 1998 by Sams Publishing

SECOND EDITION

International Standard Book Number: 0-672-31338-3

Library of Congress Catalog Card Number: 98-84860

01   00   99   98   5   4

Interpretation of the printing code: The rightmost double-digit number is the year of the book's printing; the rightmost single-digit, the number of the book's printing. For example, a printing code of 98-2 shows that the second printing of the book occurred in 1998.

Composed in Agaramond and MCPdigital by Macmillan Computer Publishing

Printed in the United States of America

Executive Editor
Lisa Wagner

Acquisitions Editor
Jamie Milazzo

Development Editor
Noelle Gasco

Technical Editor
Kevin Ortell

Managing Editor
Thomas F. Hayes

Production Editor
Karen A. Walsh

Copy Editors
Jenny Clark
Tom Stevens

Indexer
Tim Tate

Cover Designer
Karen Ruggles

Book Designer
Gary Adair

Production Team
Darlena Murray
Anjy Perry

Overview

Contents

Acknowledgments

Once again, I'm thanking Mr. Dean Miller for providing me with this writing opportunity. Dean, you must have been desperate for an author when you chose me!

The people at Macmillan Computer Publishing all take their jobs seriously. They want readers to have the best books possible. They accomplish that goal. Among the MCP editors and staff who produced this book, I want to send special thanks to Noelle Gasco who honed my writing and turned a mediocre manuscript into one we can be proud of. Karen Walsh, Kezia Endsley, Tom Stevens, and Jenny Clark also added their excellent editing skills to my work. Finally, without Jamie Milazzo, I may not have had the offer to write this book. To each of them I am most grateful.

Although they did not have a direct hand in this book, I must thank MCP's two most outstanding members, Rosemarie Graham and Grace Buechline. Rosemarie and Grace are friends I've made from past books and I want them to know I appreciate the jobs they do.

My lovely and gracious bride stands by my side night and day. Thank you once again. You, precious Jayne, are everything that matters to me on earth. The best parents in the world, Glen and Bettye Perry, continue to encourage and support me in every way. I am who I am because of both of them.

—*Greg Perry*

About the Author

Greg Perry

Greg Perry is a speaker and a writer on both the programming and the application sides of computing. He is known for his skills at bringing advanced computer topics to the novice's level. Perry has been a programmer and a trainer since the early 1980s. He received his first degree in computer science and a master's degree in corporate finance. Perry is the author or co-author of more than 50 books, including *Sams Teach Yourself Windows 95 in 24 Hours*, *Absolute Beginner's Guide to Programming*, *Absolute Beginner's Guide to C*, and *Moving from C to C++*. He also writes about rental-property management and loves to travel. His favorite place to be when away from home is either at New York's Patsy's or in Italy because he enjoys only the best pasta!

Introduction

Microsoft Corporation's Office products have an installed base of more than 22 million licensed users. Over 90 percent of the Fortune 500 companies use Microsoft Office. When developing Office 97, Microsoft conducted more than 25,000 hours of customer research. Based on that research and user feedback, Microsoft designed Office 97 to be more user-friendly as well as more integrated among applications. You won't regret your decision to learn and use Office 97.

You probably are anxious to get started with your 24-hour Office 97 tutorial. Take just a few preliminary moments to acquaint yourself with the design of this book, as described in the next few sections.

Who Should Read This Book?

This book is for *both* beginning and advanced Office 97 users. Readers rarely believe that lofty claim for good reason, but the design of this book and the nature of Office 97 make it possible for this book to address such a wide audience. Here is why: Office 97 is a major improvement over the previous Office products.

Readers unfamiliar with the Windows 95-style of windowed environments will find plenty of introductory help here that brings them quickly up to speed. This book teaches you how to start and exit Office 97 as well as how to manage many of the Windows environmental elements that you need to use Office 97 effectively. If you are new to the Internet, this book helps you get started and shows how Office 97 takes advantage of the Internet's features. This book talks to beginners without talking down to them.

This book also addresses those who presently use a Microsoft Office product. Here is how: Step-Up sidebars contained in this book explain how a specific Office 97 feature improves upon or replaces a previous Office feature. With your fundamental Office understanding, you'll appreciate the new features and added power of Office 97. Keep in mind that Office 97 is similar to previous Office versions but includes plenty of new features and improvements to keep Office gurus intrigued for a long time. This book teaches the Office 97 Professional Edition, the edition that includes all the Office 97 products and the one that sells the best.

What This Book Does for You

Although this book is not a complicated reference book, you learn almost every aspect of Office 97 from the user's point of view. Office 97 includes many advanced technical details that most users never need, and this book does not waste your time with those. You want to get up to speed with Office 97 in 24 hours, and this book helps you fulfill that goal.

Those of you tired of the plethora of quick-fix computer titles cluttering today's shelves will find a welcome reprieve here. This book presents both the background and descriptions that a new Office 97 user needs. In addition to the background, this book is practical and provides more than 100 step-by-step tasks that you can work through to gain practical hands-on experience. The tasks guide you though all the common Office 97 actions you need to make Office 97 work for you.

Can This Book Really Teach Office 97 in 24 Hours?

Yes. You can master each chapter in one hour. (By the way, chapters are referred to as hours in the rest of this book.) The material is balanced with mountains of tips, shortcuts, and methods that make your hours productive and hone your Office 97 skills.

Conventions Used in This Book

Each hour ends with a question-and-answer session that addresses some of the most frequently asked questions about that hour's topic.

This book uses several common conventions to help teach the Office 97 topics. Here is a summary of those typographical conventions:

- ☐ Commands, computer output, and words you type appear in a special monospaced computer font.
- ☐ To type a shortcut key, such as Alt+F, press and hold the first key, then press the second key before releasing both keys.
- ☐ If a task requires you to select from a menu, the book separates menu commands with a vertical bar. For example, File|Save As is used to select the Save As option from the File menu.

In addition to typographical conventions, the following special elements are included to set off different types of information to make them easily recognizable:

Special notes augment the material you read in each hour. These notes clarify concepts and procedures.

 You find numerous tips that offer shortcuts and solutions to common problems.

 The warnings are about pitfalls. Reading them saves you time and trouble.

Step-Up

Users of previous Office products advance quickly by reading the Step-Ups provided for them.

NEW TERM Each hour contains new-term definitions to explain important new terms. New-term icons make those definitions easy to find.

PART I
Working with Office 97

Hour

Hour 1

Getting Acquainted with Office 97

Microsoft Office 97 improves your work environment by offering integrated software tools that are powerful yet easy to learn and use. Offices large and small can use Office 97–based applications for many of their day-to-day computer needs as can home-based businesses and families who want simple but robust writing and analysis tools for their computer.

If you've used previous versions of Office, Office 97 takes you to the next step by adding more power and more automation than previous Office versions. Office 97 automates many of your computing chores and provides products that work in unison by sharing data between them. This hour shows you how Office 97 tackles many of the standard software requirements of today's offices.

The highlights of this hour include

- ☐ What Office 97 contains
- ☐ How the *Getting Results* book gives you a good Office 97 overview
- ☐ Which Office 97 products you use for the various tasks

☐ How the Binder tracks project data for you

☐ What the document-centric concept means to all Office 97 products

What's in Office 97?

Office 97 includes Microsoft's most powerful applications, including Word and Excel. In the past, Microsoft sold versions of these applications separately. However, the programs work so well together that Microsoft combined them in the Office 97 collection of programs. Program collections such as Office 97 are often called a *suite* of programs.

 A *suite* of programs is a collection of programs that work well together and have a similar interface. The suite is often less expensive than purchasing each product separately.

The following is a quick overview of each Office 97 program:

☐ Word 97 is a word processor with which you can create notes, memos, letters, school papers, business documents, books, newsletters, and even Internet web pages.

☐ Excel 97 is an electronic worksheet program with which you can create charts, graphs, and worksheets for financial and other numeric data. After you enter your financial data, you can analyze it for forecasts and generate numerous what-if scenarios.

☐ PowerPoint 97 is a presentation program with which you can create presentations for seminars, schools, churches, and business meetings. Not only can PowerPoint 97 create the presentation overheads, it can also create the speaker's presentation notes.

☐ Access 97 is a database program with which you can organize data collections. No matter what kind or how much data you must organize, Access 97 can analyze, sort, summarize, and report on that data.

☐ Outlook 97 is a contact manager and scheduler that organizes your contact addresses, phone numbers, and other information in an address-book format. Use Outlook 97 to track your appointments, schedule meetings, generate to-do lists, keep notes, manage all your Internet email, and keep a journal of your activities.

☐ Bookshelf Basics contains online reference materials that provide definitions, synonyms, and quotations.

All the Office 97 products share common features and common menu choices. For example, Figure 1.1 shows the Word 97 screen, and Figure 1.2 shows the Excel 97 screen. Both screens display the open File menu. As you can see, the two program interfaces look virtually identical even though the programs accomplish entirely different tasks. Also, information created in one program can be inserted into another program. For example, if you create a financial table with Excel 97, you can put that table in a Word 97 letter that you send to your Board of Directors and embed the table in a PowerPoint 97 presentation to stockholders. After you learn one program in the Office 97 suite, you'll be comfortable using all the others due to the common interface.

Figure 1.1.

The Word 97 interface behaves like that of Excel 97.

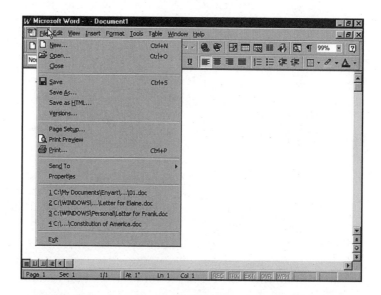

Figure 1.2.

The Excel 97 interface behaves like that of Word 97.

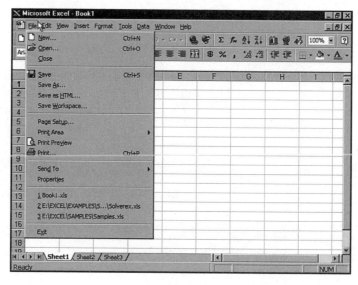

The Office 97 products are general purpose, meaning that you can customize applications to suit your needs. For example, you can use Excel 97 as your checkbook-balancing program and as your company's interactive balance-sheet system.

 You can integrate Office 97 into your network system. This way, Office 97 provides useful features whether you are networked to an intranet, to the Internet, or to both. You can share Office 97 information with others across the network.

All Office 97 products come with Word 97, Excel 97, and Outlook 97; however, Office 97 comes in the following flavors:

☐ The Office 97 Standard Edition comes with only PowerPoint 97 in addition to the three common products.

☐ The Office 97 Professional Edition, described in this 24-hour tutorial, adds the Access 97 database program, the PowerPoint 97 presentation program, the Binder 97 document-managing program, and the Bookshelf Basics reference program to the suite.

☐ Office 97 Small Business Edition (SBE) adds Publisher 97, Financial Manager 97, and AutoMap Streets Plus to the original three products. Office 97 SBE is especially well-suited to the business traveler who works with a laptop while on the road.

Step-Up

If you've mastered some of the advanced programming techniques behind earlier versions of Office products, you'll be glad to know that every program in the Office 97 suite supports Visual Basic 5, Microsoft's cross-program application programming language. Word 97 does not, however, support Word Basic (the programming language that Microsoft included with previous versions of Word) because Word Basic is incompatible with other applications. Visual Basic used to exist in earlier Office products as Visual Basic for Applications (VBA).

Introducing Word 97

When you need to write any text-based document, look no further than Word 97. Word 97 is a word processor that supports many features, including

1

- [ ] Integrated grammar, spelling, and hyphenation tools (see Hour 7, "Managing Documents and Customizing Word 97")
- [ ] Wizards and templates that create and format documents for you (see Hour 4, "Using More Powerful Features")
- [ ] Automatic corrections for common mistakes as you type (see Hour 5, "Welcome to Word 97")
- [ ] Advanced formatting capabilities (see Hour 6, "Formatting with Word 97")
- [ ] Numbering, bulleting, and shading tools (see Hour 6)
- [ ] Multiple document views so that you can see a rough draft of your document or the look of a final printed page as you write (see Hour 6)
- [ ] Drawing, border, and shading tools that let you emphasize headers, draw lines and shapes around your text, and work with imported art files (see Hour 22, "Office 97's Synergy")
- [ ] Web-page development for Internet users so that they can turn their documents into web pages (see Hour 24, "Creating Web Pages with Office 97")

Figure 1.3 shows a Word 97 editing session. The user is editing a business letter to send to a client.

Figure 1.3.

Word 97 helps you create, edit, and format letters.

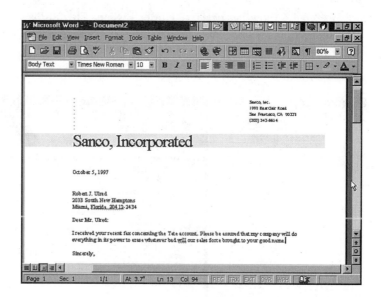

Introducing Excel 97

Although Excel 97 can be used for non-numeric worksheets, the primary goal for Excel 97 is to help you organize and manage financial information such as income statements, balance sheets, and forecasts. Excel 97 is an electronic worksheet program that supports many features, including:

☐ Automatic cell formatting (see Hour 9, "Excel 97 Workbooks")

☐ Worksheet proofing tools, such as spell checking (see Hour 10, "Using Excel 97")

☐ Automatic row and column completion of value ranges with AutoFill (see Hour 10)

☐ Automatic worksheet formatting to turn your worksheets into professionally produced reports (see Hour 12, "Formatting Worksheets to Look Great")

☐ Built-in functions, such as financial formulas, that automate common tasks (see Hour 11, "Editing Excel Worksheets")

☐ Powerful maps, charts, and graphs that can analyze your numbers and turn them into simple trends (see Hour 12)

☐ Automatic worksheet computations that let you generate multiple what-if scenarios and decide between different courses of action (see Hour 9)

Figure 1.4 shows an Excel 97 editing session. The user is getting ready to enter invoice information for a sale. As you can see, Excel 97 can start with a predesigned form. If you've worked with other worksheet programs, you might be surprised at how fancy Excel 97 can get.

Figure 1.4.

Excel 97 helps you create, edit, and format numeric worksheets.

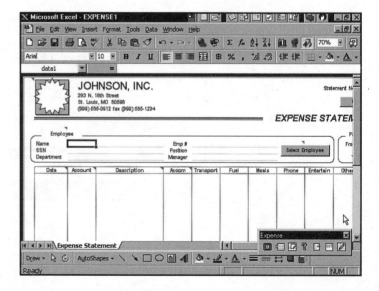

Introducing PowerPoint 97

Before PowerPoint 97, users had no way to generate presentations without making a tedious effort to design each color slide using some kind of graphics drawing program. Although presentation products similar to PowerPoint 97 now exist, PowerPoint 97 is recognized as a leader. PowerPoint 97 supports many features, including

- ☐ The capability to turn Word 97 document outlines into presentation notes (see Hour 22)

- ☐ Automatic proofing tools such as spelling and hyphenation (see Hour 18, "Access 97 Basics")

- ☐ Sample slide and slide collection templates that provide you with a fill-in-the-blank presentation (see Hour 13, "PowerPoint 97 Presentations")

- ☐ A slide projector that displays your presentation on your screen (see Hour 14, "Editing and Arranging Your Presentation")

- ☐ Complete color and font control of your presentation slides (see Hour 15, "PowerPoint 97 Advanced Features")

- ☐ A collection of clip art files, icons, sounds, and animations that you can embed to make presentations come alive (see Hour 15)

- ☐ Numerous transitions and fades between presentation slides to keep your audience's attention (see Hour 15)

- ☐ The capability to save presentations as web pages that you can then present on the Internet (see Hour 24)

Figure 1.5 shows a PowerPoint 97 editing session. The user is getting ready for a presentation and has only a few minutes to prepare ten color slides for the meeting. With PowerPoint 97, a few minutes is more than enough time!

Introducing Access 97

Access 97 provides one of the most comprehensive relational database systems available today. If you want to organize large collections of data, such as customer and inventory records, Access 97 makes your job simple. Access 97 goes far beyond other databases in power and ease of use by supporting features that include

- ☐ Simple table-creation wizards and data-entry tools that let you set up and enter database information easily (see Hour 18)

- ☐ Report-generation that enables you to track and publish your data (see Hour 21, "Advanced Access 97")

- ☐ Information retrieval query tools that let you quickly get to the data you need (see Hour 20, "Retrieving Your Data")

☐ Automatic proofing tools such as spelling and hyphenation of data (see Hour 19, "Entering and Displaying Access 97 Data")

☐ The capability to filter data rows and columns so that you see only data you want to see (see Hour 20)

☐ Sorting of data by any value (see Hour 21)

☐ The capability to produce custom labels for any printer (see Hour 21)

☐ Complete relational database support to reduce data redundancies (see Hour 18)

☐ Automatic summary provisions such as totals, averages, and statistical variances (see Hour 21)

☐ The capability to save databases in web pages so that Internet users can view your database's information (see Hour 24)

Figure 1.6 shows an Access 97 editing session. The user is editing employee records. Notice that Access 97 accepts and tracks all kinds of data, including numbers, text, and even pictures embedded as objects.

Figure 1.5.

PowerPoint 97 helps you create, edit, and format presentations.

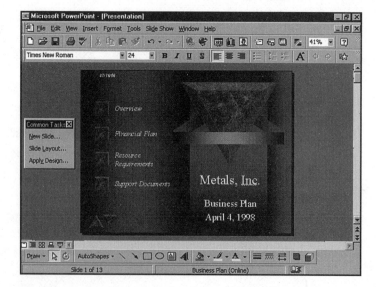

Introducing Outlook 97

Outlook 97 is a simple-to-use tool that manages your business and personal meetings, to-do lists, contacts, and appointments. Outlook 97 provides many features, including

☐ The capability to track your contact information, including multiple phone numbers and computerized email addresses (see Hour 17, "Communicating with Outlook 97")

Figure 1.6.

Access 97 manages your database data.

□ The capability to track your computer activities in a journal (see Hour 17)

□ Management of your email, phone calls, and to-do lists (see Hour 17)

□ The capability to schedule appointments (see Hour 17)

□ The capability to plan people and resources you need for meetings (see Hour 16, "Outlook 97 Basics")

□ The capability to sound an alarm before an important event (see Hour 16)

Figure 1.7 shows an Outlook 97 calendar screen. The user is getting ready to schedule a meeting on a particular day. As with all the Office 97 programs, you can modify screen elements in Outlook 97 so that they appear in the format most helpful to your needs.

Step-Up

Outlook 97 replaces Microsoft Schedule+. Outlook 97 is a completely new program that adds new personal information features but retains all those of Microsoft Schedule+.

Introducing Bookshelf Basics

Bookshelf Basics provides an online guide to the following references:

□ *The American Heritage Dictionary*

□ *The Original Roget's Thesaurus*

□ *The Columbia Dictionary of Quotations*

Figure 1.7.

Outlook 97 tracks appointments and events.

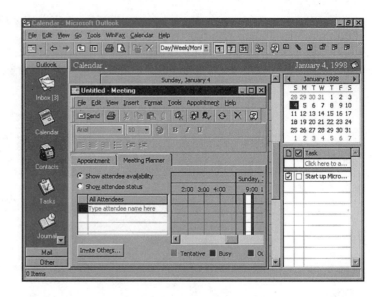

Suppose that you're working in one of the other Office 97 products and you need a definition. Choose Bookshelf Basics from the Office 97 Shortcut bar, and Bookshelf Basics provides a definition for whatever word you need. Figure 1.8 shows a Bookshelf Basics screen in which the user is looking up a reference for Italy.

Bookshelf Basics provides full multimedia support.

Figure 1.8.

The Bookshelf Basics dictionary provides encyclopedia references, maps, Internet locations, as well as simple definitions.

Click the speaker icon to hear the word *Italy* spoken

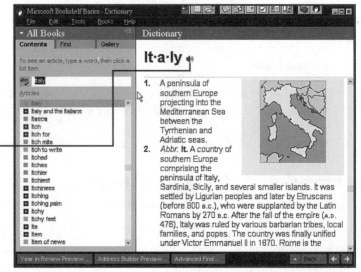

1

Microsoft unabashedly supplies Bookshelf Basics in Office 97 as a sales preview for the full version of *Microsoft Bookshelf*, which contains nine reference works including an encyclopedia, Internet reference, and an online atlas. You might want to join Microsoft's subscription program that sends you a new *Microsoft Bookshelf* each year.

A Quick Tour of Office 97

Office 97 includes an electronic version of *Getting Results*. This electronic book does not operate like an electronic manual; *Teach Yourself Microsoft Office 97 in 24 Hours* teaches you far more about Office 97 than *Getting Results* does. Nevertheless, *Getting Results* gives you a graphical demonstration of Office 97.

If you want to take a few minutes to browse *Getting Results*, click the Getting Results button on the Office Shortcut bar (the row of buttons you see at the top of your Windows screen and shown in Figure 1.9).

Figure 1.9.
The Office Shortcut bar gives you access to Office 97 products.

The Getting Results button

Depending on your installed options, the Office Shortcut bar shown in Figure 1.9 might look different from yours.

You can move your Office Shortcut bar to another location by dragging the bar to a different place on your Windows desktop.

Hour 2, "Reviewing Windows and Office 97 Fundamentals," explains more about the Office Shortcut bar. For now, you do not need to understand the rest of the buttons on the bar.

When you click the Getting Results button, Office 97 displays the first page of the electronic *Getting Results* book from one of Microsoft's Internet web pages. Click a topic to browse it in more detail from the web. As you move your mouse pointer over the screen, the pointer changes to a hand cursor, which lets you know when you can click for additional information. When you click a topic, Office 97 automatically turns the electronic page to show you more of the book's information.

Binding Your Work

If you've ever used a PC program you've probably created *data files* that hold information. For example, Word 97 data files act as documents and Access 97 data files act as databases. All the Office 97 products refer to their data files as *documents*.

 A *data file* contains the information you produced with a program.

If you want to use one of the Office 97 products to create multiple data files, you have these options:

- ☐ Create your files one at a time, saving the files before clearing your workspace and creating the next file.
- ☐ Create your files one at a time, but keep each file in memory. For example, you can edit multiple documents at the same time in Word 97 (Ctrl+F6 switches between the documents).

The common theme in these multiple-file options is that you use the same program to create and edit the files. A problem can arise when working with a suite of programs such as Office 97. Suppose that you're working on a project requiring two worksheets, three proposal documents, a database, and a color presentation. Office 97 includes a *binder* that lets you keep track of all work within a particular project, even if you must use separate Office 97 programs to create each of the project's files. To work with the complete collection of files within the project, you only need to open the single bound project and select the individual files with which you want to work from within Binder.

 A *binder* tracks Office 97 data files that you want grouped together in a project even when different Office 97 programs created each data file.

As you learn in Hour 22, the Office 97 Binder is critical for holding multiple jobs that you want to track as a single group. When you start the Microsoft Binder program, you can add existing data files from any Office 97 product as well as create new Office 97 data files.

Figure 1.10 shows a binder that includes five data files (three Word 97 files, one Excel 97 file, and one PowerPoint 97 file). The icon along the left side of the screen indicates the file's data type. To work with any file in the binder, click that file name; Office 97 opens the program that you need to edit the file.

Figure 1.10.
The Office 97 Binder keeps track of your project's data files.

The icons let you know what program was used to create the file

Selected Binder file

A preview of the selected Binder file

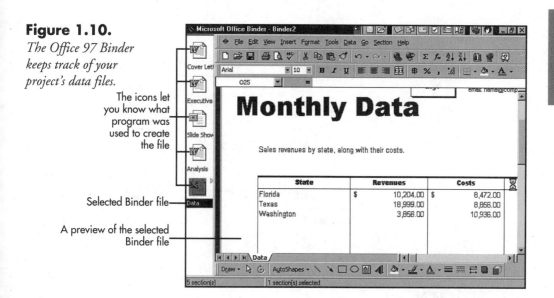

Getting Acquainted with Document Files

All Office 97 products use a *document-centric* model. Whether you write a letter or a book (or create an Access 97 database or an Excel 97 worksheet), the text you write appears in a document. As you will learn in Hour 2, document is just an Office 97 term for file. Figure 1.11 shows the many kinds of Office 97 documents with which you'll work.

NEW TERM   *Document-centric* refers to the way that all Office 97 products work with documents instead of traditional and distinct kinds of data files such as database files, worksheet files, and presentation files. The document-centric concept lets Office 97 products work uniformly with each other's files. Although each Office 97 product stores its document in a different format from the other Office 97 programs, document-centricity keeps terms uniform throughout the products.

When you create a document, name it just as you label a file folder before you put it in a file cabinet. The document file's extension tells Office 97 which application (such as Word 97 or Excel 97) was used to create that particular document.

You can use either uppercase or lowercase letters for your document names. Although neither Windows nor Office 97 considers Proposal.doc to be different from PROPOSAL.DOC, the document names are easier to read when you mix the case. If you let Office 97 add the extension, as you should usually do when you name documents, Office 97 adds a lowercase extension, such as .doc.

Figure 1.11.

*All Office 97 products
interact with documents.*

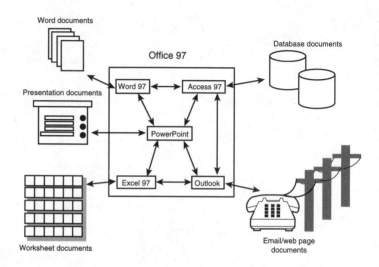

Summary

This hour introduces the Office 97 programs by showing you a little of what each program can accomplish. Before learning Office 97 specifics, you need to get the big picture. This hour provides that big picture and introduces the Office 97 tools that you'll use.

All Office 97 programs share a common interface. After you learn one Office 97 program, the others are easy to master. Some users find that they can use Office 97 for all their computer needs.

The next hour covers the Windows basics you need for Office 97. Take a moment to browse the next hour even if you've used Windows before because much of the material is specific to the Office 97 environment.

Q&A

Q I've used Word and Excel. Do I need the other Office 97 products?

A Only you can answer that question because only you know whether you need a program to keep track of your appointments and contacts (Outlook 97) or your database (Access 97). Only you know whether you'll be called to present a topic in a meeting or at a conference (PowerPoint 97).

If you only need word processing and worksheet computing, you may not need the other Office 97 products and you only need to install those programs that you want to use. However, if you've truly mastered Word and Excel, you'll be glad that Microsoft kept the same uniform interface throughout all the Office 97 products. This enables you to use what you already know.

1

Q Why don't I see the Office Shortcut bar?

A Your Office 97 installer probably failed to install the Office Shortcut bar. Simply rerun the Office 97 Setup program and install the Office Shortcut bar. The Setup program acts like most other Windows-based installation programs, but if you feel uncomfortable running the Setup program, ask whoever installed your Office 97 to help you.

Q Isn't a dictionary easier to use than Bookshelf Basics?

A If you had to start a Bookshelf Basics program every time you needed a definition, a paperback dictionary would probably be easier to use than Bookshelf Basics.

As you see in Hour 3, "Introducing Office 97 Features," when you're working on a Word 97 document (or any other Office 97 data file) and you need an extended definition for the word you just typed, you only need to click the word and press a Bookshelf Basics button to read Bookshelf's definition for the word. This on-line reference is much quicker than going to a dictionary every time you need a definition.

Q Suppose that I want to keep track of names and addresses. Which Office 97 product would I use?

A This is actually a trick question. Word 97, Excel 97, Access 97, and Outlook 97 all track names and addresses! Word 97 keeps track of names and addresses for mail merging (sending the same letter to many people); Excel 97 includes a simple database feature that can track items such as names and addresses; Access 97's primary purpose is to track virtually any data in an organized list; and Outlook 97 records all your name and address records. Generally, use Outlook 97 for your names and addresses (all the other Office 97 products can read Outlook 97's data) and save the other Office 97 products for their primary purposes.

Q Why are Office 97 programs simple after I learn one well?

A The Office 97 programs share common interfaces. After you learn how to use one Office 97 program you understand the interface of the others.

Q How can I keep track of four Word 97 documents that belong together for a project?

A Either create the four documents and save them in the same directory or create a new binder for the documents. If you think you might need to add a different kind of Office 97 file (other than a word-processed file) at a later time, use a binder to bind Office 97 documents that require different Office 97 programs.

Hour 2

Reviewing Windows and Office 97 Fundamentals

If the Office 97 Windows environment is new to you, this hour briefly covers some of the fundamentals you need to use Office 97 effectively. This hour does not give you an in-depth Windows tutorial. Instead, it reviews the tasks and features that directly relate to Office 97.

Although the Windows 95 interface has been around for a while, many companies are slow to upgrade from older Windows interfaces (such as Windows for Workgroups 3.11) to Windows 95 or Windows NT (the Office 97 operating environments). Therefore, even if you have used previous versions of Windows, you might need this hour's refresher so that you can hit the ground running with Office 97.

The highlights of this hour include

- ☐ What the Windows 95 interface provides
- ☐ What improvements Office 97 brings to the Windows 95 interface

☐ How to access the Start menu

☐ Why the Open dialog box is so crucial to your Office 97 work

☐ Where to find ToolTips

☐ How to use dialog box tabs

☐ How to preview your documents before printing to save time and paper

☐ Why you should master consistent Windows terminology while learning Office 97 with *Teach Yourself Microsoft Office 97 in 24 Hours*

☐ How Windows and the Internet combine to give you worldwide data access

Basic Windows Elements

Although this book does not assume you are a Windows guru and teaches Office 97 from the ground up, it does assume you possess those basic Windows skills that you can pick up in less than an hour with the Windows Tour (available from the Start menu's Help option). Therefore, you won't find any instructions for using the mouse except where the mouse specifically works in a unique way with Office 97.

Just to keep terminology straight throughout the book, take a moment to study the callouts in Figure 2.1. When this book mentions the Control menu or the window's Close button, you'll know exactly what is meant.

Figure 2.1.

Common window element descriptions.

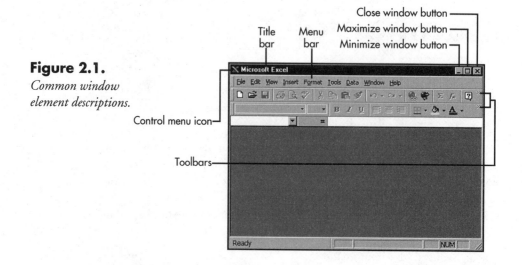

When you maximize a window's size by clicking the Maximize window button, that button changes to the Resize window button.

You might save time by skimming through this material if you're already familiar with many of this hour's topics, such as ToolTips. By presenting all the required Windows interface elements in one hour, the remaining hours are devoted to Office 97 without Windows reviews. You'll be better able to concentrate on the differences and improvements in Office 97.

2

The Windows 95 Interface

If you use Windows NT 4.0, Windows 95, or any later version of those operating systems, the interface that your Windows version uses is called the *Windows 95 interface* because it has been around since the first version of Windows 95. The most prominent features of the Windows 95 interface are the Start button and the Start menu (see Figure 2.2).

The *Windows 95 interface* is the user interface all versions of Microsoft operating systems have used since Windows 95 was released. The interface makes Windows 95 simple to learn and use.

The *Start button* is the button labeled Start from which you display the Windows 95 Start menu. The *Start menu* is the menu from which you can start any Windows program or shut down your PC.

Your Windows screen might differ slightly from Figure 2.2 because of the programs and icons you have installed on your computer. In addition, the *wallpaper*—the screen's background picture—might differ from the figure's. Two things should be similar: You should see the Start menu when you click the Start button, and you should see two commands, New Office Document and Open Office Document, at the top of your Start menu.

NEW TERM *Wallpaper* is the graphic background on your Windows 95 interface.

The Start menu provides access to all your computer's programs. If you want to start any program, click the Start button, select Programs, and follow the Start menu path to the program. You can start more than one program if you want to share work between two or more programs, such as between Word 97 and Access 97. As you start and run programs, the Windows 95 *taskbar* displays all the program icons on task buttons. Click the task buttons to switch between running programs just as you click the remote control to switch between television programs.

Figure 2.2.
Click the Start button to see the Windows 95 Start menu.

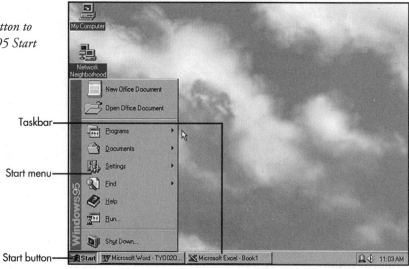

Taskbar

Start menu

Start button

 NEW TERM   The *taskbar* at the bottom of your screen displays all programs currently running.

> You can also switch between running programs by pressing Alt+Tab.

Office 97 provides you with a shortcut to all the Office 97 programs. Select New Office Document if you want to create a new Office 97 document (as you'll recall from Hour 1, "Getting Acquainted with Office 97," an Office 97 *document* is any data file you create or edit with Office 97) by using any of the Office 97 programs. Select Open Office Document if you want to work on an existing Office 97 document. To *open* a document means that you want to work with the document somehow, just as when you open a file cabinet drawer you want to work with a file from the cabinet.

NEW TERM   To *open* a document is to load it into your program workspace so that you can work with it.

When you open an Office 97 document, Windows displays an Open dialog box such as the one in Figure 2.3.

> All Office 97 programs, and most other recent Windows programs, use an Open dialog box resembling that pictured in Figure 2.3. This common interface enables you to learn new programs quickly.

Figure 2.3.

*The common Open
dialog box.*

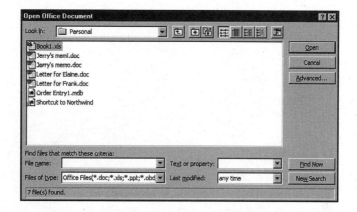

2

As you use Office 97 more, you learn which icons (pictures that represent
items on your screen) go with which Office 97 products. When you
display the Open dialog box, the icons indicate which Office 97 program
created the document listed. For example, the flying W icon represents
documents created by Word 97.

NEW TERM   *Icons* are small colorful pictures that represent items on your Windows screen.

The Open dialog box is simple or complex, depending on what you need to do with it. Most
of the time, you see the Office 97 document that you want to open and you simply double-
click the document's name to load it. The Open dialog box is smart enough to know which
Office 97 product created the document; therefore, if you click a PowerPoint 97 document,
the Open dialog box starts PowerPoint 97 and loads the selected document into PowerPoint
97 for you.

Each time a new Office 97 product is introduced in an hour in this book, that hour introduces
the program's initial screens and describes how you can begin to create documents from
within that product. For now, concentrate on getting an overall feel for the Windows 95
interface.

Following is a summary of other common tasks you can perform from the Open dialog box:

☐ If you want to open a document located in a directory or disk drive other than the
one showing, or even on a different computer on a network across the Internet,
click the Look In drop-down list box and select the location.

☐ You can limit the files shown to specific Office 97 programs by selecting from the
drop-down list box labeled Files of Type. For example, the Open dialog box
displays only Access 97 documents if you select Databases.

☐ The toolbar buttons across the top of the Open dialog box display the files in a different format, giving you more or less detail about the documents that appear. (Rest your mouse pointer on each toolbar button to see what that tool does.)

Step-Up

As you use Office 97, you'll notice that it consistently maintains a chiseled appearance on its menus and toolbar buttons that previous Office products did not have. For example, as you move your mouse pointer over menu bar items, Office 97 indents the menu bar item to show the depression that would occur if you were to click the item. You'll notice small changes in the design that improve the distinctness of the screen elements. If you've used Internet Explorer 3 or 4, you'll notice that the Office 97 products often have an Internet Explorer-like look and feel. As you learn throughout this book, Office 97 integrates well with the Internet, and that similarity to Internet Explorer is intentional.

ToolTips

As you work with the Office 97 products and dialog boxes, such as the Open dialog box, you'll need to use the toolbar buttons across the top (and sometimes the bottom and sides) of your screen. Office 97 fully supports *ToolTips*. Figure 2.4 shows an Excel 97 ToolTip describing the button to which it is pointing.

Figure 2.4.

ToolTips indicate what the buttons do.

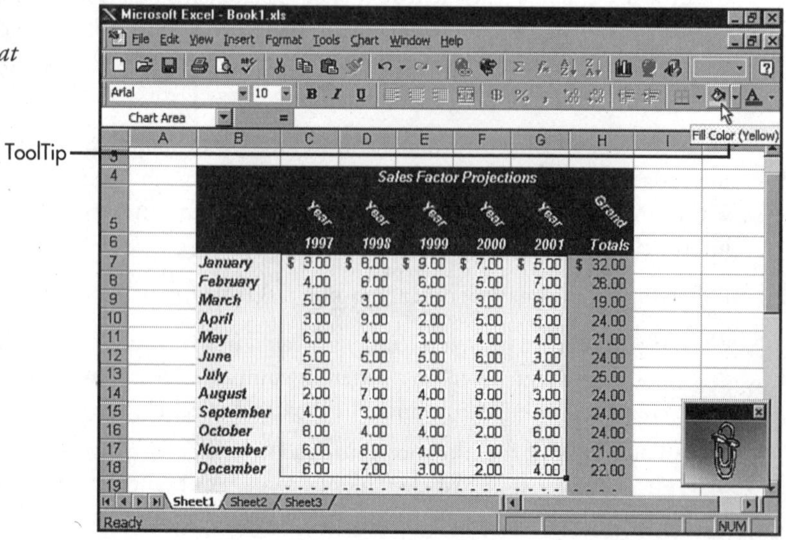

ToolTips are floating toolbar button descriptions that appear when you rest your mouse pointer over any toolbar button.

As you read this book, you won't find long boring tables that describe every toolbar button. Let the ToolTips guide you! Although many of the buttons are obvious, you might need to use ToolTips to locate a particular button.

The Office 97 Shortcut Bar

The Start menu is not the only way to start an Office 97 product. In fact, you'll probably forsake that menu and select from the *Office 97 Shortcut bar*. Figure 2.5 shows a typical Office 97 Shortcut bar, which automatically appears at the top of most Office 97 user screens.

The Office 97 Shortcut bar offers pushbutton access to any Office 97 product. You can open or create an Office 97 document by clicking the appropriate button. The Office 97 Shortcut bar always stays *active* and appears on your screen even if you work non-Office 97 programs. Therefore, you'll always be able to access Office 97 programs and documents from wherever you are.

 The *Office 97 Shortcut bar* displays a toolbar on your screen at all times from which you quickly can start Office 97 programs and open Office 97 documents.

 A window is *active* when its title bar is highlighted and its controls are available for you to use.

Figure 2.5.

Start Office 97 programs quickly with the Office 97 Shortcut bar.

Click here for options

Office 97 Shortcut bar

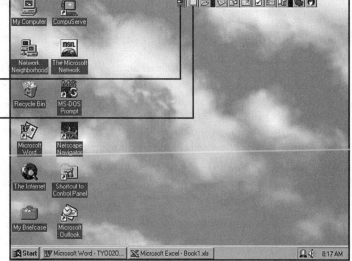

If you click the four-colored icon button on your Office 97 Shortcut bar (no ToolTip exists for this button), the Office 97 Shortcut bar displays a menu from which you can modify the Office 97 Shortcut bar's appearance or remove it from your screen. This icon is called the Shortcut bar *control icon*.

> If you use certain Office 97 programs more often than others, you might want to select the Shortcut bar's Customize option and add those specific program icons to the Office 97 Shortcut bar. If the Office 97 Shortcut bar contains buttons you rarely use, such as the New Journal Entry button, use Customize to remove any of the existing buttons.

To get rid of the Office 97 Shortcut bar, perform these steps:

1. Click the Office 97 Shortcut bar's colored control icon to display the drop-down menu.
2. Click Exit. Windows displays the dialog box shown in Figure 2.6.
3. If you want to remove the Office 97 Shortcut bar just for this session, click Yes. If you want to keep the Office 97 Shortcut bar from appearing in subsequent Windows sessions, click No.

Figure 2.6.

You can control when the Office 97 Shortcut bar appears.

The Office 97 Shortcut bar appears automatically (unless you remove it) because Office 97 installs the Office 97 Shortcut bar startup command in your Start menu's Startup folder. If you click Yes to keep the Office 97 Shortcut bar from reappearing, Windows removes the command from your Startup folder.

> You can add the Shortcut bar startup command back to your Startup folder by selecting the Start menu's Settings I Taskbar option. Click the Start Menu Programs tab and select the Remove button. Scroll to the Start menu entry you want to remove, click to select the entry, and then click Remove to delete the entry from your Start menu.

Dialog Boxes

You've probably worked with dialog boxes before. Earlier in this hour, you saw the Open dialog box. Dialog boxes give you access to a set of related *controls* and selection options that not only let you issue commands, select items, and set options, but also display information.

 Windows contains *controls* such as buttons, labels, and scrollbars that display data values, prompt you for information, and enable you to enter new information and manage the windows.

Starting with Windows 95, many dialog boxes took on an added dimension. Instead of containing a single set of controls, such as command buttons and text boxes, dialog boxes contain several sets of controls. Each set appears on a tabbed page in the dialog box. Figure 2.7 shows one such dialog box. Notice the tabs across the top of the dialog box.

Figure 2.7.

Windows 95 dialog boxes often contain several pages.

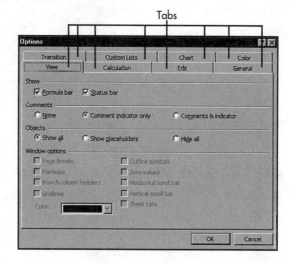

When you click one of the tabs, you display a different page that contains an additional set of dialog box controls within the dialog box. The use of the tabbed pages in dialog boxes gives you access to much more information from a single menu command.

 Tabbed dialog boxes contain pages that hold a set of controls and are common in Office 97 and other Windows programs.

Printing from Office 97

Because it is a Windows program, Office 97 uses the Windows *printer subsystem* for printing, so you'll always see the same print options throughout the Office 97 suite of products.

Windows controls all printing from Windows programs. Therefore, no matter what kind of printer you connect to Windows, Office 97 requires only that you inform Office 97 of the print type or location of the printer.

Windows lets you direct printed output to any printer device, including fax/modems that you might have connected to your computer. Windows always defaults to your system's primary printer, but you can override the default printer by selecting a different target printer.

The most common way to initiate the print process is to select File | Print. Office 97 opens the Print dialog box shown in Figure 2.8.

Figure 2.8.

The Print dialog box controls all Office 97 printing.

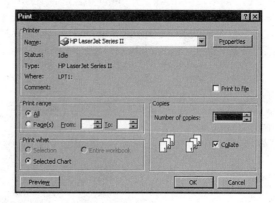

> Your Print dialog box might look different depending on your printer hardware.

The Office 97 products always contain a Print toolbar button that you can use to print, but the Print toolbar button does not display the Print dialog box. Therefore, if you want to select a printer that differs from your usual Windows default printer, or if you want to select different print options, you'll need to use the Office 97 File | Print menu command to display the Print dialog box before you print.

From the Print dialog box you can change several options, including

- [ ] The number of copies
- [ ] The range you want to print, such as selected pages or only a portion of text from a single page
- [ ] The collation selection of output papers
- [ ] The target printer

Before printing, you'll almost always want to preview your printed output on the screen. Although Office 97 products are generally *WYSIWYG*-based (What You See [on the screen]

Is What You Get [on the page]), you rarely see an entire page at once unless you use an extremely high-resolution monitor and graphics adapter. Therefore, when you click the Preview button in the Print dialog box (or select File|Print Preview from the menu bar), Office 97 displays the printed page on your screen, as shown in Figure 2.9. If your output looks correct, you can send it to paper.

 WYSIWYG (pronounced *wizzy-wig*) is an acronym for *What You See Is What You Get*, and refers to the concept that your screen shows your output as it will look when printed on paper.

When previewing any Office 97 document, your mouse pointer changes to a magnifying glass. If you click the glass over any portion of the preview, Office 97 magnifies the preview to make the text more readable (at the expense of displaying less of the preview). Click the magnifying cursor once again, and the preview reverts back to its original full-page state.

Figure 2.9.

Preview your output before printing it.

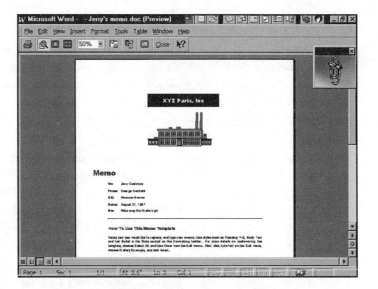

A Word on Shortcut Keys

Often, a menu option or toolbar button has an associated *shortcut key* (sometimes called an *accelerator key*) that you can press to trigger the same operation. For example, if you display Word 97's File menu, you see that Ctrl+S is an equivalent shortcut key for the File|Save option. The Office 97 suite of applications uses a consistent shortcut key interface across all programs. Therefore, Ctrl+S saves a document in every Office 97 program. When you learn one Office 97 program's shortcut key, you know the other programs' equivalent keys as well.

A *shortcut key* is a keystroke, often combined with the Ctrl key, that enables you to access a menu option without having to use the menu. *Accelerator key* is another name for shortcut key.

The primary goal of this book is to acquaint you with Office 97 as quickly as possible, showing you the basics as well as useful shortcuts and tricks to make your Office 97 life simple. Generally, Office 97 offers several ways to accomplish the same task. This book does not discuss a lot of the shortcut-key equivalents. You see shortcut-key equivalents when selecting from Office 97 menus, and you learn those shortcut keys as you use Office 97.

If a shortcut key seems obvious (for example, Ctrl+S for the Save operation) and generally easier to use (as opposed to an equivalent menu option or toolbar button), this book teaches you the shortcut key for the task. If, however, the shortcut key is not the best way to trigger a task, this book does not waste your time with the shortcut-key description.

As you use Office 97, you'll discover the shortcut keystrokes that you prefer. Everybody has different preferences.

Windows and the Internet

As Microsoft releases new versions of Windows, you'll see more integration between Windows and the Internet. The Internet's slow speed (for dial-up modem-based users) is keeping the Internet from truly integrating into your Windows desktop, but the day is not far off when quick Internet access will be available. Microsoft is preparing for that day by making the Windows operating system as well as products such as Office 97 as compliant and compatible with the Internet as possible.

If you are a PC user who has not yet worked on the Internet, this book discusses the Internet throughout these 24 hours. You never have to access the Internet to use Office 97 because Office 97 is standalone software designed to be used on a PC whether or not that PC is connected to the Internet. Nevertheless, the presence of the Internet runs throughout Office 97; you don't have to use the Internet features, but if you want them, you'll be surprised at how easily Office 97 helps bridge the Internet-to-PC connection.

With every copy of Windows sold today or distributed on a PC bundled with software, Microsoft gives you a free Internet *browser* called *Internet Explorer*. In addition, you'll probably run across a competitor to Internet Explorer named *Netscape Navigator*. After you locate a provider for Internet access, you'll be able to surf the web like a pro.

 A *browser* is a program that lets you traverse the Internet and view graphical and textual content that you find.

NEW TERM To *surf* the Internet means to view Internet pages that you find while you use the Internet. *Browse* is another word for *surf* in Internet terminology.

Hours 23, "Office 97 and the Internet," and 24, "Creating Web Pages with Office 97," explore some of the ways you can use Office 97 along with the Internet to accomplish your job. The appendix, "Internet Explorer 4 and Outlook Express," examine's Microsoft's newest browser, Internet Explorer 4. Office 97 comes with Internet Explorer 3, so that's the version used throughout this book. If you like Internet Explorer 3 and you want to upgrade to version 4, this book's appendix explains how you can do so free of charge.

Summary

This hour quickly summarized the fundamental Windows skills that you need before diving into Office 97. If you've used the Windows 95 interface before, you'll feel right at home with Office 97. One of the primary reasons for covering this material early in the book is to establish a level of terminology that all readers understand.

The next hour moves from the standard (the Windows 95 interface) to the superstandard by explaining and demonstrating Office 97's neatest features. Whether you're an Office 97 novice or expert, you'll be blown away by what Office 97 can do!

Q&A

Q I'm used to Windows 3.1, so can I begin using this book?

A Yes. Although the Windows 95 interface is new, most of your Windows 3.1 skills will still work for you. You'll see the Windows 95 improvements as soon as you begin to use Office 97.

However, you likely lack skills to use some of the more advanced Windows 95 interface features, such as Explorer, until you learn more about the Windows 95 interface—more than this book can cover. (The Windows 10-minute online tour, available from the Start menu's Help option, should explain enough to get you started.) Nevertheless, to use Office 97 to its fullest, you don't need to know any more about the Windows 95 interface than you learn in this hour.

Q I'm new to Windows. What are some good introductory Windows books?

A *Teach Yourself Windows 95 in 24 Hours, Second Edition; Using Windows 95, Second Edition; How to Use Windows 95, Second Edition;* and *Easy Windows 95, Second Edition.*

Q What are some ways that Office 97 can help me be more efficient with the Internet?

A Office 97 provides ample Internet support. If you type an Internet web page address in a Word 97 document, for example, the address becomes an actual link to that web address; you can view that web site by clicking the address inside the document. Jump to any web page just by typing the page's address in the Excel 97 toolbar address area. Create a web page lightning-fast by saving a Word 97 document as a web document.

If all this sounds intimidating because you've never used the Internet, don't fear. The Internet is simple, and Office 97 makes the Internet even simpler. Moreover, you don't have to access the Internet to take advantage of most of the features in Office 97.

Hour **3**

Introducing Office 97 Features

This hour previews the most impressive Office 97 features. If you're new to the Office environment, this hour whets your appetite for Office 97.

Office 97 attempts to move beyond the normal Windows-based help system. If you've used Windows programs in the past, you've probably read online documentation, clicked hypertext links to other related topics, and searched for keywords with which you need help. Office 97 includes all these standard online help tools, but takes that help to a new level of functionality. Office 97 provides some rather unusual help with the Office Assistant and the plain-language Answer Wizard. Every product in the suite of Office 97 programs includes these helpful guides. In a way, Office 97 looks over your shoulder and offers advice about a better way of doing things.

In addition to improving the Windows online help system, Office 97 helps disabled users by providing several accessibility options. These options magnify the screen's views and offer keyboard shortcuts that the user can define and control.

Perhaps the biggest add-on product that Office 97 provides is Bookshelf Basics. Bookshelf Basics gives you an online reference to several reference books and includes several multimedia options. In this hour you'll learn how to run Bookshelf Basics as a standalone application (in Hour 22, "Office 97's Synergy," you will learn how to integrate the Bookshelf Basics entries into other Office programs).

The highlights of this hour include

☐ What Office Assistant is

☐ How to select a different Office Assistant style

☐ When Office Assistant offers help that you didn't even know you needed

☐ How to use group-related options that Office 97 supports, such as revision marks

☐ Which data types Office 97 supports

☐ How to make Office 97 easier to use

☐ How to select from the Bookshelf Basics books

☐ Where to locate a huge assortment of drawings, photos, sounds, and videos that you can include in your documents

The Office Assistant

When you start any Office 97 program, the first feature you'll notice is the *Office Assistant*, an online cartoon character that hangs around as you work. Figure 3.1 shows the Office Assistant (named *Clippit*), which appears when you start Office 97.

 New Term *Office Assistant*, an animated cartoon character, offers advice as you use Office 97.

 If you see a different cartoon character, your Office Assistant is set to display a different character. The next section explains how to change the Office Assistant's animated character.

Step-Up

The Office Assistant replaces the TipWizard found in many of the earlier Office products.

Figure 3.1.
The Clippit Office Assistant helps you use Office 97.

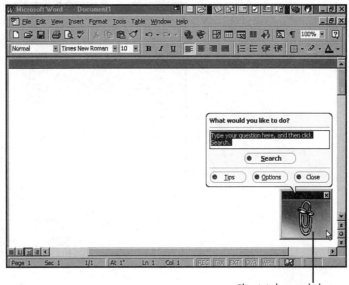

Clippit is here to help you

Keep your eyes on the Office Assistant as you work because you'll be amused at the contortions it goes through as it provides advice. If you have your speakers turned on, the Office Assistant makes noises when offering help to draw your attention.

Move the Office Assistant to a different screen location by dragging its window. If the Office Assistant is about to cover an area in which you are typing, it automatically moves out of the way.

Suppose that you want help italicizing Word 97 text. You can search through the online help system (via the Help menu), or you can click Office Assistant and type a question, such as **How do I italicize text?**, and press Enter. Office Assistant analyzes your question and displays a list of related topics (as shown in Figure 3.2). Click the topic that best fits your needs, and Office Assistant locates that help topic and displays the Help dialog box.

The Office Assistant looks over your shoulder and watches your actions. If you do something and Office Assistant can provide a better way, a yellow light bulb that you can click for shortcut information displays. For example, if you create a numbered list using menus, Office Assistant displays the light bulb to let you know that you can create a numbered list by clicking a button on the toolbar.

Figure 3.2.

Office Assistant offers lots of advice.

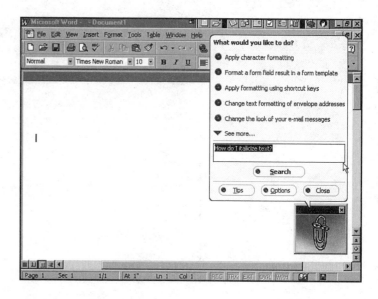

Customizing Office Assistant

If you work on a slow computer, you might want to disable Office Assistant to keep things moving a little faster. When you right-click Office Assistant, a pop-up menu appears with these options:

- [ ] **Hide Assistant:** Gets rid of Office Assistant. Display Office Assistant again by clicking the toolbar's Office Assistant button.
- [ ] **See Tip:** Displays a tip of the day.
- [ ] **Options**: Displays Figure 3.3's Office Assistant dialog box, from which you can control the behavior of the Office Assistant (such as Office Assistant's response to pressing the F1 key).
- [ ] **Choose Assistant:** Enables you to change to a different animated Office Assistant character. As you work with Office 97, check out all the Office Assistants because they are fun to see. You'll learn how to change the Office Assistant character in the steps that follow.
- [ ] **Animate:** Causes Office Assistant to dance around its window; Office Assistant likes to show off! Select Animate a few times to see Office Assistant's contortions. As Office Assistant offers advice, it also moves through these animations. For example, if you attempt to exit a program without saving your work, Office Assistant knocks on its window to get your attention (you'll even hear the knocking!).

Figure 3.3.

Control the way that Office Assistant behaves.

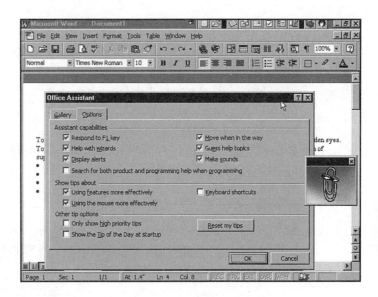

Office 97 includes several Office Assistants to help you do your job. They differ in animation, but not in their advice. Suppose you get tired of Clippit and decide that you want to see a different Office Assistant. Try this:

1. Right-click Office Assistant.

2. Select Choose Assistant. Office Assistant displays an Office Assistant Gallery screen.

3. Click Next to cycle through the Office Assistants. Each Office Assistant goes through a song and dance to convince you that it's the best. Figure 3.4 shows the Power Pup Office Assistant.

Figure 3.4.

The Power Pup Office Assistant sniffs out answers for you.

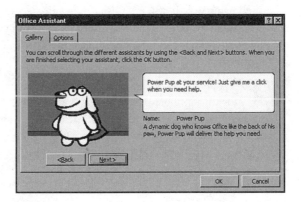

4. When you come to an Office Assistant you like, click the OK button to begin using that Office Assistant.

Here are the Office Assistants from which you can choose:

- ☐ **Clippit:** An animated paper clip that contorts in all shapes to point you to solutions.
- ☐ **The Dot:** A bouncing happy dot that draws your attention.
- ☐ **The Genius:** An Einstein-like 3D character.
- ☐ **Hoverbot:** A futuristic robot.
- ☐ **Office Logo:** A twirling colorful Office 97 logo that spins when your attention is needed.
- ☐ **Mother Nature:** An environmentally correct guide for erasing mistakes and answering questions.
- ☐ **Power Pup:** A super-hero puppy that sniffs out answers for you.
- ☐ **Scribble:** A feline guide that purrs when you (not she) need attention.
- ☐ **Will:** A Shakespearean bard whose ancient advice still works for today's computers.

> Microsoft makes several additional Office Assistants available for you to download free from the Internet. Check out Microsoft's download area at
> http://www.microsoft.com/officefreestuff/office/assistants.htm.

Using Office 97 to Share Information with Others

Although many people will use Office 97 on single-user computers, Microsoft understands that today's office worker needs the ability to share information globally. Today's computers are often networked to other computers, either through a network, an Internet connection, or an intranet connection.

NEW TERM A *network* is a collection of two or more computers linked together to share programs and data. An *intranet* is an internal network system that uses an Internet browser, such as Microsoft's Internet Explorer, to access information from other computers on the local area network.

As long as you use Microsoft Exchange, Windows Messaging, Microsoft Mail, or cc:Mail, you can create a Word 97 document and send it to users on your mail system. When you send a document, the receivers can read the document and even make changes to the document using Word 97. Word 97 keeps track of revisions, and each reviewer's notes appear separate from the others. Using Word 97's Tools | Track Changes menu, you are able to accept or reject any of the reviewer's comments when the document gets back to you.

> Office 97 lets you integrate all Office 97 products. Therefore, if you want to send a report with an Excel 97 worksheet graph to someone over the network, embed that graph into a Word 97 document (as explained in Hour 22) and send the Word 97 document. The graph travels along with the document.

Office 97 supports these three document-routing options:

- ☐ **Send a document:** Sends a copy of your document to your list of reviewers. Each reviewer can make changes to his copy, and then return the document to you.

- ☐ **Route a document:** Sends a single copy of your document to each reviewer in turn. Every subsequent reviewer is able to read the preceding reviewers' comments and add his own. The document finally gets back to you after the final reviewer makes revisions.

- ☐ **Post a document:** Sends a copy of your document to a public folder that everyone on your receiver list can read. Posting is useful when you have a company-wide policy or message that you want everyone to read. Posting requires that Microsoft Exchange Server be run with a Public Folder shortcut. Your network administrator should be able to help set up a public folder.

Word 97 keeps track of who made each revision. You can have the reviewers make changes to a copy or to the original document. To determine who made a revision, point to the edit and the editor's name appears over the edit, along with the date the edit was made.

> If the reviewers insert sound objects into the routed document, they can review the document with speech as well as with editing marks!

Figure 3.5 shows a screen from Word 97 with revision marks. The revisions appear on your screen in color—a different color for each editor who made a revision—so the revisions are easy to distinguish from the original text. Word 97's accept or reject Tools | Track Changes menu options let you quickly incorporate or delete any and all revisions made by the editing team.

Figure 3.5.

Revision marks enable a team of editors to revise the same document electronically.

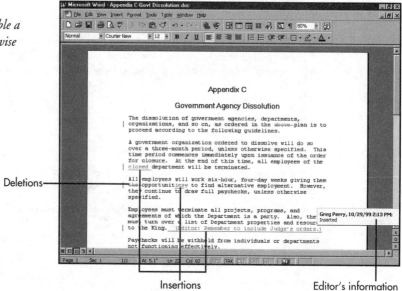

Deletions

Insertions   Editor's information

Both Word 97 and Excel 97 currently support revision marks. You can use the Tools | Track Changes menu options to see revision marks, hide revision marks (to see what the document will look like if you incorporate all revisions), and accept or reject revision marks.

You can right-click a revision mark and view a pop-up menu that lets you easily accept or reject the revision mark.

Working with Multiple Data Types

Office 97 handles today's data needs. In the past, you worked primarily with text in word processors and with numbers in electronic worksheets. Today's multimedia computers require much more data support from programs. For example, a database might hold text, numbers, pictures, sounds, and even Internet hyperlink connections! Using OLE, COM, and ActiveX technologies (the advanced data-sharing and linking tools Office 97 uses to track all kinds of data), your documents really come alive. You are no longer bound by outdated data limitations.

Suppose that you are creating a web page in Word 97, and you want to insert a *hyperlink* to another web site as in Figure 3.6. The Insert menu enables you to do just that because a web address's hyperlink is just another kind of data—just as text and numbers are two kinds of data—that the Office 97 products support. Such multi-data support frees you from the boundaries of yesterday's software and enables you to work from a global computing perspective.

NEW TERM   A *hyperlink* is an underlined word or phrase that you can click to display a different document or document section. Hyperlinks often describe web page locations, but can also refer to other data and documents on your PC or on a network of computers.

Figure 3.6.

The Office 97 products recognize web addresses and insert hyperlinks where you need them.

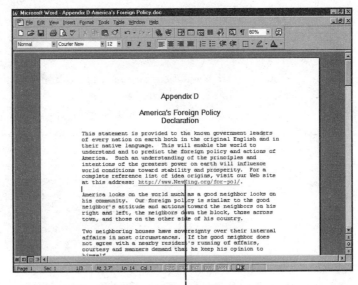

Hyperlink to a web site

Some of the Office 97 products, such as Word 97, Excel 97, and Outlook 97, automatically turn web addresses that you type into hyperlinks if the addresses begin with www and end with com. You, therefore, don't have to select from the Insert menu to embed hyperlinks in those sites. Throughout this 24-hour tutorial, you'll learn more ways to work with the multiple data formats that Office 97 supports.

Making Office 97 Easier to Use

Several accessibility features make Office 97 easier to use. You'll become familiar with many of these features as you work with Office 97. Following is a sample of some of these features:

☐ The Change document magnification option magnifies documents for easier viewing (see Figure 3.7). Even the toolbar buttons are larger to make them easier to find.

☐ The Office 97 programs contain many *AutoComplete* features with which you can begin typing items such as dates, times, days of the week or month, names, and any other AutoText entries you set up. Office 97 completes the entry for you. For example, if you begin typing a month name, such as Nov, Word 97 displays a small box with November above your month abbreviation. If you press Enter, Word 97 completes the month name for you! If you type a full month name, such as March, Word 97 offers to complete your entry with the current date, such as March 7, 1999. You can accept the complete date by pressing Enter or ignore it by typing the rest of the sentence as you want it to appear.

NEW TERM *AutoComplete* is an Office 97 feature that completes text entries it recognizes as you type them.

☐ You can rearrange toolbar buttons and customize toolbars so they contain only the buttons you use most frequently.

☐ You can assign shortcut keys to just about any task in any Office 97 product. Suppose that you often need to color and boldface an Excel 97 value. Create a shortcut keystroke and press it whenever you want to apply the special formatting.

Figure 3.7.

Magnify your document to make it easier to read.

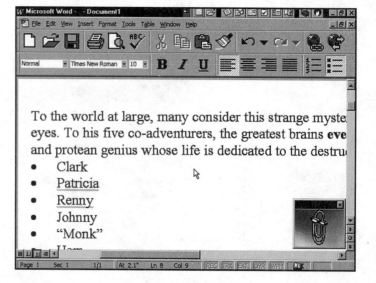

Bookshelf Basics

Office 97 comes with Bookshelf Basics, which is a three-volume electronic reference set. Bookshelf Basics is a subset of the complete Microsoft Bookshelf product, which you can purchase separately. Even though Bookshelf Basics supplies only a subset of Microsoft Bookshelf, the subset is a welcome and free add-on Office 97 product.

> Previous versions of Office did not come with Bookshelf Basics.

Bookshelf Basics is less of a standalone program than Word 97, Excel 97, Access 97, PowerPoint 97, or Outlook 97. In Hour 22, you'll learn how to access Bookshelf Basics from the primary Office 97 programs. Sometimes, however, you'll want to use Bookshelf Basics by itself for research or just to pass the time.

3

To start Bookshelf Basics, click the Office Shortcut bar's Bookshelf Basics button, or select Bookshelf Basics from the Microsoft Reference option on your Windows Start | Programs menu. Bookshelf Basics opens with a screen similar to Figure 3.8.

Figure 3.8.

The opening Bookshelf Basics screen.

> Depending on how your version of Office 97 is set up, Bookshelf Basics might present you with a Preview of the Day screen, much like the screen shown in Figure 3.9. The previews give you glimpses of the full-featured Microsoft Bookshelf product. You can order the full version by clicking the preview's Subscribe/Upgrade hypertext link or by phone, fax, mail, or modem. Click the Main hypertext link to return to Bookshelf Basics.

When you start Bookshelf Basics, you see the All Books label in the upper-left corner of the screen. Bookshelf Basics is letting you know that the search list of articles is a collection of all topics from all books within Bookshelf Basics (Bookshelf Basics includes a dictionary, a thesaurus, and a book of quotations, as well as a preview of the other Microsoft Bookshelf books). If you search for a subject, Bookshelf Basics looks through all the books.

If you want to limit the search to one of the three primary books within Bookshelf Basics, such as *Columbia Dictionary of Quotations*, click the All Books label and select Quotations from the list that appears to convert the article list to a set from that book only.

Figure 3.9.

The Preview screen shows you a glimpse of the full Microsoft Bookshelf program.

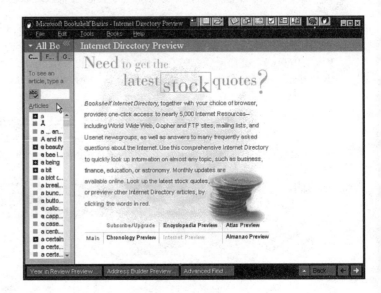

Getting a Definition

Suppose that you want to know the definition of the word *amerce*. Perform these steps:

1. Click the Contents tab of the All Books list.

2. Type the letters of the search word. As you type, the article list updates to show words from the dictionary that begin with the typed letters. As soon as you type the first four letters, you see an article entry for *amerce*. Although you can scroll the article list to search, scrolling is time-consuming due to the large number of dictionary entries.

3. Click the plus sign next to *amerce* to display both entries. When multiple entries appear, the plus sign expands the article list to show all details. If only a single entry appears, click the green box next to the entry to see that definition.

4. Click *amerce* on the expanded list to see the definition shown in Figure 3.10.

When searching for multiple definitions, you can click Back to look through the list of words you've found. Print the definition by selecting File | Print Article. Listen to the word by clicking the speaker icon next to the entry.

Figure 3.10.

Finding a definition for
amerce.

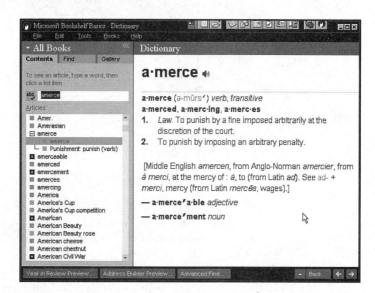

If you need help with the pronunciation symbols, click the phonetic spelling (which appears in red) next to the word's entry to display the Pronunciation Key dialog box (see Figure 3.11).

Getting a Synonym

To search the Bookshelf Basics thesaurus for a synonym, such as all words related to the word *tactile*, perform these steps:

 A *synonym* is a word with a meaning similar to that of another word.

1. Select Thesaurus from the All Books item to limit your search to *Original Roget's Thesaurus*. Bookshelf Basics updates the article list to show only entries from the thesaurus. If you looked up the definition for *amerce* in the previous section, you notice that Bookshelf Basics automatically selects to find synonyms for *amerce*.

2. Type the word whose synonym you want to find (in this case, **tactile**). Like the dictionary, the Bookshelf Basics thesaurus updates the article list to display thesaurus entries for your search word as you begin typing the word.

Figure 3.11.
The dictionary offers standard pronunciation help.

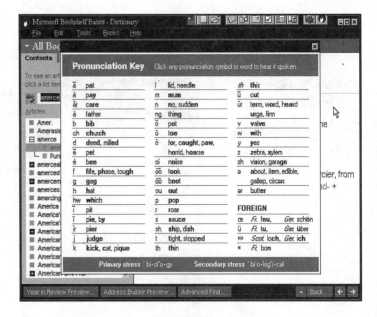

3. Click tactile to display the synonym entry. As Figure 3.12 shows, Bookshelf Basics sometimes displays your synonym list with a different lead-in synonym, one that has the most common usage of the word you originally used.

If you click any of the red synonyms in the list, Bookshelf Basics displays that entry's synonym list.

Figure 3.12.
Seeing the synonyms for tactual.

Getting a Quotation

To search the Bookshelf Basics book of quotations for a quote by author (John Adams, for example) or by subject, perform these steps:

1. Select Quotations from the All Books item to limit your search to *Columbia Dictionary of Quotations*. Bookshelf Basics updates the article list to show only entries from the quotations book. If you looked up the synonyms for *tactile* in the previous section, you notice that Bookshelf Basics automatically selects to find quotations relating to the word *tactile*.

2. Type **Adams, John** to select the article of quotes by John Adams. Notice that more than one quotation by Adams appears.

3. Click the plus sign to expand the quotes by John Adams.

4. Click the third entry to see what John Adams said about democracy (see Figure 3.13).

3

Figure 3.13.
Reading a quote.

 The Bookshelf Basics quote always displays the quotation's source.

Other Bookshelf Basics Options

The previous sections explain how to access specific topics within Bookshelf Basics. If you want to search for *all* occurrences of a subject, click the Find tab to let Bookshelf Basics locate information about a topic instead of you entering a word in an index list to locate its entries.

You can search for multiple words and phrases, such as *Senate and Congress*, to find all Bookshelf entries that contain your search words and phrases.

The Gallery tab is perhaps even more interesting if you are new to Bookshelf Basics. When you click the Gallery tab, Bookshelf Basics displays all the sound, image, and multimedia video entries that appear in Bookshelf Basics.

When you begin to explore Bookshelf Basics, search through the gallery to see and hear the multimedia entries. Figure 3.14 shows a volcano demonstration that you can watch.

Figure 3.14.

The Bookshelf Basics multimedia entries are fun to watch.

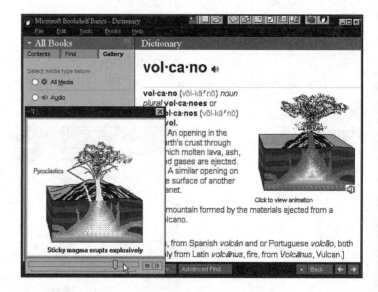

All the gallery entries appear under their particular article list when you search for them from the Bookshelf Basics books. The gallery, however, presents the sounds, images, and multimedia entries in a single place so you can browse.

The full retail version of Microsoft Bookshelf provides many more gallery entries than does Bookshelf Basics.

Clip Art

Recall from earlier in this hour how Office 97 supports several kinds of data. Not only can Office 97 work with text, numbers, and even web hyperlinks, but it can also work with sound, pictures, and moving video.

Office 97 includes a huge collection of royalty-free *clip art* files you can use when you want to embed a special data item—such as a picture or video—into a document, spreadsheet, or web page. When you need a graphic to spice things up, or when you want to include an attention-getting sound file in an Outlook 97 email message, select Insert | Picture | Clip Art to access the Office 97 clip art collection called *Microsoft Clip Art Gallery*. The gallery includes several hundred sounds, pictures, and drawings arranged by category, as Figure 3.15 shows.

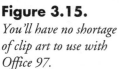 *Clip art* is a data file that you can include in your own documents.

Figure 3.15.
You'll have no shortage of clip art to use with Office 97.

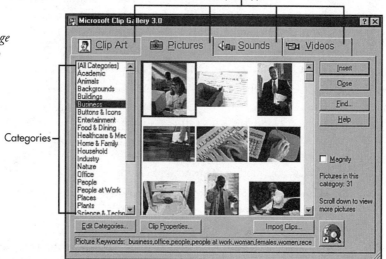

Perhaps one of the most impressive features from the Microsoft Clip Art Gallery is that you can click the Connect to the Web button to link to Microsoft's clip art web site and search for even more files to use in your documents.

Summary

This hour introduced some of the more fun features of Office 97, including the Office Assistant, the Bookshelf Basics, accessibility features, and clip art files. By routing documents to your coworkers over your network (or over the Internet using Office 97's built-in Internet support), you can all work on the same documents and track revisions as each of you review Office 97 material.

The next hour, "Using More Powerful Features," discusses some of Office 97's more powerful features.

Q&A

Q What help functions does Office 97 support?

A Office 97 supports all the help features you've come to expect from a Windows program, including tying help to the F1 function key. This hour showed you the Office Assistant because it's new to Office 97 and provides functionality you've probably never seen in a help system.

Perhaps the best thing about Office Assistant is that it provides help when you don't even request it. If Office Assistant can provide a better way to do something, it quietly lets you know by displaying the yellow light bulb. You can ignore Office Assistant's help, or click the light bulb to see what Office Assistant suggests.

Q What if I want to use Office Assistant only when I need help?

A Right-click Office Assistant to display the pop-up menu and select Hide Assistant. The Office Assistant window disappears. When you want to use Office Assistant again, click the toolbar's Office Assistant button. You might want to display the Office Assistant's Options dialog box (right-click Office Assistant and select Options) to change the way Office Assistant responds to you. The Options dialog box lets you modify the timing of Office Assistant's responses.

Q Why does Office 97 provide accessibility options when the accessibility options already appear in Windows?

A Office 97 extends Windows accessibility options. In addition, Office 97 provides more advanced keyboard shortcuts, such as the capability to finish typing common or user-defined entries. You can also increase the size of the Office 97 icons on the toolbars as well as increase the viewing area of the data.

Q How can I prevent Office Assistant from getting in the way when I enter data in an Office 97 product?

A You can drag the Office Assistant window out of the way or close it completely. Keep in mind, though, that Office Assistant automatically moves if you are about to enter data at its current screen location. The Office Assistant comes in two sizes; you can drag a corner inward to shrink the window to its smaller size.

Q Why would I *route* a document instead of *sending* a document if coworkers needed to make revisions?

A Use the document routing option when you want to send the same document to multiple coworkers and let each coworker see the revisions made. When you send a document, Office 97 sends a copy to each of the recipients, who then make revisions to that single copy and return it to you. Office 97 users often route when they have more time to wait for revisions and when they want to send a document through a predetermined chain of organizational command.

Q Can I add my own collection of clip art files to the Microsoft Clip Art Gallery?

A Certainly. Not only can you add your own sound, video, graphic, and picture files to the Clip Art Gallery, but you also can add your own categories to organize the gallery in the way that works best for you. If you see a category or clip art image that you'll probably never use, you can also remove that category or image from the gallery to make subsequent browsing through the gallery more efficient. Hour 15, "PowerPoint 97 Advanced Features," explains in detail how to use the Clip Art Gallery.

3

Hour 4

Using More Powerful Features

This hour offers a glimpse into Office 97's most powerful features. You find out that these features are not difficult to use or understand. You also learn how two of the most powerful Office 97 features, templates and wizards, *reduce* your workload.

In addition to templates and wizards, this hour introduces you to using Office 97 with the Internet. Throughout Office 97 you'll find Internet connections that let you support Office 97 with Internet files almost as easily as if the Internet were part of your own computer system.

The highlights of this hour include

- ☐ How and when to use templates
- ☐ How to use wizards to create documents
- ☐ How to follow the wizard's instruction
- ☐ How to use the Internet with Office 97
- ☐ How to send your Office 97 data files via faxes and Internet email addresses

Templates

A *template* is nothing more than a formatted outline of a document. Suppose that you follow a monthly budget, and you prepare monthly statements to follow. You like to include your savings account interest calculations, so you determine that Excel 97 will function well as the creation tool for your statements.

 A *template* is an outline that holds the format of a document, database, or other Office 97 data file.

When you create your monthly statements, you have three options:

☐ Create each monthly budget from scratch.

☐ Modify a saved monthly budget to change the details for each subsequent statement.

☐ Create a monthly budget template and fill in the details for each statement.

Obviously, the first option requires the most work. Why create a new statement for each budget, adding the titles, date, time, details, summaries, creditors, and new investment information if many of those details remain the same from statement to statement?

The second option is not a bad idea if the statements are fairly uniform in design and require only slight formatting and detail changes. Some people feel more comfortable changing an existing statement's details than creating statements from scratch or using a template. New Office 97 users might prefer to change an existing statement until they get accustomed to Office 97's programs.

 Although templates are great for Office 97 newcomers, you do not *always* want to start with them. Sometimes, it's easier to understand an Office 97 program if you create your first few data files (documents, databases, electronic worksheets, and so on) from scratch. For example, until you've created an Access 97 database from scratch and until you've learned all the terminology related to such data, the Access 97 templates do not make a lot of sense to you. After you master the fundamentals of the Office 97 programs, you can leverage the power that templates provide.

When you get used to Office 97, however, you discover that the template method makes the most sense for repetitive statement creation. The template literally provides a fill-in-the-blank statement. You don't have to format the same information from statement to statement, and you're guaranteed a uniform appearance.

Using Existing Templates

Office 97 supplies several common templates, and each Office 97 product contains templates of its own. For example, when you want to create a new Excel 97 electronic worksheet, you can select from a blank worksheet or you can click the Spreadsheet Solutions tab to see four icons that represent templates. When you click a template icon, Office 97 shows you a preview of that template (as shown in Figure 4.1).

Figure 4.1.

Office 97 provides several templates that you can preview.

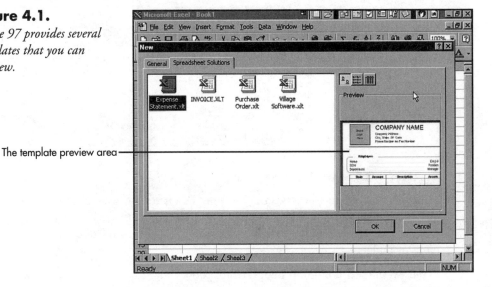

The template preview area

4

Many companies provide Office 97 templates. For example, several accounting firms provide accounting templates for Word 97 and Excel 97, and you can often find Office 97 templates on the Internet as well as on other online services.

After you select a template, the Office 97 program opens it and presents the file (as shown in Figure 4.2). Edit the template and save the details in a new file. The new file becomes your template file that you use for subsequent documents.

If you use the same template for the majority of your work, each Office 97 program lets you specify a template that you want to be the basis for *all new files you create*. For example, if you create an Excel 97 template, save the template under the name BOOK.XLT and store it in the XLSTART directory. Excel 97 automatically loads that template every time you create new worksheets.

Figure 4.2.

You can now fill in the template details.

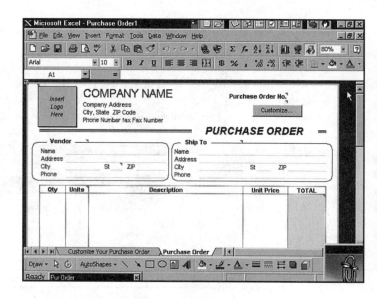

Creating New Templates

Although Office 97 supplies several predesigned templates, you won't find a specific monthly budget template that matches your exact needs anywhere in Office 97. You may want specific titles, special formatting, and unusual expense items that don't often appear in routine monthly budgets.

Because your specific monthly budget template does not exist in Office 97, you have to create your own. Generally, to create a template, follow these steps:

1. Create a properly formatted sample data file, such as a monthly budget, so that you know what design the template is supposed to produce.

2. Print the sample budget so that you can reference it later when designing the template from the sample.

3. Use File | New to create a new Office 97 Excel 97 worksheet. Select the template option to let Office 97 know you're creating a template file and not a normal data file.

4. Based on the document you created in step 1, add all titles, formatting, and footer information that does not change from statement to statement. Leave blank space for details.

5. Save the template.

If you are new to Office 97, creating the initial template may seem like a *lot* of work. (As you learn more about Office 97, you see that creating a template document gets easier.) After spending the time to create the template, however, subsequent statements become extremely simple. Instead of creating a statement from scratch, you can create the statement from the template; all you need to do is enter the details. The template supplies the proper formatting and the information that doesn't change from statement to statement.

> Office 97 supports a template-creation shortcut that you can use after you become more acquainted with Office 97. After you create the initial sample statement (or any other kind of file you want to use as the basis for a template), you can save that file as a template by selecting File | Save As and then selecting Document Template as the document's type.

> As you learn more about the Office 97 products, you learn how to add specialized *fields* to the template to make the creation of your template-based statements even easier.

 A *field* is an area of a template designed to accept certain information, such as a name or phone number. The field contains all necessary formatting and spacing, so you need only be concerned with the data.

You can save a template at any time after the creation of an Office 97 data file. You might not start out thinking that you need a template. Suppose that you create a fax cover letter and then decide that you like the letter enough to use it as a template for subsequent faxes. You can load the fax cover letter file and save the file as a template (saving two versions of the file: the original and the template).

Wizards

One reason so many users have switched to Microsoft-based Office products is Microsoft's wizard technology. *Wizards* are step-by-step guides that walk you through the development of a document or through a complicated process such as creating an Internet web page from scratch. (You learn more about Office 97's Internet integration later this hour and in Hour 23, "Office 97 and the Internet.")

 A *wizard* is a step-by-step set of dialog boxes that guides you through the creation of a document or through a complicated selection process (such as a report's design).

You probably don't have the means to create Office 97 wizards from scratch unless you have an extremely advanced programming background. However, you probably won't ever need to create a wizard yourself; Office 97 can usually supply one for you.

Although each wizard differs in its goal, all follow a similar pattern. Wizards display a series of dialog boxes, and each dialog box asks for a set of values. As you fill in the dialog boxes, you answer questions to help the program perform a specific job.

Generally, each dialog box within a wizard contains Next and Back buttons, which you can click to move back and forth through the wizard. If you change your mind after leaving one dialog box, you can back up to that dialog box and change its values.

Microsoft supplies you with several wizards you can use to create Office 97 documents. For example, if you use Word 97 to create a résumé, you can select the Résumé Wizard. Figure 4.3 shows the Résumé Wizard's opening dialog box.

Figure 4.3.

The opening Résumé Wizard dialog box.

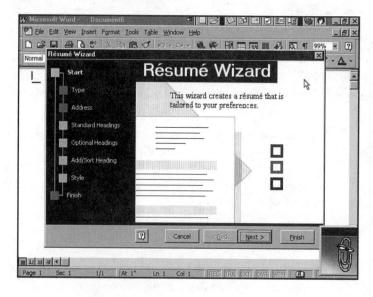

Many wizards contain opening dialog boxes that display information about the wizard. Figure 4.3 informs you that you selected the Résumé Wizard. If you click the Next button, the wizard asks which of the following kinds of résumés you want to create:

☐ Entry-level résumé

☐ Chronological résumé

☐ Functional résumé

☐ Professional résumé

Clicking Next again displays a dialog box that requests your name and address information for the top of the résumé. Office 97 is smart enough to automatically pull your name from the Office 97 registration information, but you can change the name if you create résumés for other people.

Continue through the wizard, clicking Next after you fill in each dialog box. Often, wizard dialog boxes present you with a selection of styles, such as the ones shown in Figure 4.4.

Figure 4.4.

Wizards help you determine which styles you want to use.

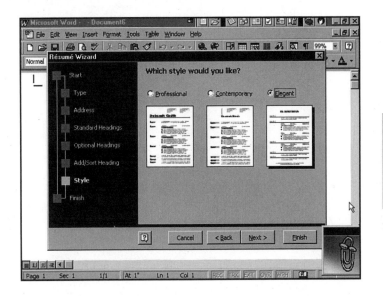

Every wizard's final dialog box includes a Finish button. Click this to complete the wizard and generate the document based on the wizard.

Notice that the wizard applies formatting to the résumé in response to your dialog box answers. You don't have to center titles or format different parts of the résumé. The wizard designs exactly the kind of résumé you specify.

Don't worry if you have no idea how to use the Word 97 Résumé Wizard! The goal of this section is simply to familiarize you with wizards so that you know what to expect. The next part of the book explains how to use Word 97 to create and edit documents. When you become familiar with Word 97's environment, you'll be able to run the Word 97 Résumé Wizard and any other wizard available from Word 97.

Generally, wizards create shells of documents, such as Word 97 template documents or Access 97 databases, that contain no data. It's your job to enter the details.

Sometimes, Office Assistant (covered in Hour 3, "Introducing Office 97 Features") lends a hand and asks whether you want help (as shown in Figure 4.5). Even though the wizard is finished and your résumé is ready for details, the Office Assistant offers a few services to make your résumé complete, such as offering a cover letter and changing the résumé's style.

Figure 4.5.

The Office Assistant lends a hand after you complete a wizard.

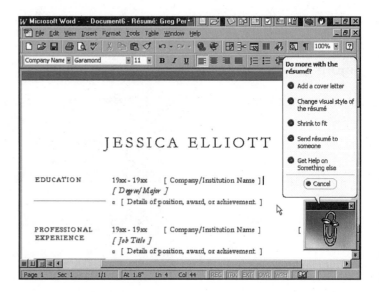

After a wizard designs a document, you are free to make whatever changes you need.

Some wizards are less complicated than Word 97's Résumé Wizard. For example, Access 97's Table Wizard creates a single table of data within a much larger database. The Table Wizard asks you fewer questions than the Résumé Wizard.

Get Ready for the Internet and Office 97

Microsoft did not make the Internet interface really stand out; instead, the Internet interface appears as just one of a long line of Office 97 features so that you can access the Internet from within the Office 97 environment. The seamless web integration lets you get to Internet information much easier than before. The Internet interface between the various Office 97 products differs a little, but the Internet interface is always underneath Office 97, ready to handle the connection.

The Web Toolbar

All Office 97 programs contain a Web toolbar button that you can click to display the Office 97 Web toolbar shown in Figure 4.6. The buttons give you web access from within an Office 97 program.

Figure 4.6.

Access the Internet from this Office 97 Web toolbar.

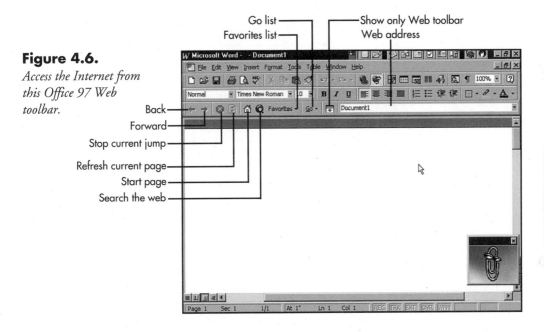

 If you've used Internet Explorer, you'll recognize the format Microsoft uses for the Web toolbar. Several of the Web toolbar buttons match those in Internet Explorer, and the drop-down list box contains a list of your most recently accessed web *URLs*.

NEW TERM   *URL*, short for *Uniform Resource Locator*, uniquely identifies an Internet site.

If you're logged on to the Internet when you click a Web toolbar button, such as the Start Page button, Office 97 takes you directly to your Start page, substituting your web browser for the current Office 97 program on your screen. If you're not logged on to the Internet before using the Web toolbar buttons, Office 97 initiates your logon sequence for you (with a login dialog box such as the one in Figure 4.7).

Figure 4.7.

*Office 97 helps you log
on to the Internet.*

If you use Internet Explorer as your web browser, type the name of any
Office 97 data file in the URL Address drop-down list and Internet Explorer
displays your properly formatted Office 97 data file.

Web Hyperlinks

In the previous hour, you learned that as you create Word 97 documents, Excel 97
worksheets, Access 97 databases, and PowerPoint 97 presentations, you can use the
Insert|Hyperlink menu command (an Insert Hyperlink toolbar button also appears on the
Web toolbar) to display the Insert Hyperlink dialog box shown in Figure 4.8.

The Insert Hyperlink dialog box lets you insert a hyperlink to another file on your disk, on
your network, or on the Internet. A hyperlink is an electronic address within one document
that describes a separate location, and that location might reside on the Internet or on your
own PC. If the file is an Office 97 document with a named bookmark, specify that location
at the bottom of the Insert Hyperlink dialog box to jump directly to that location in the
document. The jump takes place when the user of your document clicks the hyperlink.

If you're giving a PowerPoint 97 presentation and need to reference
something on the web, simply insert a hyperlink jump to that web site and
click it during the presentation. PowerPoint 97 jumps to the web and
displays the page.

A web site does not have to exist yet for you to insert a hyperlink to it. For
example, you may be creating an in-house reference manual for your
company's new web site. You can insert a hyperlink to an address on
your company site before the site actually appears on the Internet.

Figure 4.8.
Create a hyperlink location to jump to.

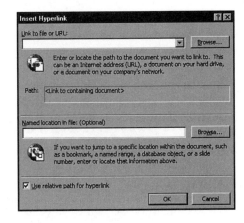

Creating Web Pages By Using Word

One of the major improvements to Word 97 is its capability to effortlessly create web pages. Just use Word 97's formatting and text-entry capabilities to create a web page. Select File|Save as HTML to save the file as a fully compatible web page. For help creating your web page, start the Web Page Wizard shown in Figure 4.9.

4

Figure 4.9.
Use the Web Page Wizard for help with web-page design.

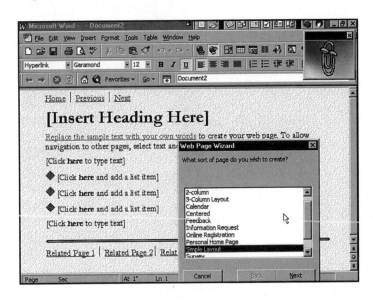

NEW TERM *HTML* stands for Hypertext Markup Language and refers to a formatting language used to display web pages.

When creating web pages with Word 97, the Show Web Page Preview toolbar button shows a preview of the web page with all the HTML codes displayed.

You can even use the Internet as your Office 97 data repository. Not only can you access the Internet web pages from the Web toolbar, but you can also edit web pages as if they were on your own PC. If you want to edit a document located on an FTP or HTTP site, just enter the document's URL when you open the document. You can also save to HTTP and FTP sites by using any of the Office 97 Save commands.

Sending Information to Other Locations

Office 97 gives you the freedom to send information from one location to another. Some Office 97 products present you with a File | Send To option that sends your data to one of the following locations:

☐ **Mail Recipient:** Produces the Send dialog box (shown in Figure 4.10), in which you can select an email recipient from your Outlook 97, Outlook Express, or Windows Messaging address book.

Step-Up

Windows Messaging used to be called Microsoft Exchange.

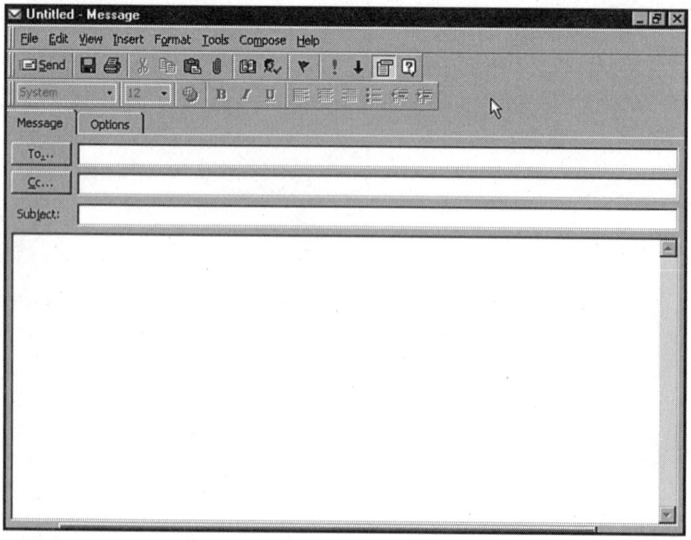

Figure 4.10.

Send a letter or worksheet to someone via email.

☐ **Routing Recipient:** Produces the Routing Slip dialog box (shown in Figure 4.11), in which you can select one or more recipients from your Windows Messaging or Outlook 97 address book to receive the data file.

☐ **Exchange Folder:** When selected, sends your data file to an Exchange Folder.

☐ **Fax Recipient:** Faxes your data file to whatever fax recipient (or recipients) you select. You must have Microsoft fax or a compatible faxing software available on your computer to fax an Office 97 data file to someone.

Figure 4.11.

Route a letter or worksheet to several people for their review.

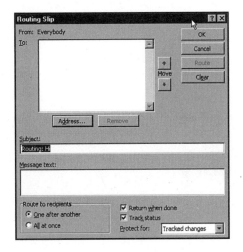

4

Suppose that you're writing a business proposal in Word 97, and you realize that you're missing a sales figure that you need. Without leaving Office 97 and starting your regular email program, you can create a new note using Word 97's File | New command and ask for the sales figure in the document you create. Send that note to your corporate office's email address with Word 97's File | Send To | Mail Recipient menu option.

Improved Online Help

Even Office 97's online help extends far beyond your disk and Office 97 CD-ROM. When you want to know something about Office 97 (or any other Microsoft product), select Help | Microsoft on the Web, and then select from one of the several web sites Office 97 locates for you. (Figure 4.12 shows the list of web-based help areas that Office 97 provides.)

Figure 4.12.

Need more help? Office 97 takes you to the web for additional Microsoft resources.

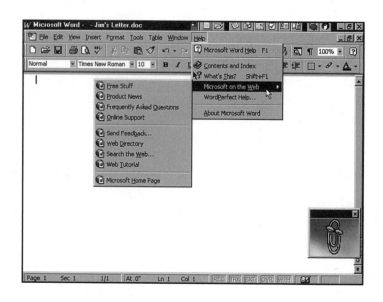

Summary

This hour explored three of the most powerful features in the suite of Office 97 products: templates, wizards, and Office 97's Internet interface.

Previous versions of Office supported templates and wizards, but Office 97 expands and improves the templates and wizards. With Office 97, you have more selection. Some of the newer wizards help you create web-based home pages.

Office 97 doesn't stop with just home pages. To Office 97, your computer is not limited by your hard disk and CD-ROM drive. You can work with any document on any computer connected to yours, whether the other computer is on your local area network or across the globe on the Internet. Office 97 also provides direct links to several web sites and offers a Web toolbar, from which you can access the Internet's HTTP and FTP sites.

Hour 5, "Welcome to Word 97," introduces Word 97. You'll soon see why Word 97 is considered to be the most powerful word processor available.

Q&A

Q What is the difference between a template and a wizard?

A A *template* is a formatted shell, design, or empty data file. For example, an Excel 97 accounts-receivable template would contain no data but would contain all the titles, fields, and formatting necessary for an accounts-receivable worksheet. After you load the template, you're able to add specific data easily without having to format titles and totals.

A *wizard* is more than a formatted shell. A wizard is a step-by-step guide that presents a series of dialog boxes. As you fill in each dialog box, the wizard builds a data file for you. You can create complex documents like professional résumés, newsletters, and web pages by answering a few simple questions within the dialog box series.

Q What if I don't have Internet access?

A If you don't, you're the only person in the free world without it! Seriously, without Internet access, you lack only the capabilities to access Internet sites and send email through Office 97's Internet email; otherwise, you can use all that Office 97 offers. If you want to get Internet access, plenty of companies will gladly sign you up. Microsoft offers Internet access through its Microsoft Network online service, and you can access everything you need by using Microsoft's Internet Explorer that comes with Office 97. Microsoft Network (MSN) offers free trial memberships for a month, so you can try the service risk-free.

Q Why is using a template not always the best approach when an Office 97 newcomer needs to create a data file?

A Sometimes you need to understand the Office 97 products a little before you can understand and fully appreciate templates. For example, if you've never created an Access 97 database and do not know the common terms related to database work, you might want to create your first Access 97 database from scratch. After you become familiar with Access 97 (as you do after completing this book's Part VI, "Tracking with Access 97"), the templates make more sense.

Q True or False: A template is a file.

A True.

Q True or False: A wizard is a file.

A False; a wizard is a step-by-step guide that helps you generate files.

Q True or False: A wizard generates a template file.

A False, but that's a trick question for two reasons. First of all, you haven't learned enough about using Office 97 to know the answer. In addition, *sometimes* a wizard creates a template, but not always. If you use a wizard to generate a data file from scratch, the wizard generally creates a template-like data-file shell that contains no data but contains all the formatting you need to create the final detailed document. Many wizards, however, simply walk you through a series of dialog boxes to complete a task such as logging you on to the Internet.

4

PART II
Processing with Word 97

Hour

Hour 5

Welcome to Word 97

This hour introduces you to Word 97. If you've never used a previous version of Microsoft Word, you'll soon see why Word is the most popular word processor on the market. With Word 97, you can create documents of any kind with amazing ease. Word 97 helps you painlessly create letters, proposals, business plans, resumes, novels, and even graphics-based multicolumn publications, such as fliers and newsletters.

The highlights of this hour include

- ☐ How to start Word 97
- ☐ How to edit by using Word 97
- ☐ How to edit multiple documents at once
- ☐ When to use the Find and Replace text features
- ☐ How to modify Word 97's automatic editing tools
- ☐ How to quit Word 97 properly and why this is important

Starting Word 97

You can start Word 97 in several ways:

- [ ] Click the Office 97 Shortcut bar's New Office Document button and double-click the Blank Document icon to create a new document. (Click the General tab if it is not already selected to see the Blank Document icon.)

- [ ] Click the Office 97 Shortcut bar's New Office Document button and open a Word 97 template or start a Word Wizard. Hour 4, "Using More Powerful Features," explains how to use templates and wizards.

- [ ] Click the Office 97 Shortcut bar's Open Office Document button and select an existing document you want to edit.

- [ ] Use the Windows Start menu to start Word 97 by selecting Microsoft Word from the Programs menu.

- [ ] Select a Word 97 document from the Windows Start menu's Documents option. Windows recognizes that Word 97 created the document, starts Word 97, and loads the document automatically. (The Start menu's Documents option holds a list of your most recent work.)

- [ ] Click the Office 97 Shortcut bar's Word 97 button to create a blank document. Depending on your Office 97 Shortcut bar's setup, you might not see the Word 97 button.

> If the Word 97 button doesn't appear on your Shortcut bar, click the Office 97 Shortcut bar's icon and select Customize. Click the Buttons tab and select Microsoft Word to add the button to your Shortcut bar.

Figure 5.1 shows the opening Word 97 screen. (Your screen might differ slightly depending on the options that the installer set.)

Step-Up

Microsoft did not completely revamp Word 95 to create Word 97; rather, Microsoft honed Word 95's environment to include more Internet features and usability improvements. You'll like the slicker Word 97 look. For example, you'll wonder why nobody thought to show menu bar selections as pushbuttons before (point your mouse to the File menu bar command to see this) or why nobody previously thought to display menu commands with their corresponding toolbar icons.

Figure 5.1.

Word 97's opening screen.

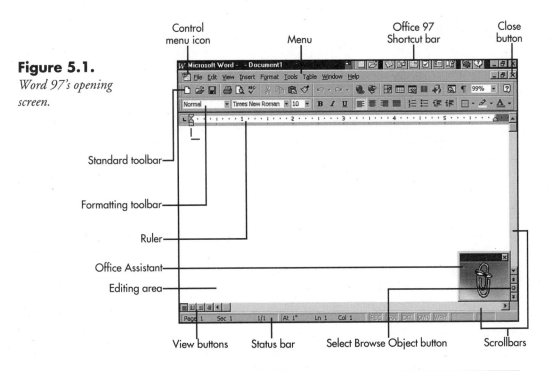

Control menu icon

Menu

Office 97 Shortcut bar

Close button

Standard toolbar

Formatting toolbar

Ruler

Office Assistant

Editing area

View buttons   Status bar   Select Browse Object button   Scrollbars

Remember the ToolTips described during Hour 2, "Reviewing Windows and Office 97 Fundamentals." If you forget what a toolbar button does, rest the mouse pointer over any button to learn the toolbar button's name.

5

Editing with Word 97

This section reviews fundamental Word 97 editing skills and brings you up to speed if you are new to word processing. In this section, you learn how to

☐ Type text into a document

☐ Delete text

☐ Copy, cut, and paste text from one location to another

☐ Locate and replace text

Entering Text

When you start Word 97, it displays a blank editing area in which you can type text to create a new document. You also can load an existing Word 97 document and make changes to that document. If you've started Word 97 through the Start menu's Documents option, Word 97 starts with the open document you selected.

> If you want to work with an existing document, you must *open* that document as described in Hour 2. You *save* the document to transfer your work to a disk file for long-term storage. You can *close* a document if you want to clear that document from the editing area; if you have not first saved changes, Office 97 gives you a chance to save your work before closing the document.

The text you write appears in the editing area. The flashing vertical bar (called the *cursor* or *insertion point*) shows where the next character will appear. As you type, remember these basic editing points:

- [ ] Don't press Enter at the end of a line. As you type close to the right edge of the screen, Word 97 automatically wraps the text to the next line for you.

- [ ] Press Enter at the end of each paragraph. Each subsequent press of the Enter key adds an extra blank line before the next paragraph.

- [ ] If you type a web address in your document, Word 97 automatically changes that web address to a hyperlink that you can click to jump to that page if you (or someone who reads your document file) have Internet access.

> You can turn off the automatic Web address feature so that Word 97 treats web addresses like regular text, by selecting Tools | AutoCorrect, clicking the Auto Format As You Type tab, and unchecking the Replace as You Type Internet and Network Paths with the Hyperlinks Option.

 The flashing vertical bar that shows where your next typed character will appear is called the *cursor* or *insertion point*.

> If you click the Show/Hide toolbar button, Word 97 displays nonprinting characters such as spaces, tabs, and returns (as shown in Figure 5.2). The nonprinting characters show you exactly where paragraph marks, tabs (indicated by right arrows), and spaces (small dots) occur in your document.
>
> Some writers prefer to show nonprinting characters during the entire editing session; others prefer to keep the screen clear of clutter. You can customize Word 97 to show only a subset of the nonprinting characters. Hour 7, "Managing Documents and Customizing Word 97," shows you how to customize Word 97.

Figure 5.2.

Display nonprinting characters.

Show/Hide toolbar button

Insert mode is Word 97's default start-up mode. When in *insert mode*, new typing appears at the text cursor, and new text pushes existing characters to the right (and down the page if needed). When in *overtype mode*, new text replaces existing text.

 Word 97 uses *overtype mode* when you want typed characters to replace existing characters.

 Word 97 uses *insert mode* when you want to insert newly typed characters before existing characters.

The Word 97 Status bar indicates Word 97's insertion mode. If the letters OVR are visible, Word 97 is in overtype mode. If OVR is grayed out, Word 97 is in insert mode.

To change modes, select the Tools|Options Edit page and click the Typing Replaces Selection option.

Step-Up

Unlike previous Microsoft Word products, Word 97 does *not* let you toggle between insert and overtype modes by pressing the Insert key!

Not only can you insert text, but Word 97 also lets you insert blanks. Suppose you forget a space or want to insert three spaces before the start of a paragraph. Move the cursor to the place you want the blanks (to the left of text that you want to shift right) by pointing and

5

clicking the mouse pointer to anchor the cursor in position. Press the spacebar as many times as you need to shift the existing text right.

Navigating Word Documents

When you first type a document, you might enter the rough draft all at once and edit the text later, or you might be the kind of writer who likes to edit as you go. No matter how you write, you need to be able to move around a Word 97 document quickly, locating text that you want to change or read. Much of the time you navigate through a Word 97 document using these general practices:

☐ Use the four arrow keys to move the text cursor around the editing area.

☐ Click the scroll bars until you locate text you want.

☐ Click your mouse pointer anywhere inside the editing area to move the text cursor to that location.

☐ If you type more text than fits in the editing area, use the scrollbars, arrow keys, PageUp, PageDown, Ctrl+Home, and Ctrl+End keys to scroll to the portions of text that you want to see.

> If you open an existing document, press Shift+F5 to jump directly to the last edit you made. Keep pressing Shift+F5 to jump to each of your previous edits.

To quickly navigate through a lot of text, press Ctrl+G (the shortcut for Edit|Go To) to display the Find and Replace dialog box (shown in Figure 5.3) with a Go To page. When you type a page number and press Enter, Word 97 immediately takes you to that page.

Figure 5.3.

Quickly jump to any page.

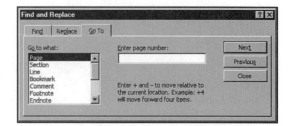

> The skills you learn here also apply to the other Office 97 products. Therefore, when you learn these skills in Word 97, you already know them for the other Office 97 products.

Selecting Text

Word 97 is more of a document processor than a word processor; Word 97 enables you to work with multiple words, paragraphs, pages, and complete documents. Earlier in this hour, you learned how to insert and delete individual characters; you now learn how to select entire sections of text you can move or delete.

When you or Word 97 highlights (*selects*) text, you can perform tasks on that selection. For example, you might want to select two sentences and underline them for emphasis.

Highlighted text that you want to work on as a single block is called a *selection* or *selected text*. Some people call a selected text section a *block* of text.

You can select text using your keyboard or mouse. Table 5.1 shows the mouse-selection operations.

Table 5.1. Word 97's text-selection options.

To select this	Do this
Any text	Click the mouse at the start of the text and drag the mouse to the end of the text. (Figure 5.4 shows a partial paragraph selection.)
Word	Double-click the word.
Sentence	Press Ctrl and click the sentence.
Line	Click to the left of the line.
Paragraph	Double-click to the left of the paragraph or triple-click anywhere inside the paragraph's text.
Entire document	Press Ctrl and click to the left of the document.

To select with your keyboard, move the text cursor to the beginning of the selection, press the Shift key, and move the text cursor (with the arrow keys or other cursor-movement keys you learned about in the section titled "Entering Text") to the final selection character. When you release the Shift key, the selected text appears.

Ctrl+A selects your entire document. When you want to apply global formatting or clipboard-related tasks (you'll learn about the clipboard in the next section) to the entire document, Ctrl+A makes quick work of selecting the entire document.

5

Figure 5.4.

A partial text selection.

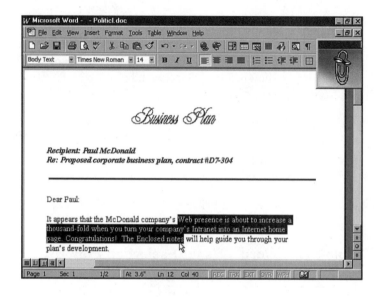

Deleting Text

No matter which mode you're in (insert or overtype), press Delete to delete any character at the text cursor's position. Any characters to the right of the deleted character shift left to close the gap. Press the Backspace key to reverse the text cursor and erase the previous character.

> Here's a tip that even advanced Word 97 gurus often forget: Ctrl+Backspace erases the word to the *left* of your text cursor, and Ctrl+Delete erases the word to the *right* of your text cursor. Remember these shortcuts when you must remove a large section from a sentence or paragraph.

> The Del key on your numeric keypad's period is identical to the Delete key. On some keyboards, no Delete key appears, so your only option is to press Del. Make sure NumLock is off (the keyboard's indicator light will be off) before pressing Del; otherwise, a period appears where you wanted to delete a character.

The section found earlier this hour titled "Selecting Text" illustrates how to select multiple characters. After selecting multiple characters, press Delete to delete the entire selection.

Copying, Cutting, and Pasting

After you select text, you can copy or cut and move that text to a different location. One of the most beneficial features that propelled word processors into the spotlight in the 1980s was their capability to copy and move text. In the medieval days (before 1980), people had to use scissors and glue to cut and paste. Now, your hands stay clean.

NEW TERM To *copy* is to reproduce selected document text and send it to the clipboard. You then can paste that copied text from the clipboard into another document.

NEW TERM To *cut* is to send selected document text to the clipboard and remove that text from the document. You then can paste that cut text from the clipboard into another document.

Windows uses the *clipboard* during the copy, cut, and paste processes. The clipboard is an area of memory reserved for text, graphics, and whatever other kind of data you need to place there.

NEW TERM The *clipboard* is an area of Windows where you temporarily store data that you can paste elsewhere.

> The clipboard contents are temporary! Windows replaces the clipboard contents as soon as you send new contents to the clipboard. Also, when you exit Windows, Windows erases the clipboard.

To copy text from one place to another, select the text, copy the selected text to the clipboard by selecting Edit | Copy (or by pressing Ctrl+C or clicking the Copy toolbar button), and paste (that's computer lingo for *insert from the clipboard*) the clipboard contents in their new location. To paste, select Edit | Paste, press Ctrl+V, or click the Paste toolbar button. You can paste the same text again and again wherever you want it to appear.

NEW TERM To *paste* is to send the clipboard contents to a location inside your document.

When you *cut* text from your document (select Edit | Cut, click the Cut toolbar button, or press Ctrl+X), Word 97 erases the text from your document and sends it to the clipboard where you can paste the clipboard contents elsewhere. In effect, cutting and pasting moves the text.

NEW TERM To *cut* text means to delete the selected text and send that text to the Windows clipboard where you later can paste the text elsewhere.

5

You also can move and copy by using your mouse. Select the text you want to move, click the selection, and drag the text to its new location. To copy with your mouse, press Ctrl before you click and drag the selected text. Word 97 indicates that you are copying by adding a small plus sign to the mouse cursor during the copy.

Finding and Replacing Text

Word 97 locates text for you. When searching through extremely long documents, Word 97's search capabilities come in handy. For example, suppose that you're writing a political letter and you want to correct a congressional district's seat name. Ask Word 97 to find all occurrences of the word *district* by following these steps:

1. Select Edit | Find. Word 97 displays the Find and Replace dialog box (shown in Figure 5.5).

Some people prefer to use the Ctrl+F shortcut key; others click the Select Browse Object button on the vertical scrollbar (refer to figure 5.1) and click the binoculars to display the Find and Replace dialog box. The Select Browse Object button has a round dot to distinguish it from the scrolling arrows. Use whatever method you can remember because you often search for (and replace) text in word-processing sessions.

Figure 5.5.

Enter text that you want Word 97 to locate.

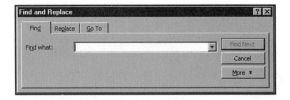

2. Type the word or phrase you want to find in the Find What text box. For example, type **District** to locate that word. By default, Word 97 searches from the top of the document and does not worry about exactly matching your find text with its occurrences in the document.

3. When Word 97 locates the first occurrence of the search word, Word 97 highlights the word (as shown in Figure 5.6). (As you saw in the section titled "Selecting Text," this highlighted text is said to be *selected*.)

Figure 5.6.

Word 97 found a match.

Selected text—

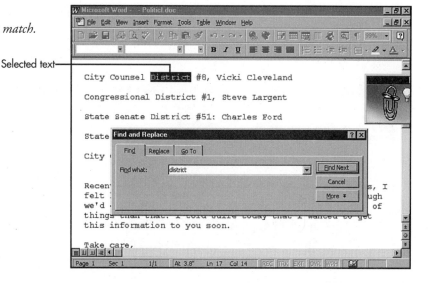

4. If the selected text is the text you wanted to find, click the Cancel button or press Escape to return to your document. Word 97 keeps the selected text highlighted so that you can identify the found text. To remove the selection, press an arrow key or click anywhere in the editing area. If the selected text is not the text you want, click the Find Next button in the Find and Replace dialog box to search for the next occurrence of the text.

5

Instead of pressing Esc to get rid of the Find and Replace dialog box, you can click anywhere in your document's text to send your cursor back to the document and keep the Find and Replace dialog box on your screen. Doing so enables you to edit found text and quickly search for additional matches by clicking the Find button in the dialog box when you're ready to find the next occurrence of the text.

As you probably can guess from the name of the Find and Replace dialog box, Word 97 not only finds but also replaces text. Suppose that you wrote a lengthy business proposal to an associate you thought was named Paul McDonald. Luckily, before you sent the proposal over your corporate network (using Microsoft Outlook as shown in Hour 16, "Outlook 97 Basics"), you realized that Paul's last name is spelled *Mac*Donald.

Tell Word 97 to change all *McDonalds* to *MacDonalds* by following these steps:

1. Select Edit | Replace. Word 97 displays the Find and Replace dialog box (shown in Figure 5.7) with the Replace tab displayed.

Figure 5.7.

Make Word 97 find and replace text for you.

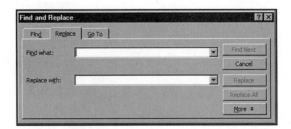

2. Type the word or phrase you want to find in the Find What text box. Unless you change the default (you learn how to do this in the next section), you don't need to worry about distinguishing between uppercase and lowercase letters.

3. Press Tab to move the text cursor to the Replace with text box.

4. Type the replacement text (in this case, `MacDonald`). Use the correct case because Word 97 replaces the find text with your exact replacement text.

5. If you want Word 97 to replace all occurrences of the text, click the Replace All button. When Word 97 finishes replacing all the occurrences, it indicates how many replacements were made.

    If you want to replace only one or a few of the occurrences (for example, there might be another person with the name McDonald in the business plan whose name is spelled that way), click the Find Next button, and Word 97 locates the next occurrence of the text. Upon finding a match, Word 97 selects the text and gives you a chance to replace it by clicking Replace. To skip an occurrence, click Find Next instead of Replace after a match is found that you want to ignore.

6. Press Escape or click Cancel when you're finished.

If you want to delete all occurrences of a word or phrase, leave the Replace with text box blank when you click Replace All.

Be careful when using Replace All because it could change more than you expect. To be safe, locate each replacement and click Replace individually so that you can see the context of the found text before you decide to replace it with something else. If you do use Replace All but then realize that Word 97 replaced too much, use Word 97's undo feature to reverse the replacement.

Advanced Find and Replace

Both the Find and Replace pages inside the Find and Replace dialog box (see the previous section) contain More buttons. If you want more control over your text searches and replacements, click the More buttons when you want to find or replace text. The dialog box expands to show more·options, as Figure 5.8 shows.

After you click the More button and the dialog box expands, the More button becomes a Less button that you can click to return to the simpler Find or Replace pages.

Figure 5.8.
Advanced options let you control your find-and-replace operations.

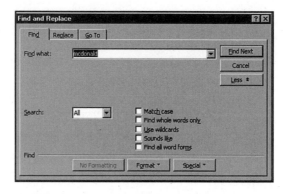

Table 5.2 describes each of the advanced find-and-replace options.

Table 5.2. The advanced Find and Replace dialog box options.

Option	Description
Search	Determines the scope of the find and replace. Select All to search the entire document starting from the beginning, Down to search the document from the text cursor's current position down in the document, and Up to search the document from the text cursor's current position up through the document.

continues

Table 5.2. continued

Option	Description
Match Case	Finds text only when the text exactly matches the capitalization of your search text.
Find Whole Words Only	Matches only when complete text words match your search phrase. For example, if this box is checked, Word 97 does not consider *McDonald* a match for *McD*. If unchecked, *McD* matches *McDonald*, *McDonald's*, and *McDonalds*.
Use Wildcards	Uses an asterisk (*) to indicate zero or more characters, or a question mark (?) to indicate a single character in your search. For example, if you search for *Mc** and click this option, Word 97 matches on *Mc*, *McDonald*, and *McDonald's*. If you search for *M?cDonald*, Word 97 considers *MacDonald* a match but not *McDonald*.
Sounds Like	Bases the match on words or phrases that phonetically match the search phrase but are not necessarily spelled the same way as the search phrase. Therefore, Word 97 would consider both *to* and *too* matches for the search phrase *too*.
Find All Word Forms	Matches on similar parts of speech that match the search phrase. Therefore, Word 97 would not consider the verb *color* to be a match for the noun *color* when you check this option.

Word 97 cannot conduct a word-form search if you've checked either the Use Wildcards or Sounds Like options.

AutoCorrecting and AutoFormatting

Word 97 is smart. Often, Word 97 fixes problems without you ever being aware of them, thanks to Word 97's *AutoCorrect* feature. AutoCorrect uses a Microsoft-created technology called *Intellisense* to hunt constantly for errors. As you type, Word 97 analyzes the errors and makes corrections or suggested improvements along the way.

NEW TERM   *AutoCorrect* is a Word 97 feature that corrects your document as you type it.

The Office Assistant is always there to guide you, but AutoCorrect is more integral to Word 97 as well as to the other Office 97 products. If AutoCorrect recognizes a typing mistake, it immediately corrects the mistake.

Following are just a few of the mistakes AutoCorrect recognizes and corrects as you type:

- [ ] AutoCorrect corrects two initial capital letters at the beginning of sentences. `LAtely, we've been gone` becomes `Lately, we've been gone`.
- [ ] AutoCorrect corrects sentences that don't begin with an uppercase letter by capitalizing the first letter for you.
- [ ] AutoCorrect capitalizes the names of days and months that you forget to capitalize.
- [ ] AutoCorrect corrects a sentence that you accidentally type in the Caps Lock key mode. For example, `lATELY, WE'VE BEEN GONE` becomes `Lately, we've been gone`.
- [ ] AutoCorrect replaces common symbols' predefined characters. For example, when you type `(c)`, Word 97 converts the characters to a single copyright symbol.
- [ ] AutoCorrect replaces common spelling transpositions, such as *teh* with *the*.

If AutoCorrect corrects something that you don't want corrected, press Alt+Backspace and AutoCorrect reverses itself.

All the AutoCorrections in this list are preset. You can add your own, as you'll want to do when you run across common words and phrases that you often type. For example, you'll most certainly want to add your initials to the AutoCorrect table so that you only need to type your initials when you want to enter your full name in a document.

To add your own AutoCorrect entries, perform these steps:

1. Select Tools|AutoCorrect. Word 97 displays the AutoCorrect dialog box shown in Figure 5.9.
2. Type the AutoCorrect shortcut, such as an abbreviation, in the Replace text box.
3. Press Tab.
4. Type the AutoCorrect replacement text in the With text box.
5. Press Enter.

After you enter a new AutoCorrect entry, you can begin using the AutoCorrect feature immediately.

5

Step-Up

The AutoCorrect dialog box presents four tabs that let you control on-the-fly AutoCorrecting, on-the-fly AutoFormatting, regular AutoFormatting, and AutoText entries. These were available on separate menus in previous Word versions.

Figure 5.9.

*Add your own
AutoCorrect entries.*

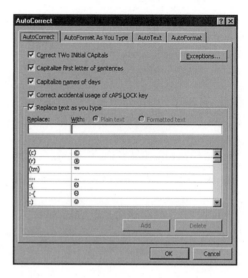

In addition to AutoCorrect entries, Word 97 also automatically formats special character combinations within your document as you type. Word 97 converts common typed fractions, such as 1/2, to their single character equivalent. You can control exactly which *AutoFormat* features Word 97 uses by selecting Tools | AutoCorrect and clicking the AutoFormat As You Type tab. Figure 5.10 shows you what options you can control.

Figure 5.10.

*Word 97 formats your
text as you type.*

NEW TERM   *AutoFormat* is a feature within Word 97 that changes the format of some text, such as fractions and dates, as you type.

Editing Multiple Documents

With Word 97, you can work with multiple documents. For example, you could be typing a letter to a friend and remember that you have to send a memo to your out-of-state office before the mail runs. Instead of closing your letter, click the toolbar's New button to create a blank document. The new document appears on top of your letter. Switch between the letter and your memo by selecting the filename from the menu bar's Window option. In most instances, only one document is active (visible on the screen) at one time. When you issue a Close or Save command, Word 97 closes or saves the active document.

Select Window | Arrange All to show both (or as many as you currently have open) documents at once (see Figure 5.11). When you display both documents, you can scroll each document individually, rearrange the window sizes to give more or less space to one of the documents, and copy and paste text between the documents. (The section that appeared earlier this hour titled "Copying, Cutting, and Pasting" explained how to copy, cut, and paste text within a document, between windows, and between applications.)

Figure 5.11.
Word 97 lets you edit two or more documents at once.

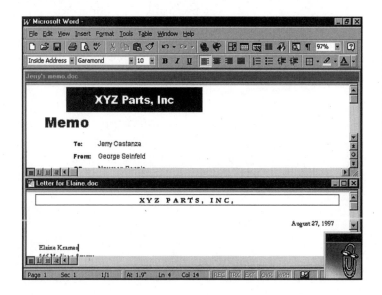

5

If you display multiple document windows, the window with the highlighted title bar and window buttons is the active window. It often helps to hide the ruler (select View | Ruler) to make more room to display your documents within multiple windows.

Word 97 documents end with the .doc filename extension, as in Proposal.doc and Sales Notes.doc. (Filenames can have spaces in them.) You don't have to type the extension when opening or saving documents; Office 97 automatically attaches the correct extension.

Correcting Mistakes

At any point you can *undo*, or reverse, your most recent edit or edits. Click the toolbar's Undo button (this performs the same action as selecting Edit | Undo, and is easier to use in most cases). If you delete a character or even an entire paragraph, for example, click Undo. Word 97 puts the deleted text right back where it was originally!

NEW TERM An *undo* is the reversal of an edit.

As you edit documents, Word 97 changes its Edit | Undo menu option to reflect your last change; for example, if you delete text, the Edit menu's first option becomes Undo Clear, indicating that you can undo the clearing of text that you previously performed.

Word 97 keeps track of multiple edits. Therefore, if you realize that the last three edits you made were wrong, click Undo three times and Word 97 reverses those three edits no matter what the edits were. If you go too far, press the Redo toolbar button, and Word 97 replaces the undo—in effect, undoing the undo! It gets confusing! If you click the arrows next to either the toolbar's Undo or Redo buttons, Word 97 displays a list of up to 100 recent changes, which you can choose to undo or redo.

NEW TERM The reversal of an undo is a *redo*.

Word 97 can reverse any and all replacements you make with the Find and Replace dialog box.

In addition to undoing wrong edits, Word 97 works in the background to keep your documents as safe as possible. Table 5.3 describes Word 97's automatic file-saving features. (You can control these features through the Tools | Options dialog box. You learn all about the Options dialog box in Hour 7.) Therefore, if you turn off your PC before saving your work, you still have the edits to the point of the most recently saved document.

Table 5.3. Word 97's file-saving features.

Feature	Description
Automatic backup	When you begin editing an existing document, Word 97 saves a copy of the original document with the original name and the .bak extension (for *backup*). No matter how much you change (or mess up) your document, the original version is always safely stored until your next editing session on that document.
AutoRecovery	Automatically saves enough of your document to restore the complete document at that point. Subsequently, if your power goes out or your computer system crashes before you have a chance to save your document and exit Word 97, and provided that you've turned on the AutoRecovery option, Word 97 recovers the document the next time you start Word 97. Ordinarily, you would lose your last edits and possibly your entire document. As long as you've turned on the AutoRecovery option, Word 97 recovers the document the next time you start Word 97. The more frequently you set AutoRecover's timer, the more likely you will be able to recover your most recent edits if a power failure or system crash occurs.

5

Step-Up

The AutoRecovery feature replaces the AutoSave feature found in previous versions of Word.

The Office Assistant is always around if you need help. When you click the small Office Assistance window, Office Assistant displays a list of subjects related to what you're currently trying to do. If you don't want Office Assistant's help, close the Office Assistant's window by clicking the Close button. Office Assistant stays out of your way. If your typing starts to get close to Office Assistant, Office Assistant moves to another area of the screen.

Click the Office Assistant's Close button (the button with the *X* in the upper-right corner) to close the Office Assistant if you don't want the help it provides.

Quitting Word 97

When you're finished with Word 97, you can quit by performing any of the following:

- ☐ Select File|Exit.
- ☐ Press Alt+F4.
- ☐ Double-click the Control menu icon.
- ☐ Close the window.

 Always quit Word 97 and shut down Windows (by selecting Start I Shut Down) before turning off your computer, or you might lose your work.

Summary

This hour introduced Word 97, Office 97's word-processing product. As you saw in this hour, Word 97 makes entering text simple, and Word 97 even corrects mistakes as you type.

One of Office 97's many productivity factors is that the products in the Office 97 suite often work in a similar manner. Therefore, many of the skills you learned in Word 97 this hour carry over to the other products. If you have used Word in the past, you've already seen some of the improvements Microsoft made with Word 97.

The next hour delves further into Word 97 and shows you how to format your document's text. In addition, you see how the Word 97 templates and wizards practically create your documents for you.

Q&A

Q How can I eliminate the wavy lines beneath some of the text I type?

A The red and gray wavy lines indicate that Word 97 found a spelling or grammatical error. Word 97 is not perfect, just helpful, and sometimes Word 97 incorrectly flags such errors when they are not really errors. You learn in Hour 7 how to handle the errors and teach Word 97 what is correct.

Q Does it matter whether I press Tab or several spaces when I want to move text to the right?

A In some cases, you see that pressing Tab and the spacebar several times produces the same results, but you should reserve Tab presses for those times when you want to indent or align several lines of text. You can more easily adjust tab spacing later if you want to change the indention.

Q I create special charts and tables with Word 97, and I don't always want AutoCorrect to do its thing. How can I keep AutoCorrect from making certain corrections?

A Select the AutoCorrect corrections you need from the Tools|Options menu. If you want AutoCorrect to make a particular correction most but not all the time, you can always reverse a single AutoCorrect correction by pressing the toolbar's Undo button as soon as Word 97 makes the AutoCorrect change.

5

Hour 6

Formatting with Word 97

This hour demonstrates Word 97's formatting features, which add style and flair to your writing. Not only can Word 97 help your writing read better, it can help your writing *look* better as well.

Word 97 supports character, paragraph, and even document formatting. You can control every aspect of your document. If you don't want to take the time to format individual elements, Word 97 can format your entire document automatically for you. When you begin learning Word 97, type your text before formatting it so that you get your thoughts in the document while they're still fresh. After you type your document, you can format its text.

The highlights of this hour include

- ☐ Which character formats Word 97 supports
- ☐ What fonts are all about
- ☐ Why you should not get too fancy with most document formats
- ☐ How to apply paragraph formats
- ☐ When different views are helpful
- ☐ Where to see a preview of your printed document
- ☐ How to format an entire document with a predefined style

Simple Character Formatting

When you want to emphasize text to make a point, you can *format* your text. The three standard character formatting styles are underline, boldface, and italicized text. Figure 6.1 shows a document with boldfaced and italicized text on the top half and with underlined text on the bottom half.

These special formatting styles are called *character formats* even though you can apply them to multiple characters, paragraphs, and complete documents as easily as you can apply them to single characters. The character formatting styles attach themselves to whatever text you select for the formatting.

NEW TERM   A *format* is the shape, size, and position that you can apply to selected text, margins, headers, footers, page numbers, and virtually any other element of a document.

Figure 6.1.

Character formatting improves your documents.

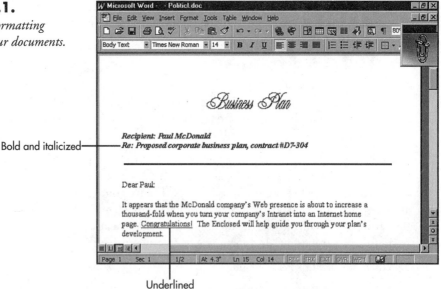

Bold and italicized ──────

Underlined

Express but don't impress. You learn how to add a lot of fancy styles in this hour. Too many styles make your documents look busy and take away from your writing goals. Add only enough fanciness to add appeal to your writing.

To apply boldface, italic, or underlining, for example, select the text that you want to format and click the Bold, Italic, or Underline toolbar buttons. To apply formatting to a single word, first click within the word and then click the appropriate toolbar button.

> The shortcut keys Ctrl+B (boldface), Ctrl+I (italic), and Ctrl+U (underlining) apply character formatting, and your hands don't have to leave your keyboard to click the mouse. Press one of the shortcuts before you type the text you want to format. When you want to stop formatting, press the same shortcut key to deactivate the formatting.

Applying Fonts

One of the most common formatting changes you can make is to change the font used in your document. A *font* determines the way your characters look, from their size to their curliness to their elegance. Fonts have different names, such as *Courier New* and *Schoolbook*.

NEW TERM   The *font* is a collection of letters, numbers, and special characters that contain the same typeface, thickness, and size. Consider *font* to be synonymous to *character*.

Consider your daily newspaper. The banner across the top of the page probably looks like old Gothic letters; the headlines are more standard type. Either might or might not be boldfaced, underlined, or italicized (although a newspaper rarely applies underlining styles). Throughout your paper, the articles might contain the same font as the headline, but the headline font may be larger and heavier than the articles'.

The size of a font is measured in *points*. One point is 1/72nd of an inch. As a standard rule of thumb, a 10- or 12-point size is standard and readable for most word-processed writing. As you type and move your text cursor throughout a document, Word 97 displays the current font name and size on the formatting toolbar. To change any selected text's font name or size, click the drop-down arrow to the right of the Font Name box, or use the Font Size drop-down list to select a new value.

NEW TERM   A *point* is a font character measurement that equals 1/72nd of an inch.

Instead of using the toolbar to apply font and other format changes, you can set formats in the Font dialog box. When you select Format|Font, Word 97 displays the Font dialog box (shown in Figure 6.2). You can also display the Font dialog box by right-clicking selected text and choosing Font from the pop-up menu.

Not only can you set multiple character formats from one location (the Font dialog box), but Word 97 displays a preview of the font in the dialog box's Preview area. Therefore, you can select various font names, sizes, and styles and see the results before actually closing the dialog

6

box to apply those changes. When the previewed text looks the way you want, select OK and apply those changes to your selected text.

Figure 6.2.

Set many character formats in the Font dialog box.

Step-Up

Notice that the Font dialog box supports character formats that previous Word versions did not support: double strike-through, shadow, outline, emboss, and engrave.

If you select the Hidden character format in the Font dialog box, the hidden text appears on your screen but does not print. Hidden text is great for notes to yourself and explanatory information that supports the surrounding text that you want to print. If you use hidden text, be sure to check the Hidden text option in the Tools | Options View page. Otherwise, the hidden text won't show up on your screen.

Applying Color

One special character format that you can apply almost as easily as the three from the previous section is color. When you click the drop-down arrow next to the Font Color toolbar button, Word 97 displays the small Font Color dialog box (shown in Figure 6.3). Click a color, and Word 97 changes your selected text to that color.

Figure 6.3.

You can change the color of text.

> **Step-Up**
>
> The Font Color toolbar button did not appear on previous versions of Word's formatting toolbar. In addition to text, you can apply color to the document's background by selecting Format | Background.

Remember that Office 97 now easily links with the Internet and the Internet's fancy and colorful World Wide Web pages (see Hour 24, "Creating Web Pages with Office 97"). When you use Word 97 to create a colorful web page, the Font Color button comes in handy.

The Highlight tool on the toolbar does outline text in color but is not a color-formatting tool. Instead, the Highlight tool works great for marking important text that you want to reference later or make stand out to the next reader. When you select text and click the Highlight tool (click the Highlight tool's drop-down arrow to change the highlighting color), Word 97 highlights the text as though you marked your screen with a yellow highlighter pen.

Paragraph Formatting

Some formats work on characters; others are better suited for paragraphs. This section describes the essentials for formatting your paragraphs so that your documents look the way you want them to look.

6

As with all the formatting commands, you can apply a paragraph format *before* typing to apply the formatting to all subsequent paragraphs that you type.

Justifying Text

Perhaps the most common paragraph formats are the justification formats. When you *justify* text, you determine the text's alignment. Word 97 supports these justification options:

☐ Left-justification aligns (makes even) text with the left margin.

☐ Center-justification centers text between the left and right margins.

☐ Right-justification aligns text with the right margin.

☐ Full-justification aligns text with both the left and right margins.

NEW TERM   To *justify* means to align the text flush with the left or right margin (or both as done in a newspaper column) so that it does not show a ragged edge.

The simplest way to justify text is to click anywhere inside the paragraph that you want to justify (or select multiple paragraphs if you want to justify several) and click the toolbar's Align Left, Center, Align Right, or Justify (for full justification) buttons.

Although you can justify multiple paragraphs and even complete documents, a single paragraph is the smallest amount of text you can justify—hence, the term *paragraph format*.

Newspaper, magazine, and newsletter columns are usually fully justified. The text evenly aligns with the left and right margins.

NEW TERM   *Paragraph format* refers to a format that you can apply to one or more selected paragraphs.

Setting Margins and More

The Page Setup dialog box (shown in Figure 6.4), displayed by selecting the File | Page Setup command or by double-clicking the top of the ruler, lets you control your paragraph and page margins. Enter values for your top, bottom, left, and right margins so that your text does not print past the margin limits.

Figure 6.4.

The Page Setup dialog box lets you set margins, page size, and page layout.

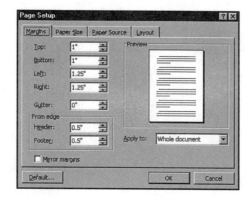

Many printers, especially laser printers, cannot print flush with the edge of the paper. Generally, one-half inch is the minimum margin size these printers allow.

The *gutter* value, if you indicate one, shifts all other measurements away from the inside margin of your page.

NEW TERM The *gutter* is an area of a page you reserve if you plan to bind your document.

The Header and Footer values determine how far from the top and bottom of your pages the header and footer appear if you supply a header or a footer. (Hour 8, "Advanced Word 97," describes headers and footers.)

Using Tab Settings

Click the Tabs command button in the Paragraph dialog box to display the Tabs dialog box (shown in Figure 6.5). A *tab* controls the vertical spacing for certain items in your text. The bottom line is that a tab keeps you from having to press your spacebar many times when you want to insert multiple spaces in your text. In addition, a tab is more accurate when aligning text.

Table 6.1 describes each of the options in the Tabs dialog box. After you set tabs, press your Tab key as you enter paragraph text to move the cursor to the next tab stop.

NEW TERM A *tab stop* is the location on a line where a Tab key press moves the cursor. You set tab stops by adding them on the ruler or from within the Tabs dialog box.

6

Figure 6.5.

The Tabs dialog box lets you specify multiple tab settings.

Table 6.1. The Tabs dialog box options.

Option	Description
Tab stop position	Lets you enter individual measurement values, such as .25" to represent one-fourth of an inch. After you type a value, press Set to add that value to the list of tab settings. To clear a tab stop, select the value and click Clear. Click Clear All to clear the entire tab list.
Alignment	
Left	Left-aligns text at the tab stop (the default).
Center	Centers text at the tab stop.
Right	Right-aligns text at the tab stop.
Decimal	Aligns lists of numbers so that their decimal points align with each other.
Bar	Inserts a vertical bar at the tab stop.
Leader	
None	Removes *leader* characters. A leader is a character that provides a path for the eye to follow across the page within a tab stop. By default, Word 97 displays nothing (blanks only) for tab areas.
....	Displays a series of periods inside the tabs (often used for connecting goods to their corresponding prices in a price list).
-------	Displays a series of hyphens inside the tabs.
_____	Displays a series of underlines inside the tabs.

NEW TERM   A *leader* is a character that Word 97 uses in a tab's blank area.

Later in this hour, the section titled "Making the Ruler Work for You" explains how to use the ruler to set and adjust tab settings.

Setting Indentation and Spacing

If you need to change the *indentation* (the space between the page margin and where the text aligns) or *line spacing* (the amount of blank space between lines), select Format | Paragraph to display the Paragraph dialog box (shown in Figure 6.6).

 Indentation is the space between the page margin and where a line, lines, or paragraph of text aligns.

 Line spacing is the blank space between lines (sometimes called the *leading*).

Figure 6.6.

The Paragraph dialog box holds indentation and spacing values.

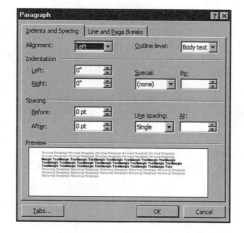

As you change the indentation, Word 97 updates the Preview area at the bottom of the Paragraph dialog box to show your setting results. You can type a Left or Right indentation value or click the arrows to change the current values. A Left indention value indents not only the first line of a paragraph, but the entire paragraph's left margin. A Right indention value indents from the right. You can set off a particular paragraph from surrounding paragraphs, such as a quoted paragraph, by indenting the paragraph by specifying either a Left, Right, or Full (using both) indention value.

Do not use the spacebar to indent text because the text will not align properly.

6

The drop-down Special values—(None), First Line, and *Hanging Indent*—determine how indentation applies itself to the paragraph. If you leave (None) selected, Word 97 indents the complete paragraph by the Left and Right indentation values that you supply. If you select First Line, Word 97 uses the value in the By field to indent only the first line of the selected paragraph.

 NEW TERM A *hanging indent* is an indentation of all lines of a paragraph except the first line.

> If you indent the first line or apply a hanging indent, your Left and Right indentation values still apply to the entire paragraph. The first line and hanging indent values specify the *additional indenting* you want Word 97 to perform on the first or subsequent paragraph lines.

The Spacing section lets you specify exactly how many points you want Word 97 to skip before or after each paragraph. You can also select multiple line spacing by selecting from the Line spacing field.

> Increase or decrease a paragraph's indentation by clicking the Decrease Indent and Increase Indent buttons on the toolbar.

Making the Ruler Work for You

As you specify indentation and tab information, the ruler updates to indicate your settings. Not only does the ruler show settings, but you also can make indentation and tab changes directly on the ruler without using dialog boxes.

Figure 6.7 shows the ruler's various tab stops and indentation handles. Click anywhere on the ruler to add a tab stop after you select the appropriate tab from the tab selection area. To remove a tab, drag the tab stop down off the ruler. By dragging an indentation handle, you can change a paragraph's indentation on-the-fly.

> Double-click the bottom of the ruler to display the Tabs dialog box, and double-click the top of the ruler to display the Page Setup dialog box.

First line indent   Hanging indent   Ruler   Right indent

Figure 6.7.

Use the ruler to set and change tabs and indents.

Click here to select a tab

Left indent

Left tab stop

Center tab stop

Right tab stop

Decimal tab stop

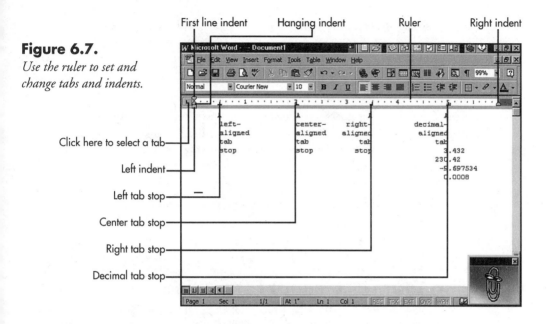

Inserting Line and Page Breaks

Lines and pages do not always break the way you need them to. For example, you may want to end a page early because you want to insert a chart at the top of the next page or start a new chapter. Perhaps you want to put a sentence on a line by itself to make it stand out from the surrounding text. The Format|Paragraph dialog box's Line and Page Breaks tab lets you control the way your document's lines and pages start and stop. When you click the Paragraph dialog box's Line and Page Breaks tab, Word 97 displays Figure 6.8's settings.

Figure 6.8.

Control the way your paragraph lines break.

A *widow* is the last line of a paragraph that prints at the top of the next page, and an *orphan* is the first line of a paragraph that prints at the bottom of a page. Usually, widowed and orphaned lines look incomplete. If you click the Widow/Orphan control option, Word 97 adjusts page breaks, if necessary, so that two or more paragraph lines always begin a page and so that two or more paragraph lines always end a page.

The Keep Lines Together check box ensures that a page break never breaks the selected paragraph. The Keep with Next check box ensures that a page break never appears between the current paragraph and the next. The Page Break Before check box forces a page break before the selected paragraph even if a page break would not normally appear for several more lines.

By enabling the Suppress Line Numbers check box, law pleadings and other documents with line numbers will not print the lines on the selected paragraph lines. If you've set up automatic hyphenation (described later in this hour), the Don't Hyphenate option deactivates automatic hyphenation for the selected paragraph.

Viewing Your Document's Formatting

Try this: Type and format some text. Press Shift+F1. The mouse pointer changes to a question mark. When you click over text, Word 97 displays all the information about that selected text, including the character and paragraph formatting applied. This is neat! (Figure 6.9 shows an example.) To get rid of the formatting description, press Shift+F1 again.

Figure 6.9.

You can find out a lot about formats!

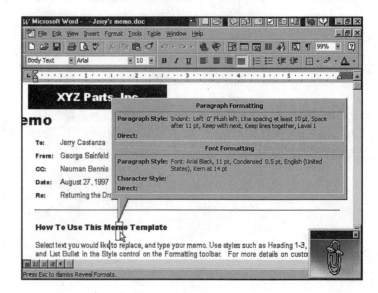

Formatting with Styles

A *style* is a collection of character and paragraph formats you can apply to your document. Each style has a name. Word 97 comes with several styles, and you can also create your own.

 A *style* is a named collection of formatting styles applied regularly on specific kinds of text such as headings.

Click the drop-down arrow on the Style toolbar field to see the names of the styles. When you select a style, Word 97 applies it to the current paragraph and subsequent paragraphs that you type. If you want to change a style's formatting or create a new style, select Format | Style to show the Style dialog box. If you want to modify the current style, click Modify; if you want to create a new style, click New.

Suppose that you routinely write résumés for other people, and you have created three separate sets of character and paragraph formats that work well, respectively, for the title of a résumé and an applicant's personal information and work history. Instead of defining each of these formats every time you create a résumé, format a paragraph with each style and store the styles under their own names (such as Résumé Title, Résumé Personal, and Résumé Work). The next time you write a résumé, you only need to click the Style toolbar button and select Résumé Title from the style list. When you then type the title, the title looks the way you want it to look without your having to designate any character or paragraph format.

Understanding Document Views

Now that you can format your document, you need to know how to display it onscreen to make the best use of the formatting during the editing process. Word 97 supports several display views that present your document in different ways. Use the View menu to select a view, or click one of the view buttons on the horizontal scrollbar above the status bar (you must be displaying the scrollbars to see the view buttons).

The Normal View

For routine document creation and editing, the Normal view presents the cleanest screen approach and shows all character and paragraph formatting. If you choose to display special formatting characters such as italicized text, you'll see those in the Normal view as well. All screen shots in this and the previous chapters show the Normal view.

The Online Layout View

If you've prepared your document for outlining by using the built-in styles (such as Heading 1 and Heading 2), the Online Layout view lets you quickly traverse your document. As Figure 6.10 shows, the Online Layout view shows your document's headings on the left and the details on the right. Jump to any document text simply by clicking the appropriate heading.

6

Figure 6.10.

Traverse a document quickly using the Online Layout view.

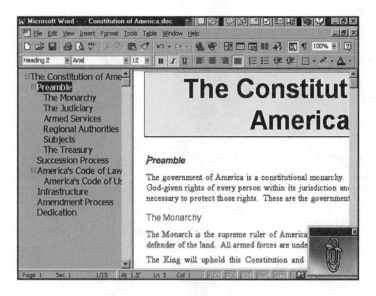

 Click and drag the screen's dividing line right or left if you want to see more of the headings or more of the detail. If you cannot read all the headings, point to a heading and Word 97 shows you that full heading title without requiring you to resize the window.

The Page Layout

If you want to view your document exactly the way it will print, select the Page Layout view. The Page Layout view shows any details, such as headers and footers, and shows you where page breaks occur.

The Outline View

The Outline view gives you true expandable and collapsible views of your document in outline form. If you prefer to write from an outline, you can. Use the predefined heading styles to create your document's outline, and then expand on the outline when you're ready to add detail. (Figure 6.11 shows a document's Outline view.)

 Surprisingly, Word 97 offers no way to print the Outline view.

Figure 6.11.

If you work with outlines, the Outline view is for you.

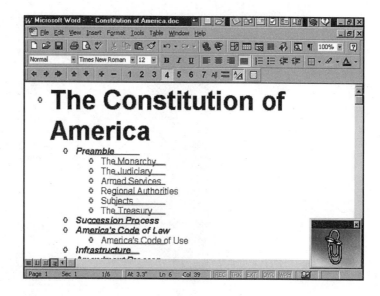

The Outline view presents the structure of the document, and shows exactly as much detail as you want to see. By clicking the heading numbers (corresponding to the styles Heading 1, Heading 2, and so on) or the plus and minus signs on the Outlining toolbar, you can see more or less detail. All the detail stays with your document, but all the detail does not appear at one time.

Full Screen View

When you need to see as much of your document as possible, select View | Full Screen. Word 97 hides the toolbars, status bars, and menus to give more screen real estate to your document. Click the Restore window or press Esc to return to the previous viewing state.

Print Preview

Print Preview shows how your document will look on paper. As Figure 6.12 shows, you can click Print Preview's Multiple Pages button to display several pages. You get a bird's-eye view of your printed document, which enables you to predict print format problems without wasting time or paper.

Click the Close button or press Esc to exit the preview.

6

Figure 6.12.

View how your printed document's pages will look.

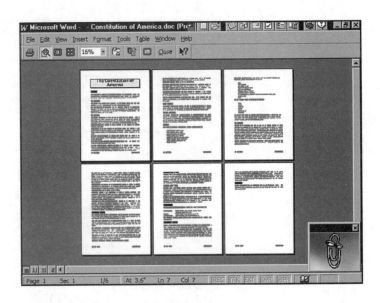

If you want a closer view of your Print Preview, click the magnifying glass mouse pointer anywhere on the preview to see the preview in more detail.

Determine Your Own View

The Zoom dialog box (shown in Figure 6.13), displayed by selecting View|Zoom, enables you to adjust the display size of your characters onscreen so that you can see more text on the screen. If your margins and font size make your document's text wider than your screen size but you want to see entire lines, shrink the percentage shown in the Zoom dialog box to squeeze more text onto your screen. You can enable Word 97 to adjust the size to fill your entire screen by selecting the Page Width option.

Figure 6.13.

Display as much of your text as you need to.

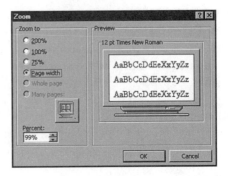

Inserting Numbers and Bullets

Word 97 makes numbered and bulleted lists easy to produce. If you've set the proper AutoFormat options (see Hour 5, "Welcome to Word 97"), follow these steps to create a properly formatted and indented numbered list:

1. Press Tab to start the first numbered item.
2. Type the number, such as 1. (follow the number with a period).
3. Press Tab.
4. Type the text that goes with the first numbered item.
5. Press Enter. The Office Assistant (if you've activated it) indicates that Word 97 converted your previous text to a numbered list. You can change it back to regular text, deactivate the numbering, or click OK to continue the list.
6. Press Cancel if Office Assistant is present. Word 97 automatically formats the first item and types the second number to prepare you for the next item.
7. Keep entering numbered items. When you finish, press Enter after a number, and Word 97 converts that final numbered line to regular text.

In other words, to create a well-formatted numbered list, just start typing the list! Word 97 formats and numbers your list after you enter the first item. If you want to convert a series of paragraphs or lines to a numbered list, select the text and click the Numbering toolbar button.

Here's another numbering trick: Before typing the numbered list, click the Numbering toolbar button. Word 97 starts the list, types the first number for you, inserts a tab, and you only have to complete the numbered item. Word 97 continues to add the numbers as you complete the list.

> One of the best features of Word 97 is that you can delete and insert numbered items from and to numbered lists, and Word 97 automatically renumbers the other items!

If you want to create a bulleted list, type the items to be bulleted, select those lines, and click the Bullets button. Again, when you add and delete items, Word 97 automatically adds or removes the bullets and formats new items.

> Control the size of the bullets as well as the styles in your bulleted and numbered lists by selecting Format | Bullets and Numbering.

6

Letting Word 97 Format for You

Instead of messing with all these character and paragraph formatting options, just let Word 97 do all the work! Type your document using no special format (except pressing Enter to end each paragraph and add blank lines), and then select Format | Style Gallery to display the Style Gallery dialog box (shown in Figure 6.14).

Figure 6.14.

Let Word 97 format everything in style.

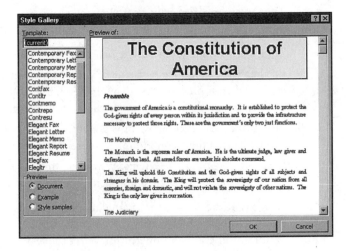

As you select from the style templates, Word 97 updates the preview window to show what your document would look like if you let Word 97 automatically format the entire document in that style. The styles range from contemporary to elegant to formal.

A Word About Word 97's Wizards

This hour has discussed formatting your text and document as you type text or after you've entered the text. Word 97's wizards, however, set up your document's format before you create your document. When you select File | New, Word 97 displays a list of wizards and templates from which you can select.

Templates contain formatting that you can use, as well as automated buttons that you can click to format certain text elements. Wizards are more interactive and produce more customized documents than do templates.

For example, select File|New, click the Publications tab, and double-click the Newsletter Wizard icon. Word 97 walks you through a step-by-step procedure to create a newsletter.

Summary

This hour explained the various format options available to Word 97 users. Keep your audience in mind; don't overdo formats or your documents look cluttered. Keep your documents readable and remember your presentation as you format.

You can apply the character formats to individual characters as well as to selected text and the entire document. Paragraph formats control the spacing and justification of paragraphs. The views enable you to see your document from various perspectives so that you can determine whether your formats work well together. Perhaps the best indicator of style is the print preview, which shows how your document will look when you print it.

The next hour moves into document management and Word 97 customization. Depending on how you use Word 97, you might want to change the way Word 97 behaves in certain situations.

Q&A

Q How can I type an italicized paragraph?

A Before typing any text that you want formatted in any way, set up the formatting. If you want to italicize a word, phrase, or an entire document that you're about to type, press Ctrl+I (or click the toolbar's Italic button) before you type, and Word 97 italicizes the text. If you've already typed a paragraph that you want to italicize, select the paragraph and press Ctrl+I or click the Italic toolbar button.

Q How can I see hidden text on both the screen and printer?

A Select Tools|Options and select the Hidden Text option to display hidden text on your screen. The hidden text still does not display on your printer. That's why it's called hidden! Nevertheless, you can print hidden text if you click the Hidden Text option on the Print page of the Options dialog box.

Q How can I see my entire page on the screen at once?

A If you have an extremely high-resolution monitor and graphics adapter card, you can probably see an entire document page when you select the full-screen view with View|Full Screen. If you want to see the toolbars, menu, and status bar, however, you probably have to adjust the zoom factor when you select View|Zoom. After you display the Zoom dialog box, click the Page Width option to enable Word 97 to fit the text within your screen width, or you can control the width using the Percent option. The only other way to see an entire page is to select the Print Preview mode; in preview mode, you can make simple margin adjustments but no text changes.

6

Q How can I make margin adjustments in Print Preview mode?

A You should adjust the margins only when displaying a single page. Therefore, if you see multiple page previews, click the One Page button to show a single page. Then click the View Ruler bar to add a ruler to the top of the page. Use your mouse to drag and adjust the left, right, top, and bottom margins. Although such margin adjustments are not as accurate as you can set from within the Page Setup dialog box, you can visually see the results as you make margin adjustments on-the-fly.

Hour 7

Managing Documents and Customizing Word 97

This hour works more globally with your documents than the previous two hours. Instead of concentrating on specific editing skills, you learn how to manage your document properties. Word 97 can keep track of several document-related items, and that tracking really comes in handy if you work in a group environment.

The proofing tools in Word 97 are powerful and work as you type. The spell checker acts as a mentor looking over your shoulder with a dictionary, supplying you with suggested spellings for mistyped words. Additionally, Word 97 helps with grammar, hyphenation, and synonyms.

The highlights of this hour include

- [ ] What document properties are
- [ ] Where to locate and change a document's properties
- [ ] How to request the spell and grammar checker

☐ Why you need to proof documents manually despite the proofing tools in Word 97

☐ How to customize Word 97 to behave the way you want

☐ How to update the file conversion capability in Word 97

Understanding Document Properties

Each Word 97 document (as well as the other Office 97 documents) has properties. A *property* is information related to a particular document, such as the author's name and creation date. If you do not specify properties, Word 97 adds its own to your document. You see the Properties dialog box (shown in Figure 7.1) when you select File | Properties.

 Information related to a certain document, such as the number of paragraphs inside the document, the document name, or the document's author, is called a *property*. Other objects, such as icons, menu items, and toolbars also have properties of their own.

Figure 7.1.

Track your document's properties.

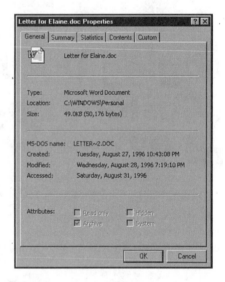

The tabs in the Properties dialog box provide the following information:

☐ **General:** Contains the document's file information, including the date and time you created, last modified, and last accessed the document.

☐ **Summary:** Tracks a document title, author (name to which software is registered by default), keywords, and comments you enter about the document.

☐ **Statistics:** Tracks the document's numeric statistics, such as character, word, page counts, and total editing time.

☐ **Contents:** Describes the parts of your document, such as the header, body, and footer.

☐ **Custom:** Keeps track of information you want in the order you specify. You can keep track of customized properties, such as the department responsible for creating or maintaining the document, a project group name that works on the document, and the person responsible for typing the document's information. As you add items to the Properties list box, indicate the item's data type (such as text or date) so that Word 97 can properly format the property value that you want to track. The Custom tab is great for departments in which many people see and edit the same set of documents.

Some properties are available elsewhere in Word 97. For example, you can find a document's statistics, such as word and paragraph counts, by selecting Tools | Word Count. Often, you can select from the menu option more quickly than displaying the document properties.

> If you create numerous documents and continually search through your disk files for particular ones, try adding search keywords to the Properties Summary page so that you can more quickly find that document using the Advanced Search option in the Open dialog box.

Using Word 97's Advanced Proofreaders

Word 97 offers these proofreading services for your writing:

☐ **Spell checker:** Checks your document's spelling either from beginning to end or as you enter it into the document.

☐ **Grammar checker:** Checks your document's grammar either from beginning to end or as you enter it into the document.

☐ **Thesaurus:** Provides synonyms when you need them.

NEW TERM   A *thesaurus* is a list of synonyms.

☐ **Hyphenation:** Automatically hyphenates words at the end of lines, when appropriate, either from beginning to end or as you enter the text into the document.

7

Step-Up

Previous versions of Word did not check grammar as you typed your documents. You could request a manual grammar check only after you typed the document.

> Word 97's built-in proofreading tools do not eliminate your proofing
> responsibilities! No matter how good Word 97 is, Word 97 cannot match
> human skills when deciphering the written language. For example, Word
> 97's spell check has no problem with this sentence:
>
> *Wee road two the see too sea the waives.*
>
> The proofreading tools work only as guides to find those problems you
> might have missed during your own extensive proofing.

Perhaps the most important reason to learn the proofreading tools is that the other Office 97 products use similar features. Therefore, after you learn how to use Word 97's proofreading tools, you also know how to use the tools for an Excel 97 worksheet or an Access 97 database.

Using the Spell Checker

Word 97 automatically checks your spelling and your grammar as you type your document. Any time you see red wavy underlines and gray wavy underlines as you type, Word 97 is letting you know about a possible spelling problem (the red line) or grammar problem (the green line).

Depending on the options you (or someone else) have set, your version of Word 97 might not check both spelling and grammar as you type. Therefore, if you don't see any wavy lines, you should check your document's spelling and grammar after you've typed the document so that you don't miss anything.

> To turn on and off the Check Spelling as You Type option, choose
> Tools | Options, and then click the Spelling & Grammar tab. On that tab,
> check the Check Spelling as You Type check box.

When you see a red wavy line, you can correct the problem in these ways:

- ☐ Edit the misspelling.
- ☐ Right-click the misspelling to display the pop-up menu shown in Figure 7.2. Word 97 offers you the following options:
    - ☐ Ignore all subsequent similar misspellings (in case you want to type foreign words or formal names but you don't want to add those words to Word 97's spelling dictionaries).
    - ☐ Add the word to Word 97's dictionary so that Word 97 no longer flags the word as misspelled.

☐ Select AutoCorrect and choose a correct word to add the misspelling to the AutoCorrect entries so that Word 97 subsequently corrects the word for you on-the-fly.

☐ Display Word 97's more comprehensive Spelling dialog box (shown in Figure 7.3).

Figure 7.2.

Select your spell-correction choice when Word 97 finds a misspelling.

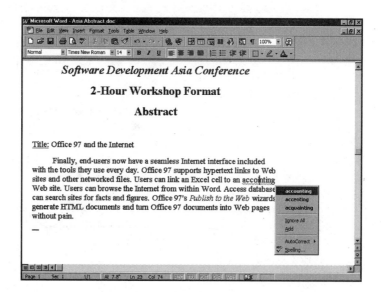

Word 97 enables you to easily remove words that you accidentally add to your spelling dictionary. Select Tools | Options and click the Spelling & Grammar tab. Click the Dictionaries button. Select the dictionary from which you want to delete (most probably the Custom.dic dictionary, which is the default unless you've created a new customized dictionary), and click the Edit button. Word 97 displays the dictionary's words in a document so that you can delete the word or words you no longer want (you can also edit any existing words or add new words). Click the Save toolbar button. You must also turn on automatic spell checking by displaying the Spelling & Grammar page once again and checking the option labeled Check Spelling as You Type.

7

☐ Ignore the misspelling and leave the red wavy line.

☐ Ignore the misspelling, but check the entire document's spelling when you finish typing the document.

Step-Up

Previous versions of Word 97 did not enable you to add AutoCorrect entries from the pop-up spelling menu as you can do in Word 97 when you right-click a spelling problem.

Figure 7.3.

The Spelling dialog box offers more options than the pop-up menu.

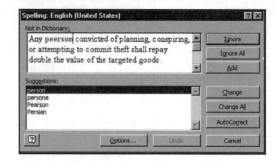

The Spelling dialog box appears when you click the pop-up menu Spelling option for a misspelled word or when you select Spelling and Grammar from the Tools menu. Table 7.1 lists the options in the Spelling dialog box.

When you check the spelling of your document from Tools | Spelling and Grammar, Word 97 checks from the cursor's current position down to the end of your document. If you want Word 97 to check your entire document's spelling in one step (assuming you've turned off the automatic spell checking that occurs as you type), move your cursor to the top of your document (by pressing Ctrl+Home) before requesting the spell check.

Table 7.1. The Spelling dialog box options.

Option	Description
Ignore	Tells Word 97 to ignore only this single occurrence of the misspelling.
Ignore All	Tells Word 97 to ignore *all* occurrences of this misspelling in this document.
Add	Adds the word to Word 97's spelling dictionary so that Word 97 subsequently knows the word's spelling.

Option	Description
Change	Changes this single misspelling to the selected correction.
Change All	Changes all the document's misspellings of the current word to the selected correction.
AutoCorrect	Adds the misspelling and selected correction to your collection of AutoText entries.
Check Grammar	Enables you to turn the automatic grammar checker on or off for this document despite the settings in effect.
Options	Displays the Spelling & Grammar options page (shown in Figure 7.4) on which you can modify the behavior of the spelling and grammar checker.
Undo	Undoes your most recent spell correction. The spell checker supports multiple undo levels so that you can undo more than one correction you've made.

Figure 7.4.

Change the spell checker's behavior from this Spelling & Grammar options dialog box.

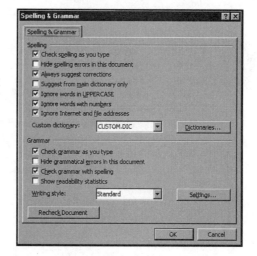

Using the Grammar Checker

When you see a gray wavy line beneath a word, Word 97 is warning you about a possible grammar problem. Figure 7.5 shows the pop-up menu Word 97 displays when you right-click a gray wavy-lined word.

7

Figure 7.5.

Word 97 displays a pop-up menu when you right-click a word with a gray wavy underline.

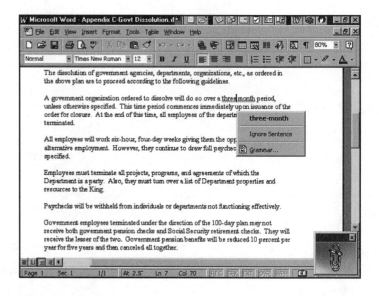

Wait until you finish your document before you check the grammar. The grammar-correction process takes a few minutes to complete. In most cases, you should turn off the automatic grammar checker to speed Word 97's response time as you type your document (to do so, select Tools | Options, select the Spelling & Grammar tab, and then uncheck the Check Grammar as You Type check box). When you finish typing the document, select Tools | Spelling and Grammar to check the grammar on the entire document. You can click the toolbar's Spelling and Grammar button to start the process as well.

Keep Office Assistant turned on when you check grammar. Microsoft added lots of plain-spoken grammar-correcting advice to the Office Assistant's repertoire of helpful topics.

As with the spelling pop-up menu, you can replace the grammar problem with the suggested word or words, ignore the suspected problem (just because Word 97 indicates a problem does not necessarily mean that one exists), or you can start the full grammar-checking system to correct that problem as well as the rest of the document.

When you check a document's grammar from the Tools | Spelling and Grammar option (to check the entire document) or by selecting the full grammar check from the pop-up menu, Word 97 displays the same Spelling & Grammar dialog box you see when you check for spelling only. However, as Figure 7.6 shows, the Office Assistant chimes in with its advice as well. The Office Assistant advice often provides very clear descriptions and examples of why your grammar might have a problem at the flagged location.

Figure 7.6.

Select your grammar-correction choice when Word 97 finds a problem.

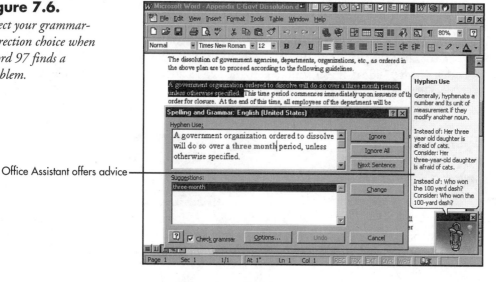

Office Assistant offers advice

Using Automatic Hyphenation

Word 97 can hyphenate your text as you type, or you can manually hyphenate your entire document. Word 97 supports three kinds of hyphens:

- Regular hyphens, which Word 97 uses to break words at the end of lines (when needed) to maintain proper document formatting. You must turn on automatic hyphenation by selecting Tools | Language | Hyphenation and checking the option labeled Automatically Hyphenate Document.

- Optional hyphens, which break special words (*AutoCorrect* becomes *Auto-Correct*, for example) only if those words appear at the end of lines (press Ctrl+- to indicate where you want the *optional hyphen* as you type the word).

NEW TERM   An *optional hyphen* breaks special terms and proper names only if those words appear at the end of a line.

- Nonbreaking hyphens, which keep certain hyphenated words together at all times; for example, if the hyphenated name *Brian-Kent* appears at the end of a line and you want to prevent Word 97 from breaking apart the names at the end of a line, press Ctrl+Shift+Hyphen to add that word's hyphen when you type the word.

NEW TERM   A *nonbreaking hyphen* keeps two hyphenated words together so that they never break at the end of a line.

You need to indicate optional and nonbreaking hyphens only when you type special words that Word 97 would not typically recognize, such as company names and special terms.

7

You can adjust the amount of hyphenation that Word 97 performs. Select Tools|Language|Hyphenation to display the Hyphenation dialog box (shown in Figure 7.7). The Hyphenation zone field enables you to determine the amount of space between the end of a line's last word and the right margin (a higher value reduces the number of hyphens that Word 97 adds). If you want to keep the hyphenation to a minimum, consider limiting the number of consecutive lines that Word 97 can hyphenate at one time by specifying a Limit consecutive hyphens to field value.

Figure 7.7.

Specify automatic hyphenation.

To hyphenate your document manually after you've created it, select Tools|Language|Hyphenation and click Manual. Word 97 prompts for your approval at each hyphen location.

If you want to stop Word 97 from hyphenating particular paragraphs, select those paragraphs, and then select Format|Paragraph, click the Line and Page Breaks tab, and check the Don't Hyphenate option.

> If you export your document text to another program or computer system (such as a desktop publishing or typesetting system) for publication, do not have Word 97 hyphenate your document. The target system that produces the final output should control the hyphenation, if possible. If you have Word 97 hyphenate your document, hyphens may appear in the middle of lines if the typesetter fails to eliminate all of Word 97's hyphens.

Using the Thesaurus

When you just can't seem to think of a particular word, you can type a *synonym* (a different word whose meaning is similar) and solicit Word 97's thesaurus for a suggestion. To see a list of synonyms, select a word (or click anywhere in the word) and select Tools|Language|Thesaurus (or press Shift+F7). Word 97 displays the Thesaurus dialog box (shown in Figure 7.8).

NEW TERM   A *synonym* is a word whose meaning is similar to another.

Figure 7.8.

Find synonyms fast.

From the Thesaurus dialog box, you can select a replacement word (Word 97 then automatically replaces the original word with the replacement), or use the replacement word list to look up additional synonyms. For example, if you cannot find a good synonym for *dissolve* but one of the replacement words for *dissolve* is *liquefy*, look up synonyms for *liquefy* by selecting the *liquefy* entry in the Thesaurus dialog box and clicking Look Up. Through this link of related words, you might find the synonym for which you're looking.

> Use the Thesaurus dialog box when you want to see *antonyms* (words with meanings that are opposite to the selected word). Word 97 supplies antonyms for some of the words as well. Click the Antonyms entry to see the antonyms.

NEW TERM *Antonyms* are words with opposite meanings.

Customizing Word 97 to Work for You

If you don't like the way Word 97 does something, you can usually customize Word 97 to act the way you want. The Tools menu contains options that enable you to customize Word 97:

- ☐ **Customize:** Enables you to change the layout of Word 97's toolbars and menus
- ☐ **Options:** Enables you to control the behavior of most of Word 97's automatic and manual editing features

Using the Tools I Customize Features

Figure 7.9 shows the Customize dialog box, which appears when you select Tools | Customize.

The Toolbars tab enables you to specify exactly which toolbars you want to see, if any, during your editing sessions. Too many toolbars can clutter your screen and take away editing space, but different toolbars are useful at different times. For example, display the Tables and Borders toolbar any time you want to create or edit tables in your documents.

7

Figure 7.9.

Customize toolbars and menus.

Most people modify the Commands tab when they want to add or remove an item from the menus in Word 97. Select the menu from the Categories list, and Word 97 displays that menu's items in the Commands list. You then can change a menu label or select one from the list that Word 97 doesn't already display for that menu item. Additionally, if you start automating Word 97 with *macros* (predefined keyboard shortcuts) or Visual Basic programs (which require some computer-programming skills), the Commands tab enables you to hook your own procedure commands to new menu items.

The Options tab controls enable you to increase the size of the toolbar icons to read them more easily (at the expense of some editing area), to determine whether you want to see ToolTips, and to determine whether you want shortcut keys attached to those ToolTips.

Using the Tools | Options Features

Tools | Options is the Library of Congress of Word 97 options. From this dialog box, you can modify the behavior of these Word 97 features:

- [ ] **View:** Changes the way Word 97 displays documents and windows.
- [ ] **General:** Determines colors, animation, behavior, and the measurement standard (such as inches or centimeters).
- [ ] **Edit:** Changes the way Word 97 responds during your editing sessions.
- [ ] **Print:** Determines several printing options.
- [ ] **Save:** Specifies how you want Word 97 to save document changes.
- [ ] **Spelling & Grammar:** Lists several spell-checking and grammar-checking settings that you can change. This is one place where you can turn these options on or off.
- [ ] **File Locations:** Enables you to set disk-drive locations for common files.
- [ ] **Compatibility:** Lists a plethora of options you can change to make Word 97 look and feel like other word processors, including previous versions of Word.
- [ ] **User Information:** Holds name, initials, and address of the registered party for use with document summaries and automatic return addresses.

☐ **Track Changes:** Determines the format Word 97 uses when you make changes to documents in a group environment or when you want to track several revisions for the same document. (Word 97 can keep track of multiple versions of a document.)

Correcting Word 97's File Conversion

If you ever work with documents from Word 95, as is the case if you share documents with other users who have not upgraded to Word 97, you should update your copy of Word 97 so that you can accurately convert your documents to Word 95.

Despite Word 97's tremendous power, one simple item that Microsoft left out of Word 97 is the Word 95 document conversion utility. If you create a document in Word 97 and give that document, on disk or via email, to a Word 95 user, the Word 95 user cannot read your document file because Word 97 saves with extra formatting features that Word 95 does not recognize.

The most surprising aspect of Word 97 is its *lack* of a Word 95 converter, especially when you consider the following:

☐ Word 95 was the version of Word that appeared right before Word 97, so many people need to work with both during an upgrade and conversion time period.

☐ Word 97 acts as if it has a Word 95 converter. If you select File | Save As to save a document, and then click the Save as Type drop-down listbox, you'll find a document type listed as Word 6.0/95 (see Figure 7.10). If you select Word 6.0/95 and save the file, however, Word 97 saves the file in another format called *RTF* (for *Rich Text Format*). Although Word 95 can read RTF files, you lose some advanced formatting styles when you load the document into Word 95 because Word 97 does not perform a true Word 95 conversion.

Microsoft offers a free solution for this problem. You need to go to Microsoft's web site, which contains the conversion utility, and update your Word 97. The conversion utility works for all Office 97 products, including Office 97 SBE, Office 97 Professional, and Office 97 Standard. The web site address is `http://www.microsoft.com/office/office97/servicerelease/` and you'll find that the patch updates several other Office 97 products and adds speed to Office 97 if your PC uses one of Intel's MMX-based CPUs. The Word 95 patch is part of the update named *Office 97 Service Release 1*.

7

Check the Microsoft site (`http://www.microsoft.com/msdownload/default.asp#sup`) often for free downloads and patches. Microsoft updates this site frequently.

Figure 7.10.

Word 97 acts as if the Word 95 conversion exists.

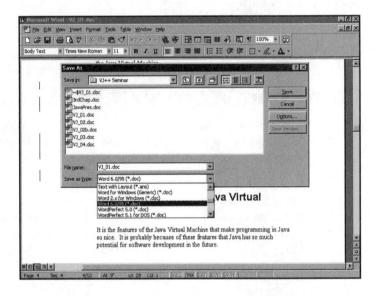

If you don't have Internet access, you can call Microsoft's product support number at (206) 882-8080 and ask for the Office 97 Service Release 1 ordering instructions.

Summary

This hour explained how to manage your documents through the use of document properties. The document properties contain count statistics as well as other pertinent information that stays with your documents. If you work in an office environment, the properties help maintain order when many people edit the same document.

Part of managing your documents is proofing them to make them more readable and correct. The proofing tools in Word 97 include a spell checker, grammar checker, hyphenation capabilities, and thesaurus. Although these tools don't replace human proofreading, they can help you locate problems.

You can customize almost any part of Word 97. This hour gives you just a glimpse of the many modifications that can be made to Word 97. Take the time to peruse the Tools | Options tabs. Even advanced Word 97 users forget some of the options that can make their editing lives simpler. Check the options screens frequently as you learn Word 97 and you'll make Word 97 work the way you want it to.

The next hour wraps up Word 97 by teaching you its more advanced capabilities.

Q&A

Q   **Does Word 97 update my document-property values for me?**

A   In some cases, Word 97 updates your document's property values. For example, as you type words into your document, Word 97 updates that document's word count. You must specify other user-specific properties, such as the document-search keywords and comments.

Q   **Why should I wait until after I create a document to proof it?**

A   Most Word 97 users prefer to turn on the automatic spell-checker but wait until their document is finished before hyphenating and checking the grammar. During the editing process, edits frequently change hyphenation locations; depending on your computer's speed, Word 97 might slow down considerably to update changed hyphens when you change lines. Additionally, the grammar checker has to work constantly as you create your document, not only slowing down your edits but also indicating bad grammar in the places where you might be typing rough-draft material.

Q   **Should I modify Word 97 settings if several people use the same computer?**

A   If you share a computer with others, you should not customize Word 97 without telling the others what you've done. As a group, you might determine that certain Word 97 options are better defined than others, but be sure to make customization changes only with the consent of others. Otherwise, the next person who uses Word 97 might think Word 97 no longer can check spelling, when in fact you've only turned off the spell checker temporarily.

7

Hour **8**

Advanced Word 97

This hour wraps up our Word 97 coverage by giving you an idea of Word 97's uncommon features and advanced capabilities. Despite their advanced nature, Word 97's advanced features are not difficult to use.

You'll find lots of tidbits throughout this chapter that you will use as you write. From inserting special characters to creating multiple-column newsletters, Word 97 offers something for everybody's writing needs.

The highlights of this hour include

- ☐ How to type special characters that don't appear on your keyboard
- ☐ How to insert the date, time, and page numbers in your documents
- ☐ When to add AutoText and when to add AutoCorrect entries
- ☐ How to prepare tables for your documents
- ☐ How to convert a single-column document into multiple columns
- ☐ What headers, footers, footnotes, and endnotes are all about

Using Special Characters

Symbols are special characters that don't appear on the standard keyboard. If you want to type special symbols, select Insert | Symbol to display the Symbol dialog box (see Figure 8.1).

 A *symbol* is a special character that doesn't appear on the standard keyboard (such as a copyright symbol).

Figure 8.1.

Find a symbol you want to insert.

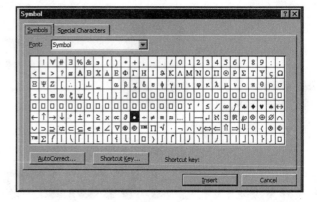

If you don't see the symbol you want to insert, select a different font from the Font drop-down list. Many fonts, such as *WingDings*, supply special symbols from which you can choose.

 If you find yourself inserting the same symbol over and over again, consider adding that symbol to your AutoCorrect table. Click the AutoCorrect button to see the AutoCorrect dialog box (in which Word 97 has already inserted the symbol); type the AutoCorrect entry that you'll use to produce the special symbol, press Enter, and you've created the AutoCorrect entry for that symbol.

In addition to adding a symbol-based AutoCorrect entry, you can assign a shortcut key to any symbol. Click the Shortcut Key button, type a shortcut keystroke (such as Alt+Shift+S), and press Enter. Word 97 then assigns that shortcut keystroke to the special symbol. Subsequently, you won't have to display the Symbol dialog box to insert special symbols.

Many special characters already have AutoCorrect and shortcut-key entries. If you want to see these predefined symbols, click the Symbol dialog box's Special Characters tab to show the Special Characters page (see Figure 8.2). Scroll through the list to see the predefined characters currently set.

Figure 8.2.
Word 97 comes pre-defined with many shortcuts for symbols.

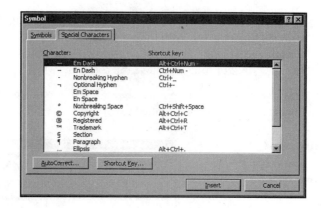

8

Inserting Dates, Page Numbers, and Comments

In addition to special characters, you can insert the date and time at the cursor's current position. Select Insert | Date and Time, and select the date and time format from Word 97's selection list. If you click the Update Automatically option, Word 97 constantly updates the date and time; if you leave the Update Automatically option unchecked, Word 97 keeps the original date and time in the document.

If you want Word 97 to insert page numbers at the top or bottom of the document's printed pages, select Insert | Page Numbers. Word 97 displays the Page Numbers dialog box. Tell Word 97 whether you want the page numbers to appear at the top or bottom of the document pages, as well as on which portion of the page they should appear (left, center, right, inside on facing pages, or outside on facing pages).

> Word 97 can format page numbers in several formats, such as 1, Page 1, -1-, Roman numerals, and even letters of the alphabet. Click Format to select from the various page number format options.

One of the most interesting items that you can insert in a Word 97 document is a *comment*. A comment does not print, but shows up on your screen highlighted in yellow so you're sure to see it.

 A *comment* is a Word 97 document message that you can see on the screen but that does not print.

Suppose that you want to remind yourself to do something later when you edit the document, such as format the title with information you'll research at another time. Just write yourself a comment! The comment acts like a yellow sticky note. The comment stays attached to your text, but you can read or remove the comment whenever you want.

To insert a comment in your text, select Insert | Comment. Word 97 displays the comment's annotation window (see Figure 8.3).

Figure 8.3.

Add comments to your writing.

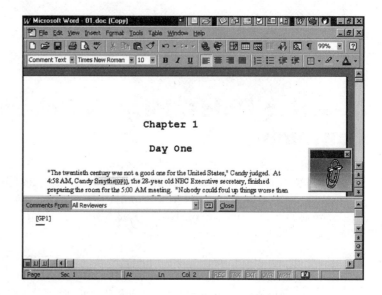

Word 97 names each of your comments using your initials (found in the document property settings). When you type your comment and click Close, Word 97 attaches the comment to your text and indicates the comment by highlighting the anchor text in bright yellow and inserting the comment name inside square brackets. Comments provide a convenient method for leaving messages for co-workers inside documents that you edit as a team.

Subsequently, when you edit your document, you see the yellow comments. If you right-click the comment, Word 97's pop-up menu enables you to edit (or read) the comment, or delete the comment from the text.

Step-Up

Microsoft substituted comments in this version for the annotations you used in previous versions of Word.

Creating and Using AutoText Entries

8

Whereas AutoCorrect is great for quickly inserting formal names and common phrases, AutoText enables you to quickly insert completely formatted multilined text. AutoText is often called *boilerplate text*, which is a publishing term used for text that appears frequently.

NEW TERM *Boilerplate text* is text that you often type, such as your company name and address.

For example, suppose that you often place your bold-faced, 16-point, name and address centered across the top of your personal letters. Instead of typing and formatting this text each time you need it, follow these steps to add the text as an AutoText entry:

1. Type and format the text you want to add to the AutoText entries. Make sure that it's exactly as you want it to be reproduced.

2. Select the text.

3. Select Insert | AutoText | AutoText. Word 97 displays the AutoText page, which shows the AutoText entries currently in effect (see Figure 8.4).

Figure 8.4.

Adding an AutoText entry makes subsequent typing easier.

4. Type an abbreviation for the AutoText entry in the field labeled Enter AutoText Entries Here. You can either type this text to activate the AutoText entry or you can select from the available options listed.

5. Press Enter.

When you subsequently type the AutoText entry's abbreviation and press F3, Word 97 replaces the abbreviation with your expanded formatted AutoText entry. AutoText entries require the F3 keystroke, whereas AutoCorrect entries automatically appear when you type their abbreviations. Nevertheless, AutoText entries can be more complex and span multiple lines, whereas AutoCorrect entries are more limiting.

Step-Up

Word 97 contains an assortment of predefined AutoText entries that previous versions of Word did not support. For example, if you type **Created on** and press F3, Word 97 adds the current date and time to the end of the Created on text in your document. Select Tools|AutoCorrect and click the AutoText tab to see the AutoText entries defined.

If you use the predefined AutoText entries often, consider adding better shortcuts. For example, add a second Created on AutoText entry called cron so that you don't have to type as much to enter the AutoText in your document. To add a cron entry that mimics that of Created on, type **Created on** and press F3 to display the current entry. Highlight the expanded words and select Insert | AutoText | AutoText. Type the new name, **cron**, and click Add to add the new entry.

Adding Tables to Your Documents

Word 97's report-creation power shines when you see how easily you can create customized tables of information inside Word 97. *Tables* are collections of information organized in rows and columns. Tables might contain numbers, text, or combinations of both. Each row and column intersection is called a *cell*. When you use both Word 97 and Excel 97, you might want to embed part of an Excel 97's worksheet into a Word 97 table. Embedded worksheets let you report financial data from within Word 97. (Hour 9, "Excel 97 Workbooks," introduces Excel 97.)

NEW TERM   A *table* is a collection of data organized in rows and columns.

NEW TERM   A *cell* is a single table entry.

Creating a New Table

8

To create a new table, perform these steps:

1. Select Table | Insert Table. Word 97 displays the Insert Table dialog box (see Figure 8.5).

Figure 8.5.

Use the Insert Table dialog box to prepare the new table.

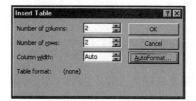

2. Specify the number of columns and rows your table will need. You can change these values later if you need to. Estimate on the high end, however, because it is easier to delete additional rows and columns than to add them.

3. Enter a column width, or leave the Column Width field set to Auto if you want Word 97 to guess the table's width. You can change a table's column width at any time (even after you enter data).

4. When creating your first table, press Enter. After you get used to creating tables, you can click the AutoFormat button to select from a list of predefined table formats, as shown in Figure 8.6.

Figure 8.6.

Word 97 can format your table automatically.

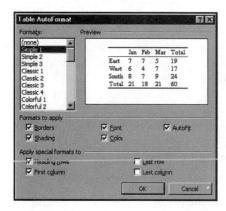

5. Click OK (or press Enter) to close the dialog box. Word 97 creates your table and outlines the table's cells in a grid format.

Word 97 contains two tools that help you build more customized tables. You can create a document with one of the table wizards when you select File | New. Also, you can draw your own tables by clicking the Insert Table toolbar button and dragging the resulting table of cells down and to the right until you've outlined the table size you prefer.

Traversing the Table

One of the easiest ways to enter data in a table's cell is to click the cell (which moves the text cursor to the cell) and type. As you type past the cell's right margin, Word 97 wraps the cell and increases the row height (if needed) to display the complete cell contents.

When you begin typing data, notice that Word 97's automatic formatting might not match the table's data; perhaps one of the columns is too narrow or too wide. Use your mouse to adjust the size of a row or a column's width by clicking and dragging one of the table's four edges in or out. You can also expand or shrink individual columns and rows by dragging their edges.

When you move your cursor to a table's row or column edge, Word 97 changes the mouse pointer to a table-adjuster cursor. When the mouse cursor changes, you can drag your mouse to resize the column or row.

Although you can click a cell with your mouse every time you want to enter or edit the contents of that cell, the table cursor-movement keystrokes come in more handy because you can traverse the table without ever removing your hands from the keyboard. Table 8.1 describes how to traverse a table's rows and columns.

Table 8.1. Moving around a table.

Press this...	To move the table's cursor here
Tab	The next cell
Shift+Tab	The previous cell
Alt+PageUp	The column's top cell
Alt+PageDown	The column's bottom cell
Alt+Home	The current row's first cell
Alt+End	The current row's last cell

8

To highlight a row, click in the margin left of the row; Word 97 highlights the entire row. Drag your mouse down or up to select multiple rows.

Inserting New Columns and Rows

Not creating enough rows or columns for your table is one of the first table problems you'll encounter. To insert or delete rows or columns, select a row or column and right-click your mouse.

Suppose that you need to insert a column. Select the column that will appear *after* the new column by pointing above the column until the mouse pointer changes to a down arrow. Select multiple columns by dragging your mouse to the right after you've selected one column. Right-click your mouse to display a pop-up menu. The menu will be different depending on whether you've selected a row or column first. Select Insert Columns, and Word 97 inserts a new column before the selected column. The right-click menu also contains a Delete Columns command.

To highlight a row, point to the margin left of the row; Word 97 highlights the entire row. Drag your mouse down or up to select multiple rows. When you right-click your mouse, the pop-up menu contains an Insert Rows and a Delete Rows command.

> After you create a simple table, click the table next to it and then select Table | Table AutoFormat to select a style (such as the shaded style in Figure 8.7). The table in Figure 8.7 is only a 3-column table, but Word 97 turned it into a professional-looking chiseled data storehouse.

Figure 8.7.
Make sophisticated tables out of simple ones.

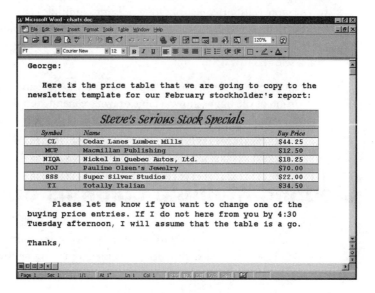

Drawing Tables Freehand

As you've seen, the Tables menu option gives you complete control over tables you create. Word 97 goes one step further to help you create exactly the table you want. The toolbar's Tables and Borders tool enables you to draw tables freehand the way you might draw using a pencil and paper. The Tables and Borders tool enables you to quickly draw tables that don't necessarily have an equal number of columns for each row.

Follow these steps to use the Tables and Borders tool:

1. Click the location in your document where you want the new table.
2. Click the Tables and Borders tool. Your mouse cursor turns into a pencil shape, and the Tables and Borders toolbar appears.
3. Click and drag the pencil cursor diagonally down and across the page. A rectangular table outline appears. When you release the mouse, the outline becomes your table's outline.
4. Continue adding rows and columns by dragging the mouse. Notice that you can draw (by dragging) a partial row or partial column. If you draw a row or column you don't want, click the Tables and Borders Eraser tool and retrace the table lines you want to delete.

You can also change the table's line style by selecting a different style from the Tables and Borders toolbar and change the line's thickness by selecting from the Tables and Borders toolbar's Line Weight listbox.

After you've drawn the table's basic outline, use the Border Color, Outside Border, and Shading Color tools to modify the table's colors. The remaining tools enable you to merge two or more cells into one, split long cells into multiple cells, change a cell's text alignment (as you might do with border columns), equally distribute columns or rows within an area, sort (alphabetically or numerically) cells within a selected row or column, and automatically sum a selected row or column.

Figure 8.8 helps to show what you can do with the freehand Tables and Borders tool. The top portion of the figure shows a table drawn freehand, and the bottom shows the results of entering the table's data and making a few simple edits using the Tables and Borders tools. Although Word has supported the design and creation of tables since its incarnation, Word 97 is the first version to make tables as simple as drawing with a pencil and paper.

Creating Multiple Columns on a Page

When you want to create newspaper-style columns—such as those that appear in newsletters and brochures—configure Word 97 to format your text with multiple columns. You can assign multiple columns to the entire document or to only a selected part of your document.

8

Figure 8.9 shows a document with three columns and a single column for the title area. Generally, you should type your document's text before breaking the document into multiple columns.

Figure 8.8.

You can format your freehand tables into professional-looking tables.

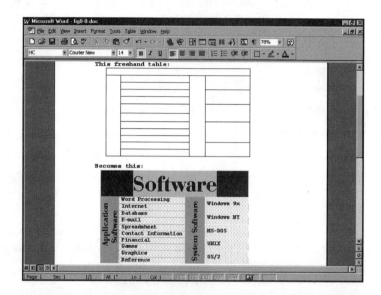

Figure 8.9.

You can use multiple columns for brochures and other pamphlets.

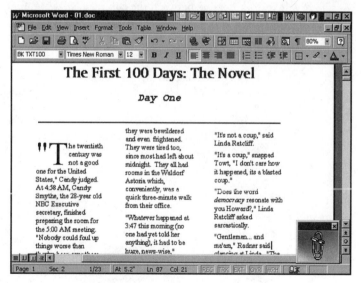

Do you like the way Figure 8.9's opening paragraph begins with the large letter T? Such opening characters are called *drop-cap* or *drop-capital* characters because they are capital letters that extend into the next line or two. To add a drop cap, select the text you want dropped and then select Format | Drop Cap.

NEW TERM A *drop-cap* is an oversized letter that begins a paragraph.

When you want to set multiple columns, follow these steps:

1. Select the text you want to convert to multiple columns. If you want to select your entire document, press Ctrl+A.
2. Select Format | Columns to display the Columns dialog box shown in Figure 8.10.
3. Click the preset column format and enter the number of columns you want to produce.
4. In the dialog box's Width and Spacing area, adjust the column width and spacing between columns if you want to adjust Word 97's default. Generally, the default measurements work well. As you adjust the columns, Word 97 updates the Preview area to give you an idea of the final result.
5. If you want a line between the columns, click the Line between option.
6. When you click OK, Word 97 formats your document into multiple columns.

To add multiple columns quickly and let Word 97 handle the spacing (which Word 97 generally does well), select the text that you want to format into multiple columns and then click the toolbar button's Columns button. Drag your mouse to the left to select the number of columns (from one to four). When you release the mouse, Word 97 formats the multiple columns.

Figure 8.10.

Set up multiple columns with the Columns dialog box.

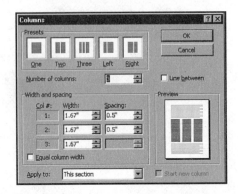

If you format your document into multiple columns that are right-justified, you'll probably need to hyphenate the document. Thin, justified columns often contain a lot of extra spaces that Word 97 inserts to maintain the right-justification. You may want to select File | Print Preview to see how your overall document looks with the narrow columns.

8

Creating Headers and Footers

A *header* is text that appears at the top of each page (or the pages you select, such as all even pages) in your document. A *footer* appears at the bottom of your pages. You don't have to add headers and footers to each page—Word 97 allows you to type them just once, and it automatically adds them to each page.

NEW TERM A *header* contains text that appears at the top of your document pages.

NEW TERM A *footer* contains text that appears at the bottom of your document pages.

To add a header or footer, follow these steps:

1. Select View | Header and Footer to display both the Header and Footer toolbar, as well as outline boxes where you can type the header and footer text. Figure 8.11 shows a document that displays the toolbar, as well as the Header entry box.

Figure 8.11.
Use the header and footer toolbar to adjust your document's header and footer.

Header entry box
Time
Date
Page Number
Header and Footer toolbar
Switch Between Header and Footer button

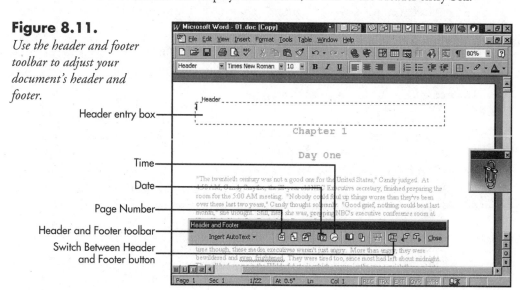

2. Type your header text. If you want to type footer text, click the toolbar's Switch Between Header and Footer button to display the footer text box and type your footer text. If you want to add page numbers, the date, or time to your header or footer text, click the appropriate toolbar buttons.

3. Click the Close button to anchor the header or footer in your document.

Word 97 normally dims header and footer text so that you can easily distinguish between the header, footer, and the rest of your document text when editing your document within the Page Layout view. If you want to specify that the header (or footer) appears only on certain pages, select the File | Page Setup option and adjust the Headers and Footers options. You must be in the Page Layout view to see headers, footers, footnotes, and endnotes in their proper places on the page.

> If you want to edit a header or footer, double-click the dimmed header or footer text while editing your document. Word 97 opens the header and footer toolbar and enables you to edit the header or footer text.

Adding Footnotes and Endnotes

A *footnote* differs from a footer in that a footnote appears only at the bottom of the page on which you include it. Word 97 inserts a footnote reference in the text where you choose to insert the footnote; if you later add text to the page so that the footnote reference moves to the next document page, Word 97 automatically moves the footnote as well, so the footnote always appears on the same page as its reference.

  Footnotes contain text that appears at the bottom of the page on which its corresponding footnote reference appears.

To insert a footnote, follow these steps:

1. Select Insert Footnote. Word 97 displays the Footnote and Endnote dialog box shown in Figure 8.12. *Endnotes* are footnotes that appear at the end of your document, rather than at the bottom of each page. Click the option you want to add—Footnote or Endnote.

  Endnotes are footnotes that appear at the end of your document, each with its own endnote reference number that appears in the document.

2. If you want Word 97 to number the footnote (or endnote) sequentially starting with 1, click OK. If you want to use a different symbol for the number, click Custom mark and enter the reference you want to use.

Figure 8.12.
Add footnotes and endnotes with this dialog box.

3. Click OK. Word 97 adds a separating line between your document and the note, adds the reference number to your document text where you inserted the footnote, and places the cursor at the bottom of the page next to the footnote reference number.

4. Type the footnote (or endnote) and click your mouse on the body of the document to resume editing.

Remember that you must display the Page Layout view to see headers, footers, footnotes, and endnotes in their proper places on the page. If you display your document in Normal view, Word 97 displays the supplemental notes in a separate window.

Summary

This hour wrapped up this book's discussion of Word 97. You learned how to add the document extras that often turn simple writing into powerful cross-referenced published works.

If you need to display tabular information, let Word 97 create and format your tables so that your data presentation looks clean. In addition, multiple columns work well for newsletters and brochures to keep the reader's attention.

To speed up your writing, use as many AutoCorrect and AutoText entries as you can. If you repeatedly type a phrase, sentence, or block of information, that text is a good candidate for AutoCorrect or AutoText.

Hour 9 introduces you to Excel 97. As you'll see, Excel 97 enables you to present numeric data as professionally as Word 97 presents your documents.

Q&A

Q Should I use AutoText or AutoCorrect?

A You must decide how much formatting and effort the boilerplate text requires. If you need to type the same text often but the text consists of only a word or two and requires no special formatting, use AutoCorrect (Tools|AutoCorrect). With AutoCorrect, Word 97 makes changes for you as you type the AutoCorrect abbreviations. (Be careful not to create AutoCorrect entries from common words, or Word 97 might replace text that you don't always want replaced.) If, however, the text is lengthy or requires special formatting that spans multiple lines, add the text as an AutoText entry. When you type the AutoText abbreviation, press the F3 key to expand the abbreviation into the formatted full text.

Q **Why can't I see my headers and footers while editing my document?**

A Perhaps you are displaying your document in Normal view. Select View | Page Layout to see headers and footers in their correct positions on the page.

Q **What is the difference between a table and a document formatted with multiple columns?**

A Both tables and multicolumn documents have multiple columns. The multicolumn document, however, is useful when you want to create a newspaper-style document with flowing columns of text and graphics. A multicolumn document might contain a table in one of its columns.

Use tables when you want side-by-side columns of related information. Use multiple columns when you want your text to snake from the bottom of one column to the top of another.

PART III

Computing with Excel 97

Hour

Hour **9**

Excel 97 Workbooks

This hour introduces you to Excel 97, Microsoft's spreadsheet program. Excel 97 is to numbers what Word 97 is to text; Excel 97 has been called a *word processor for numbers*. With Excel 97, you can create numerically based proposals, business plans, business forms, accounting worksheets, and virtually any other document that contains calculated numbers.

If you're new to electronic worksheets, you'll probably have to take more time to learn Excel 97's environment than you had to learn Word 97's. Excel 97 starts with a grid of cells in which you place information. This hour takes things slowly to acquaint you with Excel 97 and explains the background necessary for understanding how an Excel 97 working area operates.

The highlights of this hour include

- ☐ How to start Excel 97
- ☐ What workbooks and worksheets are
- ☐ How to enter various kinds of Excel 97 data
- ☐ Which keys to use to navigate through Excel 97 data
- ☐ How to quit Excel 97

Starting Excel 97

You start Excel 97 when you perform one of these actions:

- [ ] Click the New Office Document button on the Office 97 Shortcut bar and double-click the Blank Workbook icon to create a new Excel 97 document. (Click the General tab, if it is not already selected, to see the Blank Workbook icon.)

- [ ] Click the New Office Document button on the Office 97 Shortcut bar and click one of the Excel 97–based tabs to open an Excel 97 template or start a wizard. (Hour 4, "Using More Powerful Features," discussed templates.)

- [ ] Click the Open Office Document button on the Office 97 Shortcut bar and select an existing Excel 97 workbook that you want to edit. You may have to traverse directory folders to get to the workbook that you want to open.

- [ ] Use the Windows Start menu to start Excel 97 by clicking Microsoft Excel on the Programs menu.

- [ ] Select an Excel 97 document from the Documents option on the Windows Start menu. Windows recognizes that Excel 97 created the document workbook and starts Excel 97, loading the workbook automatically. (The Documents option on the Start menu contains a list of your most recent work.)

- [ ] Click the Excel 97 button on the Office 97 Shortcut bar to create a blank workbook. (Depending on your Office 97 Shortcut bar's setup, you might not see the Excel 97 button.)

Figure 9.1 shows the opening Excel 97 screen. Your screen might differ slightly depending on the options you have set.

Understanding Workbooks and Worksheets

Excel 97 enables you create and edit *workbooks*. A workbook holds one or more *worksheets* (sometimes called *spreadsheets* or simply *sheets*). A worksheet is a collection of rows and columns that holds text and numbers. Anytime you create, open, or save an Excel 97 file, you're working with a workbook. The workbook approach prevents you from having multiple files that relate to the same project—instead, you can have all worksheets related to the same project in the same workbook (in one *.xls file). Your workbook name is the Excel 97 name you assign when you save a file.

NEW TERM   A *workbook* is a collection of worksheets stored in a single file. A workbook is useful for grouping a single project's worksheets together.

Figure 9.1.
Excel 97's opening screen.

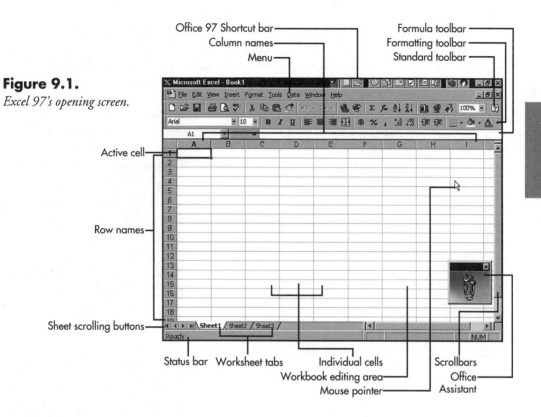

Office 97 Shortcut bar
Column names
Menu
Formula toolbar
Formatting toolbar
Standard toolbar

9

Active cell
Row names
Sheet scrolling buttons

Status bar   Worksheet tabs   Individual cells   Scrollbars
Workbook editing area   Office
Mouse pointer   Assistant

NEW TERM   A *worksheet* is an Excel 97 table-like document containing rows and columns that
holds data and formulas.

Step-Up

Excel 97 is not limited to 16 worksheets per workbook as were previous versions of
Excel.

A worksheet acts a lot like a Word 97 table, except that Excel 97 worksheets can do much
more numerical processing than Word 97 tables can.

As with Word 97 data, Excel 97 often uses the term *document* to refer to
a workbook file.

Blank Excel 97 workbooks contain three worksheets named Sheet1, Sheet2, and Sheet3 (as shown at the bottom of Figure 9.1). When you click a sheet's tab, Excel 97 brings that sheet into view. If a workbook contains several worksheets, you might have to click one of the sheet-scrolling buttons to view additional worksheet tabs. Each column has a heading; heading names start with A, B, and so on. Each row has a heading, starting with 1, 2, and so on. The intersection of a row and column, called a *cell*, also has a name that comes from combining the row name and column number, such as C4 or A1. A1 is always the top-left cell on any worksheet. The gridlines help you to distinguish between cells, but you can turn off gridlines at any time from the Tools | Options | View page option labeled Gridlines.

 A *cell* is the intersection of a row and column into which you enter text or numbers. A *cell address* is the column letter and row number location of the cell; B6 is the cell address for a cell located at column B and row 6.

 No matter how large your monitor is, you'll see only a small amount of the worksheet area. Use the scrollbars to see or edit information in the off-screen cells, such as cell M17.

Every cell in your workbook contains a unique name or address to which you can refer when you are tabulating data. The cell address of the *active cell* (the cell that the cursor is in) appears at the top-left corner of the screen, under the Font box. In Figure 9.1, the box reads A1 because the cursor is in cell A1.

When you move your mouse pointer across Excel 97's screen, notice that the pointer becomes a cross when you point it to a cell area. The cross returns to its pointer shape when you point to another part of the Excel 97 work area.

Inserting Worksheets in a Workbook

Just as Word 97 enables you to edit multiple documents in memory at the same time, Excel 97 enables you to edit multiple worksheets at once (but those worksheets must all appear in the same workbook).

To insert a new worksheet into your workbook, right-click the worksheet tab that is to fall *after* the new worksheet. Select Insert. Excel 97 displays the Insert dialog box (shown in Figure 9.2), on which you can double-click the Worksheet icon and press OK. The Insert dialog box contains several kinds of items that you can add to a workbook, but worksheets are the most common items you add. The Insert | Worksheet command also inserts a new worksheet.

Figure 9.2.
Add a new worksheet to your workbook.

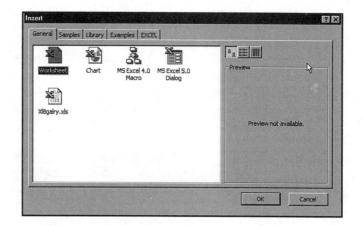

If you don't like the default worksheet names (Sheet1, Sheet2, and so on), rename them by right-clicking the sheet name and selecting Rename. Type the new name. When you press Enter, the worksheet tab displays the new name. (Notice the "Solver Example" name on the worksheet tab in Figure 9.4 as an example.)

Deleting Worksheets from a Workbook

Situations arise when you only need a single worksheet in a workbook. For example, you might want to track your monthly household budget; such a budget rarely requires multiple worksheets. For your budget, the workbook is basically the same as the worksheet, but you should pare down excess worksheets instead of wasting memory on them. Excel 97 makes it easy to delete excess sheets. Simply right-click the tab of the sheet you want to delete and select Delete from the pop-up menu.

You can keep multiple workbooks open at once and move between them by pressing Ctrl+F6 (the same keystroke that moves between multiple Word 97 documents in memory). Multiple workbooks are often difficult to keep track of until you become familiar with Excel 97 and its worksheets. Display your Window menu to see a list of open workbooks if you want to review the ones you've opened.

Working with Multiple Worksheets

To specify the maximum number of worksheets that a workbook is to hold, select Tools|Options, click the General tab, and enter a number in the Sheets in New field labeled Sheets in New Workbook. When you create a new workbook, that workbook contains the number of sheets you requested. As you can see from Figure 9.3, Excel 97's Options dialog box resembles Word 97's. Many of the options are identical in both products, as well as throughout the Office 97 suite.

Figure 9.3.

The Options dialog box lets you decide how many worksheets to include in your workbooks.

Enter the number of sheets—

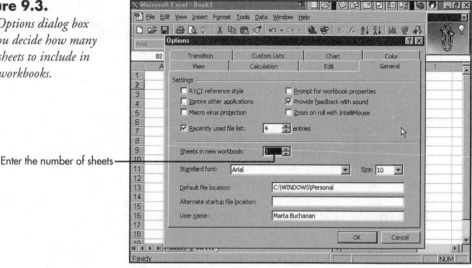

You can refer to a specific cell located within a workbook by prefacing the cell with its workbook name, followed by an exclamation point (!), to refer to a specific worksheet's cell. For example, Sheet3!G7 refers to the seventh row of column G inside the worksheet named Sheet3.

One interesting workbook feature is the capability to rearrange worksheets within a workbook, and even to move worksheets between two or more workbooks.

If you don't like the current order of the worksheets in your workbook (the worksheet tabs indicate the worksheet ordering), click and drag a worksheet's tag (the mouse cursor changes to let you know you've grabbed the worksheet) to fall before another sheet's tab. If you work with two or three particular worksheets the majority of the time, move those worksheets together so that you can move between them easily.

Make a copy of a worksheet by pressing Ctrl before you click and drag a worksheet from one location to another. Excel 97 creates a new worksheet and uses the original worksheet for the new worksheet's data. Before you make extensive changes to a worksheet, you might want to copy it so that you can revert to the old version should anything go wrong.

9

Working with Multiple Workbooks

As your workbook fills up with worksheets, you need a way to manage those worksheets and move from one to another. When you then want to copy or move information from one to another worksheet, you can easily do so.

If you need to move a worksheet from one workbook to another, open both workbooks and select Window|Arrange|Tiled to display both worksheets (as shown in Figure 9.4). Drag one of the worksheet tabs to the other workbook to move the sheet. To copy instead of move, hold Ctrl while you drag the sheet name.

Figure 9.4.

Display both workbooks if you want to move or copy worksheets or cells between them.

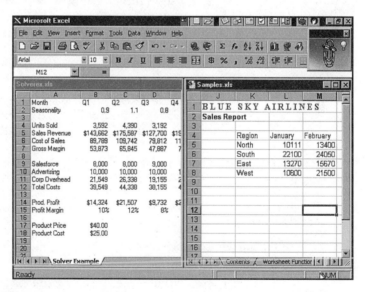

Entering Worksheet Data

Often, entering worksheet data requires nothing more than moving the cell pointer to the correct cell and typing the data. However, the various kinds of data behave differently when entered, so you should understand how Excel 97 accepts assorted data.

Excel 97 can work with the following kinds of data:

- [ ] **Labels:** Text values such as names and addresses
- [ ] **Numbers:** Numeric values such as 34, –291, 545.67874, and 0
- [ ] **Formulas:** Expressions that compute numeric results (some formulas work with text values as well)
- [ ] **Special formats:** Date and time values

As you will see in Part VII, "Combining the Office 97 Products and the Internet," Excel 97 works with data from other Office 97 products. Additionally, you can *import* (transfer) data from other non-Microsoft products, such as Lotus 1-2-3.

NEW TERM To *import* is to load data from another program into Excel 97.

Entering Text

If you want to put text (such as a title or a name) in a cell, simply place your cursor in the cell and type the text. Excel 97 left-justifies the text in the cell. As you type, the text appears both in the cell and in the formula bar. Remember that the Name box to the left of the formula bar displays the name of the cell into which you're entering data. When you press Enter, Excel 97 moves the cell pointer down one row.

> Press Tab to move the cell pointer to the right or the arrow keys to move the cell pointer in any direction after you enter data.

If you press Esc at any point during your text entry, Excel 97 erases the text you typed in the cell and restores the original cell contents.

If your text is wider than the cell, Excel 97 does one of two things depending on the contents of the adjacent cell to the right:

- [ ] If the adjacent cell is empty, Excel 97 displays the entire contents of the wide cell.
- [ ] If the adjacent cell contains data, Excel 97 *truncates* (cuts off) the wide cell to show only as much text as fits in the cell's width. Excel 97 does not remove the unseen data from the cell; however, the adjacent cell, if that cell contains data, always displays instead.

Figure 9.5 shows two long *labels* (label is another name for text data) in cells C5 and C10. The same label, which is longer than standard cell width, appears in both cells. Because no data resides in D5, Excel 97 displays all the contents of C5. The data in D10, however, overwrites the tail end of C10. C10 still contains the complete label, but only part of it is visible.

You can increase and shrink the width and height of columns and rows by dragging the edge of the column name or row number. For example, if you drag the right edge of column D to the right, the entire column D (all rows in the column) widens.

9

NEW TERM   A *label* is text data inside an Excel 97 cell.

Figure 9.5.

Excel 97 may or may not display all of a cell's contents.

No data in cell D5 to overwrite C5

Cell D10 contains data that overwrites C10

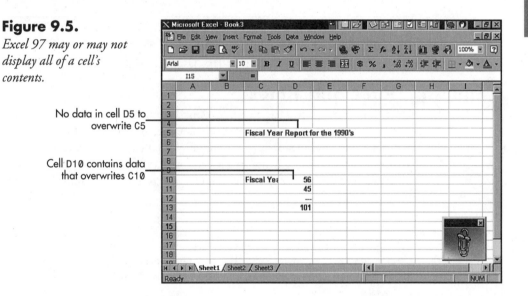

Some text data, such as price codes, telephone numbers, and zip codes, fool Excel 97. As you see in the next section, Excel 97 treats numeric data differently from text data when you type the data into cells. If you want Excel 97 to treat a number (such as a zip code) as a text entry (calculations are not performed on the cell), precede the contents with a single apostrophe ('). For example, to type the zip code 74137, type '74137; the apostrophe lets Excel 97 know to format the value as text.

Entering Numbers

Excel 97 accepts numeric values of all kinds. You can type positive numbers, negative numbers, numbers with decimal points, zero-leading numbers, numbers with dollar signs, percent signs, and even *scientific notation* (a shortcut for writing extremely large and small numbers).

The term *scientific notation* refers to a format scientists, mathematicians, and engineers often use to write extremely large and extremely small numbers and is based on powers of 10 (such as 3.049×10^{16}).

> If you type a number but see something like 3.04959E+16 appear in the cell, Excel 97 converted your number to scientific notation to let you know that the cell is not wide enough to display the entire number in its regular form. Excel 97 does not extend long numbers into adjacent cells.

Excel 97 right-justifies numbers inside cells. You can change the justification for a single cell or for the entire worksheet, as you see in Hour 10, "Using Excel 97."

Entering Dates and Times

Excel 97 supports almost every national and international date and time format. Excel 97 uses its AutoFormat feature to convert any date or time value that you type to a special internal number that represents the number of days since midnight, January 1, 1900. Although this strange internal representation might not make sense now, you use these values a lot to compute time between two or more dates. For example, you can easily determine how many days an account is past due.

> Excel 97 uses a 24-hour clock to represent time values unless you specify a.m. or p.m. To convert p.m. times to 24-hour times, add 12 to all time values after 12:59 p.m. Therefore, 7:54 p.m. is 19:54 on a 24-hour clock.

You can type any of the following date and time values to represent 6:15 p.m., July 4, 1976, or a combination of both 6:15 p.m. and July 4, 1976:

```
July 4, 1976

4-Jul-76 6:15 p.m.

6:15 p.m.

18:15

07/04/76 18:15

07-04-76 18:15
```

If you enter any of these date and time values, Excel 97 converts them to a shortened format (such as 4/4/76 18:15). You can enter only a date or a time value if you want. As with most Office 97 formats, you can change this default format with the Format menu. The shorter format often helps worksheet columns align better.

> If you use Excel 97 for financial reports and small business analysis, consider getting the Office 97 Small Business Edition. Office 97 SBE includes the Small Business Financial Manager add-on. The Small Business Financial Manager is not a separate Office 97 program but is just a worksheet data document, albeit a fancy worksheet, that includes several predesigned business reports and financial analysis routines such as what-if scenario comparisons.

Step-Up

Excel 97 contains a tracking system to track worksheet revisions. Use Tools | Track Changes to get to the tracking information.

Navigating in Excel 97

Your mouse and arrow keys are the primary navigation keys used to move from cell to cell. Unlike Word 97, which uses a text cursor, Excel 97 uses a cell pointer to show you the currently active cell. The active cell accepts whatever data you enter next. As you press an arrow key, Excel 97 moves the active cell pointer in the direction of the arrow.

 NEW TERM The *active* cell is the current highlighted cell that accepts data you type into it.

Table 9.1 lists the most commonly used navigational keystrokes used within a worksheet. Use your mouse to scroll with the scrollbars. To scroll long distances, press Shift while you scroll with the mouse.

Table 9.1. Using the keyboard to navigate Excel 97.

This key...	Moves to here
Arrow keys	The direction of the arrow one cell at a time.

continues

Table 9.1. continued

This key...	Moves to here
Ctrl+Up Arrow, Ctrl+Down Arrow	The top-most or bottom-most row with data in the worksheet.
Ctrl+Left Arrow, Ctrl+Right Arrow	The left-most or right-most column with data in the worksheet.
PageUp, PageDown	The previous or next screen of the worksheet.
Ctrl+Home	The upper-left corner of the worksheet (cell A1).
End, Arrow	The last blank cell in the arrow's direction.
Ctrl+PageUp, Ctrl+PageDown	Move to next or previous worksheet within current workbook.

Quitting Excel 97

When you're finished with Excel 97, quit by performing any of the following:

- [ ] Select File | Exit.
- [ ] Press Alt+F4.
- [ ] Double-click the Control icon.
- [ ] Click Excel 97's Close button.

Always quit Excel 97 and shut down Windows (by selecting Start I Shut Down) before turning off your computer so that you don't lose your work.

Summary

This hour introduced Excel 97, and covered Excel 97's screen and the concept of workbooks and worksheets. The workbook documents contain your worksheets, and your worksheets hold data, such as numbers and labels. As you see throughout this part of the book, Excel 97 supports a tremendous number of formatting options so that you can turn your numeric data into eye-catching, appealing output.

Although Excel 97 works best with numeric data, Excel 97 accepts text (called labels), date, and time values as well. Excel 97 is extremely lenient about how you type dates and times but immediately converts such values into a special internal number. This internal number enables you to calculate with dates when you need to determine the number of days between two dates or when you need to add a fixed number of days to a date to arrive at an ending date, such as a due date.

The next hour extends the concepts of this hour by showing you how to quickly add common data to an Excel 97 worksheet. In addition, you learn how to edit the values that you type.

Q&A

Q I'm not good at math; can I use Excel 97?

A If you were great at math, you wouldn't even *need* Excel 97! Seriously, Excel 97 does all the calculating. Your job is to place the numerical data on the worksheets so that Excel 97 can do its thing. Many people use Excel 97 for common household actions, such as tracking exercise routines and grocery lists. Excel 97 is not just for accounting and mathematical applications. You learn, in Hour 11, "Editing Excel Worksheets," how to enter formulas.

Q Do I always enter the time along with the date?

A You can enter either a time value, a date value, or both when entering such information. Excel 97 turns the information into an internal shortened format (you can change the display format if you desire to make the data look better). If you don't enter a date with a time value, Excel 97 accepts the time value only and tracks just the time. If you enter a date, Excel 97 tracks only the date.

Hour 10

Using Excel 97

This hour teaches you how to improve the accuracy of your worksheet data. You can easily edit cell contents with the tools Excel 98 provides.

After you master worksheet editing skills, you then are ready to see how Excel 97's AutoCorrect feature and the spell checker work to improve worksheets. Excel 97 can also enter values for you. When you ask Excel 97 to fill in a series of cell values, it uses some intuitive guesswork to complete any series that you begin. If you often enter a special series of numbers or labels, you can teach Excel 97 that series to eliminate typing when you use the series again.

The highlights of this hour include

- [ ] What you do to select multiple worksheet cells
- [ ] Why the spell checker and AutoCorrect are important to numeral-based worksheets
- [ ] How Excel 97 fills in a series of values for you
- [ ] When you must teach Excel 97 a new series
- [ ] How to find and replace worksheet data
- [ ] Why clearing a cell does not always equate to erasing the cell's contents
- [ ] How to use comments to describe a cell

Worksheet Editing

Some of the most important Excel 97 skills you can learn are editing skills. Entering numerical data is error-prone at its best; the faster you edit cell values accurately, the faster you complete accurate worksheets. The following sections show you the primary editing tools Excel 97 provides.

Selecting Cells

You can select a cell, a row of cells, or a column of cells just by clicking and dragging your mouse. As you drag your mouse, Excel 97 selects a rectangular region. You notice as you drag your mouse that Excel 97 displays the number of rows and columns you've selected. For example, you see the message 10R X 4C appear in the toolbar's Name box if you've selected 10 rows and 4 columns. When you release your mouse, Excel 97 displays the selection's upper-left corner.

Not only can you select a rectangular region of cells, you can also select disjointed regions. Select the first area, and then press Ctrl while you click another cell and drag the mouse. The selection highlight appears in both places on your screen. Remove any selection by clicking your mouse on any cell or by pressing an arrow key.

Spell Checking

No worksheet program included a spell checker before Excel. After all, worksheets are for numbers, right? Of course, the primary purpose for worksheets is formatting, arranging, and calculating numbers. Numbers without titles, though, are worthless in most instances. You have to present your numerical data in such a way that the worksheet users understand the significance of your data. Given the amount of text you enter on your worksheets, a spell checker makes sense. You can only wonder why worksheet makers did not add spell checkers long before Microsoft added one to Excel.

The ways that you can check your worksheet's spelling follow:

- ☐ Click the Spelling toolbar button
- ☐ Select Tools | Spelling from the menu
- ☐ Press F7, the spelling shortcut key

 Unlike Word 97, Excel 97 does not include a grammar checker. Rarely do you include complete sentences on a worksheet, so the grammar checker would be wasted overhead in most cases.

The spell checker in Excel 97 is the same one that Word 97 uses (see Hour 7, "Managing Documents and Customizing Word 97," for a quick review). The spell checker does *not*

check every worksheet in your workbook, but only the current worksheet active on your screen. If Excel 97 finds an error, you can choose to correct, ignore, or add the error so that the word no longer appears as an error (as might be the case for proper names).

AutoCorrect Worksheets

Use AutoCorrect as you type Excel 97 entries just as you used AutoCorrect in Word 97. When you type an abbreviation for an AutoCorrect entry, Excel 97 converts that abbreviated form to the complete AutoCorrect entry for you when you press the spacebar or leave the cell.

> Word 97, Excel 97, and all the other Office 97 products share the same AutoCorrect and spelling dictionaries. Therefore, when you make changes and additions in the AutoCorrect or spelling dictionaries of Word 97 or Excel 97, the other products recognize those changes.

10

To add AutoCorrect entries, perform the same steps that you do with Word 97:

1. Select Tools | AutoCorrect.
2. Type your abbreviated AutoCorrect entry in the Replace field.
3. Press Tab.
4. Type the replacement text in the With field.
5. Click OK to return to the worksheet editing area.

Cell Editing

Much of your Excel 97 editing requires that you correct numeric data-entry. Of course, if you begin to type a number (or a formula, as you learn in the next hour) in a cell but realize you've made a mistake, press Backspace to erase your mistake or press the arrow keys to move the text cursor back over the entry to correct something.

If you've already moved to another cell when you recognize that you've entered an error, quickly correct the mistake like this:

1. Move the cell pointer to the cell you need to correct (click the cell to move the pointer there).
2. Press F2, which is the standard Windows editing shortcut key. (If you've still got your hand on the mouse, you can double-click the cell to edit the cell's contents.) You know Excel 97 is ready for your edit when you see the text cursor appear in the cell.
3. Move the text cursor to the mistake.
4. Press the Insert key to change from Overtype mode to Insert mode or vice versa. As with Word 97, Overtype mode enables you to write over existing characters,

whereas Insert mode shifts all existing characters to the right as you type the correction.

5. Press Enter to anchor the correction in place.

If you want to undo an edit, click the Undo button. To redo an undo, click the Redo button. As you can see, after you've mastered one Office 97 product (as you have Word 97), you know a lot about the other products.

Finding and Replacing

Like Word 97, Excel 97 contains a powerful search-and-replace operation that can search your worksheet for values and replace those values if needed.

> The find-and-replace feature in Excel 97 works a little differently from that in Word 97. The numeric nature of Excel 97 requires a different type of find and replace. Therefore, read this section even if you've mastered the find-and-replace feature in Word 97.

Figure 10.1 shows the Find dialog box in Excel 97. You can request that Excel 97 search by rows or columns. If your worksheet is generally longer than wide (as most are), select By Columns to speed your search. Indicate whether you want Excel 97 to match your uppercase and lowercase search text exactly (not applicable for numeric searches), and select the proper Look In option of Formulas, Values, or Comments.

Use Formulas if you're searching for part of a formula (you learn all about formulas in the next hour), use Values if you want Excel 97 to search only the calculated cells (not within formulas), and use Comments if you want Excel 97 to search through cell comments. Generally, you are searching through formulas, so Excel 97 makes Formulas the default search target.

Figure 10.1.

Excel 97's Find dialog box looks for text or numbers.

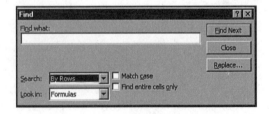

The Find Entire Cells Only option indicates to Excel 97 that a cell must contain your entire Find value and nothing else before a proper match will be made.

If you want Excel 97 to replace the found value with another value, select the Edit | Replace command to display the Replace dialog box (shown in Figure 10.2).

Figure 10.2.
*Let Excel 97 replace
values for you.*

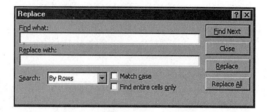

Click the Replace All button if you want Excel 97 to replace all occurrences of the found text. Otherwise, click Find Next to find the next matching value and, if that's a value you want to replace, click Replace. If it's not a value you want to replace, click Find Next to locate the next occurrence.

10

> If you want to find or replace only within a limited worksheet range, select the range before conducting the find or replace operation.

Reviewing Cut Copy and Paste in Excel 97

If you mastered the Copy, Cut, and Paste commands, in Word 97, those commands in Excel 97 are a breeze. As with Word 97 and the other Office 97 products, Excel 97 uses the Windows Clipboard to hold data that you're copying, cutting, and pasting from within or between worksheets. If you open two workbooks at the same time and display both on your screen (by selecting Window | Arrange), you can easily copy, cut, and paste between the two workbooks.

To copy data from one location to another, select the cell or cells you want to copy and click the Copy toolbar button (or press Ctrl+C) to copy the worksheet contents to your Clipboard. Ctrl+A selects the entire worksheet to copy or cut. The contents stay in the original location because you elected to copy and not cut the cells. To paste the Clipboard contents to another location, select the first cell in the target location (which may reside in another workbook) and click the Paste toolbar button (or press Ctrl+V). Excel 97 overwrites the target cells with the pasted contents, so be sure of the paste target when you paste Clipboard data.

Step-Up

Office Assistant keeps a close eye on you at all times. If you attempt to paste over data, Office Assistant issues the warning shown in Figure 10.3. You can click OK to accept the overwrite or click Cancel to stop the paste.

Figure 10.3.

Office Assistant warns you when you are about to paste over data.

	Microsoft Excel - Book1.xls

(spreadsheet screenshot showing a dialog box "Microsoft Excel — Do you want to replace the contents of the destination cells?" with OK and Cancel buttons)

	A	B	C	D	E		
3		Year	Year	Year	Year	Year	
4		1997	1998	1999	2000	2001	
5	January	3	9	9	7	5	
6	February	4	8	6	5	7	
7	March	5	3	2	3	6	
8	April	3	9	2	4	5	
9	May	6	4	3	6	4	
10	June	5	5	5	7	3	
11	July	5	7	2	8	2	
12	August	2	7	4	5	3	
13	Septeemb	4	3	7	2	5	
14	October	8	4	4	1	6	
15	November	6	8	4	2	2	
16	December	6	7	3	3	4	

Remember that the Clipboard holds its contents until you replace them with other material. Therefore, you can continue pasting the Clipboard to other worksheets as long as you keep selecting a target location and pressing Ctrl+V.

Excel 97 supports drag-and-drop editing, so after you select the cells to copy, press Ctrl and drag the selection to its new location. You must drag the selection by pointing to one of the selection edges; if you attempt to drag from the center of a selected cell set, Excel 97 changes the selection range. When you release your mouse button and the Ctrl key, Excel 97 pastes the contents to the target location. Of course, drag-and-drop editing works only when you can see both the source and the target copy and paste locations.

To cut contents and place them elsewhere, just select the cells that you want to cut and press Ctrl+X (or click the Cut toolbar button). Excel 97 removes the selection from its original location and places the selection on your Clipboard. You then can paste the Clipboard contents elsewhere. In effect, cutting and pasting performs a movement of the selected data. If you want to move the selection with your mouse, drag the selection without first pressing Ctrl as you did when copying the contents.

> If you want to drag and drop between two workbook's worksheets but you only have one worksheet displayed, press the Alt key before dragging your selection. When you drag the selection over the target worksheet's name tab, Excel 97 opens that worksheet, and you can drop the dragged contents to the open worksheet.

Clearing Data

Due to the nature of worksheets, erasing worksheet data differs from erasing word-processed data. Other information on the worksheet can heavily depend on the erased data, as you see in the next hour's lesson. When you want to erase a cell's or selection's contents, first decide which of the following kinds of erasure you want to perform:

- [ ] Erase the selection and send the contents to the Clipboard (as you learned in the previous section).
- [ ] Clear only a portion of the selection, such as its formatting, comment, or data value.
- [ ] Completely erase the selection and all formatting and notes attached to the selection.
- [ ] Erase the selected cells and their position so that other cells in the row move left or cells below move up.

> A worksheet's cell contains a lot more than just the numbers and text that you see on the worksheet screen. Not only can the cells also contain formulas and comments, but they often rely on other cells for information. Therefore, when you want to erase the selection, you must keep in mind how the selection affects other worksheet areas.

If you want to delete the selected cell's data, press Delete. Excel 97 retains any formatting and comments that you had applied before you deleted the data.

If you want to more selectively erase a cell, select the Edit | Clear command and select from one of the five options listed here:

☐ The All option deletes the entire selection, including the contents, format, and attached comments (but not the actual cell).

☐ The Formats option erases only the selection's format; you can get rid of a cell's special formatting and revert to a general format without changing or erasing the contents of the cell.

☐ The Contents option deletes the cell contents but leaves the formatting and comments intact.

☐ The Comments option deletes any special comments that appear in the selected cells.

☐ The Hyperlinks option removes any Internet-based references within the cell.

> Reverse an accidental deletion with Undo (Ctrl+Z).

Here's a quicker way to erase the values in cells: Select the cells and drag the fill handle up and to the left. As you drag the fill handle, Excel 97 grays out the cells that are erased when you release the mouse button.

To remove the selected cells as well as their contents and close the gap left by the deleted selection, select Edit | Delete to display the Delete dialog box (shown in Figure 10.4). Select Shift Cells Left or Shift Cells Up so that Excel 97 knows how to close the gap that the deletion leaves.

Figure 10.4.

Remove cell contents and close the gap.

Speed Data Entry

Excel 97 can often predict what data you want to enter into a worksheet. By spotting trends in your data, Excel 97 uses educated guesses to fill in cell data for you. Excel 97 uses data fills to copy and extend data from one cell to several additional cells.

 Data fill refers to the capability of Excel 97 to spot and continue trends in data that you've started, such as a series of numbers or dates.

One of the most common data fills you perform is to use Excel 97's capability to copy one cell's data to several other cells. For example, you might want to create a pro forma balance sheet for the previous five-year period. You can insert a two-line label across the top of each year's data. The first line would contain five occurrences of the label Year, and the second line would hold the numbers 1997 through 2000. To use the data fill feature in Excel 97 to create the five similar labels, perform these simple steps:

1. Type **Year** in the left-most cell. Don't press Enter or any cell-moving cursor keys after you type the label.

2. Locate the cell's fill handle. The *fill handle* is the small black box located in the lower-right corner of the active cell (shown in Figure 10.5).

NEW TERM   A *fill handle* is a cell pointer's box that you can drag to extend and copy the cell's contents.

3. Drag the fill handle to the right across the next four columns. As you drag the fill handle, Excel 97 displays the pop-up label Year indicating the value of the new cells.

4. Release the mouse button. Excel 97 fills all five cells with the label, as shown in Figure 10.5.

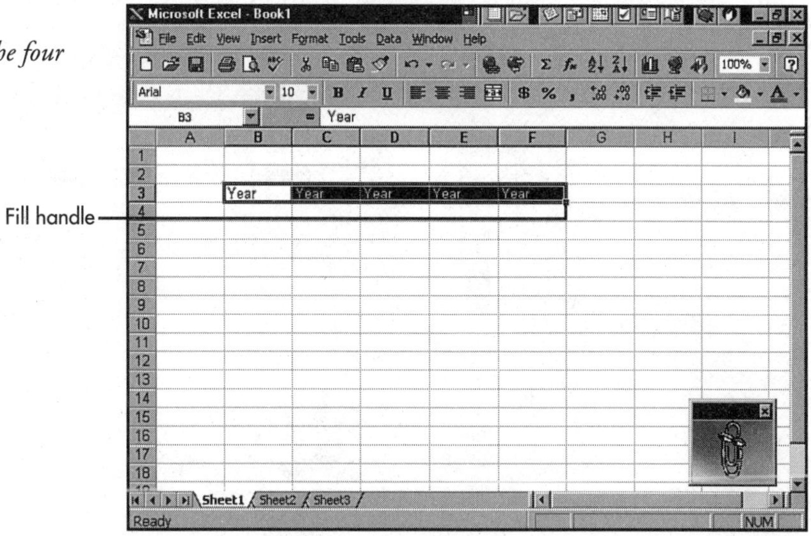

Figure 10.5.

Excel 97 filled in the four extra labels.

Fill handle ─

If you drag the fill handle down, Excel 97 copies the label down the column. Excel 97 even fills a rectangular area if you drag the fill handle across and down the worksheet. Although the Edit | Fill command performs the same function as the fill handle, dragging the fill handle is much easier than selecting from the menu. Ctrl+D performs the same operation as Edit | Fill.

Smarter Fills with AutoFill

Even if the only fill Excel 97 performed were the copying of data across rows and columns, the data fill would still be beneficial. Excel 97 goes an extra step, however: It performs smart fills with a feature known as *AutoFill*. AutoFill is perhaps the single reason why Excel took over the spreadsheet market a few years ago and has been the leader ever since. When you use AutoFill, Excel 97 examines and completes data you've entered.

NEW TERM *AutoFill* is the technique Excel 97 uses to complete data from a cell or cell selection.

For example, the five year pro forma period you were setting up in the previous section included the years 1997 through 2001. You can type 1997 under the first Year title and type 1998 under the second title. Select *both* cells using the same dragging technique you learned about in the Word 97 selection, and then drag the fill handle right three more cells. When you release the mouse button, you see that Excel 97 properly fills in the remaining years (as Figure 10.6 shows).

Figure 10.6.

Excel 97's AutoFill feature knew which years to fill.

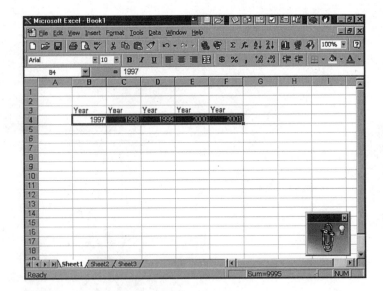

 If you had selected only one cell, Excel 97 would have copied that cell across the worksheet. Excel 97 needed to see the two selected cells to notice the trend.

The years in Figure 10.6 don't exactly align under the first row, but in the next hour, "Editing Excel Worksheets," you learn how to format data to make your titles align.

Excel 97 gets even better. If you want to use AutoFill to increment cells by a single number, as you are doing with the years, you don't really need to select two cells first. If you select any cell that contains a number, press Ctrl, and drag the fill handle, Excel 97 adds a one to each cell to which you extend. Therefore, you could fill four years from 1998 through 2001 simply by pressing Ctrl before you dragged the first year's fill handle to the right.

As you know, Excel 97 works with text as well as with numeric values. AutoFill recognizes many common text trends, including

☐ Days of the week names

☐ Days of the week abbreviations (such as Mon, Tue)

☐ Month names

☐ Month abbreviations (such as Jan, Feb)

10

Suppose that you want to list month names down the left of the pro forma sheet because you need to report each month's totals for those five years. All you need to do is type January for the first month name, and drag that cell's fill handle to the twelfth cell below. Figure 10.7 shows the result.

Figure 10.7.

Let Excel 97 fill in the series of month names.

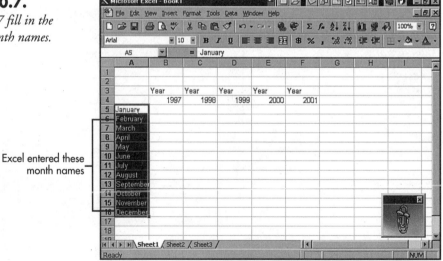

Excel entered these month names

Design Your Own Fills

In addition to the month and weekday names and abbreviations, Excel 97 can fill in any list of values. You can teach Excel 97 a new list to use with AutoFill. After you've shown Excel 97 the new list, anytime you type the first value and drag that cell's fill handle in any direction, Excel 97 fills the remaining cells with your list.

To add your own AutoFill list to Excel 97's repertoire of lists, perform these steps:

1. Select Tools | Options.
2. Click the Custom Lists tab to display the current AutoFill lists in effect.
3. Click the Add button.
4. Type your list of values for AutoFill. If you have six departments, you might enter something like Dept 1, Dept 2, Dept 3, Dept 4, Dept 5, and Dept 6. Your screen would look like Figure 10.8.
5. Click OK to add your list to AutoFill's current list.

The next time you type the label Dept 1 in a cell and drag the fill handle to the right or down the worksheet, Excel 97 fills in the remaining departments. If you fill only four cells, Excel 97 uses the first four values. If you fill six or more cells, Excel 97 fills all six departments and starts repeating the department names for any number over six.

Figure 10.8.

Teach Excel 97 new AutoFill entries.

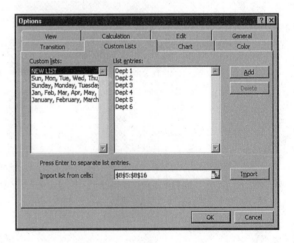

If you enter a series in a worksheet, and then decide that the series would make a great AutoFill list (in case you want to add the list to another worksheet), Excel 97 doesn't make you re-enter the list. Simply select the entire list by dragging the mouse pointer through the list. When you open the Custom Lists dialog box, click Import to add the selected range to the AutoFill entries.

AutoFill is fine for a typical range of titles and for a series of a dozen or fewer entries, but some data series consume numerous entries. When you want to enter a larger number of values in a series, perform these steps:

1. Type the first value of the series in the first cell.

2. Select the cell and all subsequent cells that will receive the rest of the series.

3. Select Edit | Fill | Series to display the Series dialog box.

4. Select Rows if you've selected cells from a row or Columns if you've selected cells from a column.

5. Select the type of series you are entering. Table 10.1 describes each of the four types from which you can choose.

6. Select the subtype. For example, if the series is a series of months, check Month.

7. Enter the Step value, which describes how each value in the series increases or decreases.

8. Enter the Stop value if necessary (you rarely need to enter one). For example, if you want to enter a series that increases every three months, you've checked the Month option, and typed 3 for the Step value, Excel 97 will know the final month and you won't need to enter it.

   Although you won't need to indicate to Excel 97 where to stop in most instances, a Stop value is useful if you check the Trend option in the Series dialog box. Excel 97 starts with your initial selected value (if numeric) and estimates the values between that starting value and the Stop value that you supply.

9. Click OK to create and enter the series of values.

Table 10.1. Types of series.

Series name	If you type...	Excel 97 can complete with
Linear	0	1, 2, 3, 4, 5
	-50, 0, 50, 100	150, 200, 250
Growth	2, 4	8, 16, 32, 64
	10, 100	1000, 10000
Date	1-Jan, 1-Apr	1-Jul, 1-Oct, 1-Jan
AutoFill	Acctg-101, Acctg-102	Acctg-103, Acctg-104
	Year '96	Year '97, Year '98

Adding Comments

As with Word 97, you can insert *comments* in a cell. The comments act like yellow sticky notes onscreen, except that the notes in Excel 97 aren't in the way when you don't want to see them. The comments don't appear in the cell; when you insert a comment, Excel 97 indicates that the comment resides within the cell by flagging the cell's upper-right corner with a red triangle. When you point to the cell, Excel 97 displays the attached comment.

NEW TERM A *comment* is a note attached to a cell that doesn't appear as part of the cell's data.

To attach a comment to a selected cell, select Insert|Comment. Excel 97 opens the box shown in Figure 10.9. Type your comment here. Excel 97 automatically places your name at the beginning of the comment. The name indicates who added the comment in case you work in a multi-user environment. (You can erase the name if you don't want to see it.) You can leave coworkers notes if you edit worksheets as a team. You can also leave yourself a note to fill in data that you might get from an outside source later.

Figure 10.9.

Add comments to cells.

Attached
comment flags

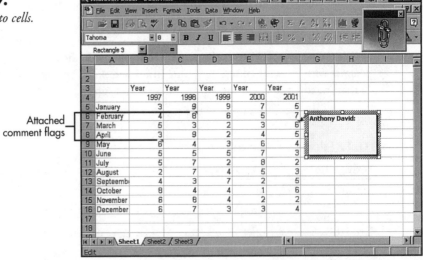

If you select a group of cells and attach a comment, Excel 97 attaches the comment only to the upper-left cell in the selection. Excel 97 cannot attach a comment to an entire selection, only to individual cells.

The earlier section in this hour, "Clearing Data," tells you how to remove comments you no longer need.

Summary

Excel 97's Copy, Cut, and Paste commands work much the same as the corresponding operations in Word 97. This hour focused more on the differences than similarities between the products. Worksheet data differs from a word processor's, and you must handle certain kinds of Excel 97 deletions differently from Word 97 deletions.

This hour taught you how to speed up your data entry by using AutoFill and AutoCorrect. After you teach Excel 97 your own special series, Excel 97 fills in that series of values for you. Although accuracy is more important than speed, you'll welcome the speedy data-entry tools Excel 97 provides.

The next hour shows how to work with ranges, formulas, rows, and columns. Now that you've covered the groundwork, you're ready to learn about Excel 97's powerhouse tools for worksheets.

10

Q&A

Q How do I know whether Excel 97 can fill a series I've started?

A Enter the first couple of values, select the cells, and drag the selection's fill handle to the right or down, depending on your desired fill direction. As you drag the fill handle, Excel 97 shows, in a ToolTips-like pop-up box, which values will fill in the series. If Excel 97 does not recognize the series, the pop-up values won't be correct. You then can teach Excel 97 the new series as explained in this hour or enter the remaining values by hand. In many instances you'll be surprised at the power of Excel 97; for example, if the first two values in your series are 10 and 20, Excel 97 guesses that you want to extend the series by 10s.

Q Why does Excel 97 sometimes select additional cells when all I want to do is extend a series?

A You are dragging the cell's contents, *not* the fill handle. Be sure that you drag the fill handle when you want Excel 97 to complete the series. If you drag with one of the cell's straight edges rather than its fill handle, Excel 97 attempts to move the cell contents from their original location to your dragging target, so be careful that you've grabbed the fill handle when you're ready for the fill.

Q Why would I want to remove formatting, but not a cell's contents?

A You learn in the next hour how to apply lots of formats to cells. For example, you can apply a date format to a cell so that Excel 97 displays a date based on the value and not a number. If you format a cell for a date and later, because of editing changes, that cell no longer holds a date but a value, you'll want to remove the date format. Excel 97 uses a general numerical format for all cells to which you don't specifically apply a different format.

Hour 11

Editing Excel Worksheets

This hour teaches you additional Excel 97 worksheet editing skills. You'll be surprised how Excel 97 helps you when you modify worksheets. For example, Excel 97 automatically adjusts cell range names and formulas when you rearrange your worksheet.

Understanding ranges is critical if you want to really master Excel 97. Therefore, be sure that you master this hour. You'll use range names and addresses in Excel 97 formulas and functions.

In addition to the editing tools, you also learn how to format worksheets to make them look better. This hour teaches the formatting essentials, so you'll be ready for the fancy stuff in the next hour.

The highlights of this hour include

- ☐ What Excel 97 does when you insert or delete rows and columns
- ☐ How ranges differ from selections
- ☐ Why range names are important
- ☐ What the fundamental math operators do

☐ How to organize formulas so that they compute in the order you want them to

☐ Which functions save you time and prevent errors

☐ How to format cells to add eye-catching appeal to your worksheet

Inserting and Deleting

As you saw in the previous hour, the requirements for Excel 97 are somewhat different from those for Word 97, even though both programs perform tasks in a similar manner and with similar menu commands and dialog boxes. The nature of worksheets makes them behave differently from word-processed documents. The next few sections explain how to insert and delete information from your worksheets.

Inserting Entire Cells

Inserting cells, as opposed to inserting data inside a cell, requires that the existing worksheet cells move to the right and down to make room for the new cell. When you want to insert a cell, perform these steps:

1. Select the cell that should appear *after* the inserted cell.

2. Select Insert | Cells to display the Insert dialog box.

3. Click either the Shift Cells Right option or the Shift Cells Down option to determine the direction of the shift. The shift makes room for your new cell.

4. Click OK to begin the shift.

Some people prefer to use the mouse to shift cells right or down to make room for new data. Press Shift and drag the cell's fill handle (or the selection's fill handle if you've selected a group of cells) down or to the right. Excel 97 grays out the areas that are left blank by the shifting. You may have to experiment with inserting cells a few times by inserting and then choosing Undo (Ctrl+Z) before you get the hang of it.

Inserting Rows and Columns

To insert a row or column (and thus move the other rows down or other columns to the right), perform these steps:

1. Select the row or column that appears *after* the inserted rows or columns by clicking its header to select the entire row or column. If you want to insert more than one row or column, select that many existing rows or columns by dragging the row or column selection.

2. Select Insert | Rows or Insert | Columns. Excel 97 shifts the existing rows or columns to make room for the new empty row or column. Instead of selecting from the menu bar, you can point to the selected row or column and display the pop-up

menu shown in Figure 11.1 by right-clicking the mouse and selecting Insert to insert the new row or column. (Excel 97 inserts multiple rows or columns if you first selected more than one row or column.)

Figure 11.1.

You can insert rows or columns with the pop-up menu.

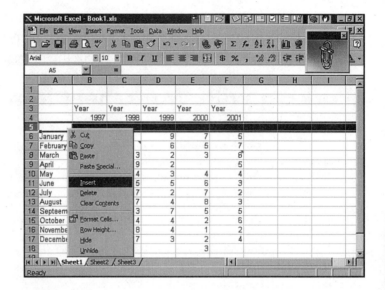

Deleting Entire Cells

When you deleted cells in the previous hour, you learned how to remove selected cells completely from the worksheet and close the gap with the Delete dialog box. The Delete dialog box not only deletes cells, but also deletes entire rows and columns.

To delete a row or column, perform these steps:

1. Select a cell that resides in the row or column you want to delete.
2. Select Edit|Delete to display the Delete dialog box.
3. Select either the Entire Row or Entire Column option.
4. Click OK to perform the deletion. Excel 97 shifts columns to the left or shifts rows up to fill in the missing gap.

If you want to delete multiple rows or multiple columns, select cells from each column or row you want to delete before displaying the Delete dialog box.

Deleting Rows and Columns

Perform these steps when you want to delete a row or column (as opposed to erasing the contents of a row or column):

1. Select the row or column to delete.
2. Right-click the selected row or column to display the pop-up menu.
3. Select Delete. Excel 97 shifts the remaining part of the worksheet to close the gap.

Working with Worksheet Ranges

A *range* is a group of cells. A selected group of cells comprises a range, but ranges don't always have to be selected. A range is always rectangular. A range might be a single cell, a row, a column, or several adjacent rows and columns. The cells in ranges are always contiguous. Even though you can *select* noncontiguous cells, ranges *always* form rectangular worksheet regions. You can perform various operations on ranges, such as moving and copying.

NEW TERM A *range* is a rectangular collection of cells.

Figure 11.2 shows three ranges on a worksheet. You can describe a range by the address of the upper-left cell of the range (the *anchor point*) and the address of the lower-right cell of the range. As you can see from Figure 11.2, multicelled ranges are designated by listing the anchor point, followed by a colon (:), followed by the range's lower-right cell address. Therefore, the range that begins at B3 and ends at F4 has the range of B3:F4.

NEW TERM An *anchor point* is a range's upper-left cell address.

You'll work quite a bit with ranges. One of the ways to make your worksheets more manageable is to name your ranges. For example, you might assign the name Titles to your column titles, Months to your column of month names, and so on.

To name a range, perform these steps:

1. Select the cells that you want to include in the named range.
2. Click the Name box at the left of the formula bar (the text box that displays cell addresses).
3. Type the *range name*.
4. Press Enter. When you subsequently select the range, you'll see that Excel 97 displays the range name instead of the range address in the Name box.

NEW TERM A *range name* is a name you assign to a range of cells. You can move a range to a new worksheet location and the range name stays the same.

Figure 11.2.

Ranges on a worksheet.

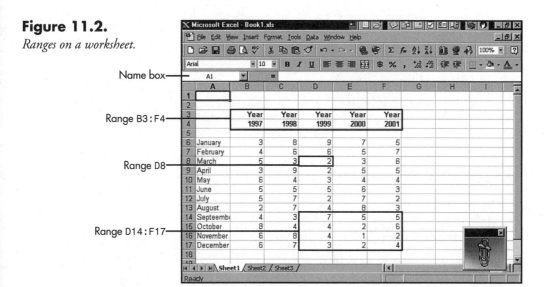

Names are easier to remember than range addresses. For example, if you create a payroll worksheet and assign the names GrossPay, NetPay, HoursWorked, TaxRate, and PayRate to the ranges that hold that data, you never again have to type the range addresses. When you want to move or copy one of the ranges or use the range as a formula, just refer to the range name and let Excel 97 figure out the correct addresses. You learn how to add ranges (including range names) to formulas in the section called "Using Formulas."

11

Here's an even better reason to name ranges: If you move a range, Excel 97 moves the name with the cells! If you tracked range addresses and not names, you would constantly have to track down the latest addresses when you referred to the range. By naming ranges, you never have to worry about keeping track of addresses because the names won't change even if the addresses do.

Use meaningful names. Although AAA works as a name for a column of net sales figures, NetSales makes a lot more sense and is easier to remember. Your range names can include between 1 and 255 characters, and can contain alphabetic letters, numbers, periods, and underscores. Although you cannot include spaces, you can mix uppercase and lowercase letters and include underscores to help distinguish between words in a single name.

If you create a large worksheet and you need to return to a named range to make some changes, click the Name box and type the name. Excel 97 instantly displays that range and selects the range for you.

Fight the urge to ignore range names when you create your worksheets. The tendency is to put off naming ranges until later, and later often does not come. By naming key ranges as you create your worksheet, you more rapidly create the worksheet and the worksheet contains fewer errors.

Using Formulas

Without formulas, Excel 97 would be little more than a word processor for tables of information. When you use formulas, however, Excel 97 becomes an extremely powerful time-saving planning, budgeting, and general-purpose financial tool.

 A *formula* is a calculation that produces a result. Formulas can include math *operators*, numbers, cell addresses, and range names.

 An *operator* is a symbol that requests a mathematical calculation such as a plus sign (+).

 Some people credit worksheet programs for the tremendous PC growth in the 1980s. Without formulas, worksheets would never have been able to create such a demand for personal computers.

On a calculator, you typically type a formula, and then press the equal sign to see the result. All Excel 97 formulas *begin* with an equal sign. For example, the following is a formula:

```
=4*2-3
```

The asterisk is an operator that denotes the times sign (*multiplication*). This formula requests that Excel 97 compute the value of 4 multiplied by 2 minus 3 to get the *result*. When you type a formula and press Enter or move to another cell, Excel 97 displays the result, not the formula, on the worksheet.

As Figure 11.3 shows, the answer 5 appears on the worksheet, and you can see the cell's formula contents right on the Formula bar area. When entering a formula, as soon as you press the equal sign, Excel 97 shows your formula on the Formula bar as well as in the active cell. If you click the Formula bar and then enter your formula, the formula appears in the Formula bar as well as in the active cell. By first clicking the Formula bar before entering the formula, however, you can press the left and right arrow keys to move the cursor left and right within the formula to edit it. When entering long formulas, this Formula bar's editing capability helps you correct mistakes that you might type.

Figure 11.3.

Excel 97 displays a formula's result on the worksheet.

The cell's formula appears here

The formula's answer is displayed here

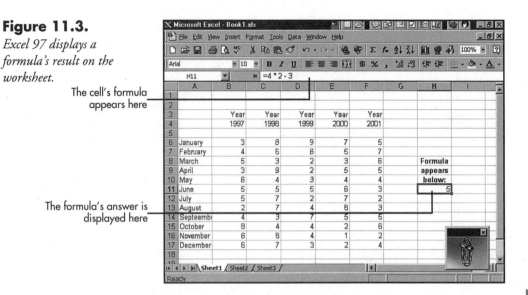

You can format a worksheet to show the actual formula instead of the answer, but you do something like that only when printing worksheet content listings that you want to study.

Excel's Primary Math Operators

Table 11.1 lists the primary math operators you can use in your worksheet formulas. Notice that all the example formulas begin with the equal sign.

Table 11.1. The primary math operators.

Operator	Example	Description
^	=7 ^ 3	Raises 7 to the power of 3 (called exponentiation)
/	=4 / 2	Divides 4 by 2
*	=3 * 4 * 5	Multiplies 3 by 4 by 5
+	=5 + 5	Adds 5 and 5
-	=5 - 5	Subtracts 5 from 5

New Term The *exponentiation* operator raises one number to a higher power.

You can combine any and all the operators in a formula. When combining operators, Excel 97 follows the traditional computer (and algebraic) *operator hierarchy model*. Therefore, Excel 97 first computes exponentiation if you raise any value to another power. Excel 97 then calculates all multiplication and division in a left-to-right order (the first one to appear computes first) before addition and subtraction (also in left-to-right order).

 The *operator hierarchy* dictates the order that operators compute in formulas: exponentiation, multiplication and division, and then addition and subtraction.

The following formula returns a result of 14 because Excel 97 first calculates the exponentiation of 2 raised to the third power, and then Excel 97 divides the answer (8) by 4, and then multiplies the result (2) by 2, and finally the subtracts the result (4) from 18. Even though the subtraction appears first, the operator hierarchy forces the subtraction to wait until last to compute.

```
=18 - 2 ^ 3 / 4 * 2
```

If you want to override the operator hierarchy, put parentheses around the parts you want Excel 97 to compute first. For example, the following formula returns a greatly different result from the previous one, despite the same values and operators used:

```
=(18 - 2) ^ 3 / 4 * 2
```

Instead of 14, this formula returns 2,048! The subtraction produces 16, which is then raised to the third power (producing 4,096) before dividing by 4 and multiplying the result by 2 to get 2,048.

Using Range Names in Formulas

The true power of Excel 97 shows when you use cell addresses and range names in formulas. All the following are valid formulas. Cell addresses or range names appear throughout the formulas.

```
=(SalesTotals)/NumOfSales
=C4 * 2 - (Rate * .08)
=7 + LE51 - (Gross - Net)
```

When you enter formulas that contain range addresses, you can either type the full address or point to the cell address. If you want to include a complete named range in a formula (formulas can work on complete ranges, as you see later this hour), select the entire range and Excel 97 inserts the range name in your formula. Often, finding and pointing to a value is easier than locating the address and entering the exact address.

If, for example, you are entering a formula for cells that are close to the formula's cell, when you get to the place in the formula that requires a close cell, don't type the cell address but point to the cell. If you've entered a formula such as =7 + , instead of typing a cell address of LE51, you can point to that cell and Excel 97 enters the cell's address for you. Immediately after typing the cell address for you, Excel 97 returns your cursor to the formula (or to the Formula bar if you're entering the formula there) so that you can complete it.

After you assign a name to a cell, you don't have to remember that cell's address when you use that cell in formulas. Suppose that you are creating a large worksheet that spans many screens. If you assign names to cells when you create them, cells that you know you'll refer to later during the worksheet's development, entering formulas that use that name is made easier. Instead of locating that cell to find its address, you only need to type the name when entering a formula that uses that cell.

To assign a range name to a cell or to a range of cells, select the cell or range and click the Name box at the left of the Formula bar. Type the name and press Enter, and Excel 97 assigns the name to that cell or range.

Relative Versus Absolute Cell Addressing

When you copy formulas that contain cell addresses, Excel 97 updates the cell addresses so that they reference *relative addresses*. For example, suppose that you enter this formula in cell A1:

```
=A2 + A3
```

NEW TERM A *relative address* is an address that references cells based on the current cell's location.

This formula contains two addresses. The addresses are relative because the addresses A2 and A3 change if you copy the formula elsewhere. For example, if you copy the formula to cell B5, B5 holds this:

```
=B6 + B7
```

The original relative addresses update to reflect the formula's copied location. Of course, A1 still holds its original contents, but the copied cell at B5 holds the same formula referencing B5 instead of A1.

An *absolute address* is an address that does not change if you copy the formula. A dollar sign, $, always precedes an absolute address. The address B5 is an absolute address. As an example, if you wanted to sum two columns of data (A1 with B1, A2 with B2, and so on) and then multiply each sum by some constant number, the constant number could be a cell referred to as an absolute address. That formula might look like this:

```
=(A1 + B1) * $J$1
```

J1 is an absolute address but A1 and B1 are relative. If you copied the formula down one row, the formula would change to this:

```
=(A2 + B2) * $J$1
```

NEW TERM An *absolute address* is an address that references cells using their specific addresses and does not change when you copy the cell holding the formula.

Notice that the first two cells changed because, when you originally entered them, they were relative cell addresses. You told Excel 97, by placing dollar signs in front of the absolute cell address's row and column references, not to change that reference when you copy the formula elsewhere.

$B5 is a partial absolute address. If you copy a formula with $B5 inside the computation, the $B keeps the B column intact, but the fifth row updates to the row location of the target cell. If you type the following formula in cell A1:

=2 * $B5

and then copy the formula to cell F6, cell F6 holds this formula:

=2 * $B10

You copied the formula to a cell five rows and five columns over in the worksheet. Excel 97 did not update the column name, B, because you told Excel 97 to keep that column name absolute (it's always B no matter where you copy the formula). Excel 97 added 5 to the row number, however, because the row number was relative and open to change whenever you copied the formula.

The dollar sign keeps the row B absolute no matter where you copy the formula, but the relative row number can change as you copy the formula.

The bottom line is this: Most of the time, you use relative addressing. If you insert or delete rows, columns, or cells, your formulas remain accurate because the cells that they reference change as your worksheet changes.

Copying Formulas

Excel 97 offers several shortcut tools that make copying cells from one location to another simple. Consider the worksheet in Figure 11.4. The bottom row needs to hold formulas that total each of the projected year's 12-month values.

How would you enter the total row? You could type the following formula in cell B19:

=B6+B7+B8+B9+B10+B11+B12+B13+B14+B15+B16+B17

After you've typed the formula in B19, you then *could* type the following formula in cell C19:

=C6+C7+C8+C9+C10+C11+C12+C13+C14+C15+C16+C17

You then *could* type the values in the remaining total cells. Instead of doing all that typing, however, *copy* cell B19 to cell C19. Hold Ctrl while you drag the cell edge of B19 to C19. When you release the mouse, cell C19 properly totals column C! Press Ctrl and copy C19 to D19 through F19 to place the totals in all the total cells. The totals are accurate, as Figure 11.5 shows.

Figure 11.4.

A total row is needed for the project's yearly values.

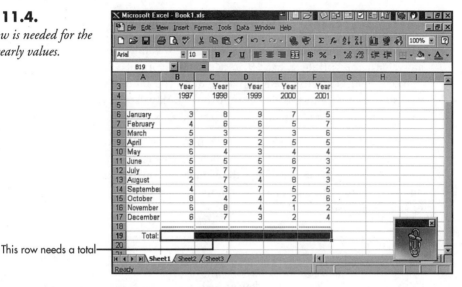

	A	B	C	D	E	F	G	H	I
3		Year	Year	Year	Year	Year			
4		1997	1998	1999	2000	2001			
5									
6	January	3	8	9	7	5			
7	February	4	6	6	5	7			
8	March	5	3	2	3	6			
9	April	3	9	2	5	5			
10	May	6	4	3	4	4			
11	June	5	5	5	6	3			
12	July	5	7	2	7	2			
13	August	2	7	4	8	3			
14	September	4	3	7	5	5			
15	October	8	4	4	2	6			
16	November	6	8	4	1	2			
17	December	6	7	3	2	4			
18									
19	Total:								
20									

This row needs a total

If cell B19 contained absolute addresses, cells C19 through F19 would all total column B!

Figure 11.5.

Relative references make totaling these columns simple.

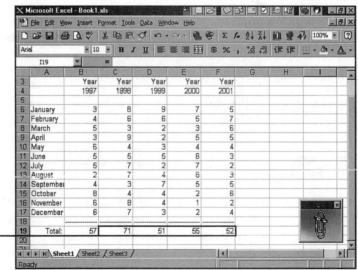

	A	B	C	D	E	F	G	H	I
3		Year	Year	Year	Year	Year			
4		1997	1998	1999	2000	2001			
5									
6	January	3	8	9	7	5			
7	February	4	6	6	5	7			
8	March	5	3	2	3	6			
9	April	3	9	2	5	5			
10	May	6	4	3	4	4			
11	June	5	5	5	6	3			
12	July	5	7	2	7	2			
13	August	2	7	4	8	3			
14	September	4	3	7	5	5			
15	October	8	4	4	2	6			
16	November	6	8	4	1	2			
17	December	6	7	3	2	4			
18									
19	Total:	57	71	51	55	52			
20									

Copied from B19

11

Recalculating Worksheets

After you set up formulas, your job is done; Excel 97's, however, has just begun. If you change any value in the worksheet, Excel 97 recalculates all formulas automatically! Therefore, Excel 97 keeps your worksheet fresh and accurate as you modify values. You can use the same worksheet each month and change only the monthly data. If you leave the formulas intact, Excel 97 computes and displays the correct answers.

You can turn off the automatic recalculation and manually recalculate when ready if you use a slow computer and want to save time when editing a large worksheet. Select Tools | Options and click the Calculation tab. Click the Manual option to force manual recalculation. If you now change the data, Excel 97 does not recalculate your worksheet until you press F9 (the Calculate Now shortcut key).

Excel 97 has a small bug that can keep some cells from recalculating in extremely large worksheets. Microsoft offers a patch to correct this problem at the following web address: www.microsoft.com/ OfficeFreeStuff/Excel/dlpages/XL8P1.htm.

Working with Functions

The previous sections explain how to enter a formula once, using relative addresses, and copy that formula to other cells. Although you only have to type the formula one time, this kind of totaling formula is tedious to type and introduces greater chance for error:

=B6+B7+B8+B9+B10+B11+B12+B13+B14+B15+B16+B17

Fortunately, Microsoft includes several built-in *functions* that perform many common mathematical calculations. For example, instead of writing a formula to sum a row or column of values, use the Sum() function.

 Functions are built-in calculations and data manipulations that perform the work of formulas to return values.

Function names always end with parentheses, such as Average(). A function accepts zero or more *arguments*. The arguments, if any, go inside the parentheses. Always separate function arguments with commas. If a function contains only a single argument, you do not use a comma inside the parentheses. Functions generally manipulate data (numbers or text), and the argument list inside the parentheses supplies the data to the function. For example, the Average() function computes an average of whatever list of values you pass in the argument list in Average(). Therefore, all the following compute an average from the argument list:

```
=Average(18, 65, 299, $R$5, 10, -2, 102)
=Average(SalesTotals)
=Average(D4:D14)
```

 An *argument* is a value on which a function operates (most often indicated by cell addresses). Arguments appear inside the parentheses of a function.

As with many functions, Average() accepts as many arguments as needed to do its job. The first Average() function computes the average of seven values, one of which is an absolute cell address. The second Average() function computes the average of a range named SalesTotals. No matter how many cells comprise the range SalesTotals, Average() computes the average. The last Average() function computes the average of the values in the range D4 through D14 (a columnar list).

The Sum() function is perhaps the most common function because you so often total table columns and rows. In the previous section, you entered a long formula to add the values in a column. Instead of adding each cell to total the range B6:B17, you could more easily enter the following function:

```
=Sum(B6:B17)
```

If you copy this Sum() function to the other cells at the bottom of the yearly projections, you achieve the same results as the added values, but the worksheet is easier to maintain if you need to make modifications later.

 Suppose that you want to track 24 biweekly totals instead of 12 monthly ones. Insert 12 additional blank rows, change the row titles (to something like JanWk12, JanWk34, FebWk12, and so on), and enter the biweekly values. You won't have to change the total calculations! When you insert rows within the Sum() range, Excel 97 updates the range inside the Sum() function to contain the 12 new values.

Use AutoSum for Speed

Before looking at a table of common functions, Excel 97 helps you with summing functions by analyzing your selected range and automatically inserting a Sum() function if needed. Here's how to do that:

1. Select the range that you want to sum. For example, if you want to sum the months over the projected years for this hour's sample worksheets, select the row with the January label, as shown in Figure 11.6.

2. Click the AutoSum toolbar button. Excel 97 guesses that you want to sum the selected row and inserts the Sum() function in the cell to the right of the row.

3. Make any edits to the summed value if Excel 97 included too many or not enough cells. You can click the cell and press F2 to edit the sum. Usually, no edits are required.

Figure 11.6.

Getting ready to request a sum.

AutoSum button——

Excel 97 places the Sum() function here

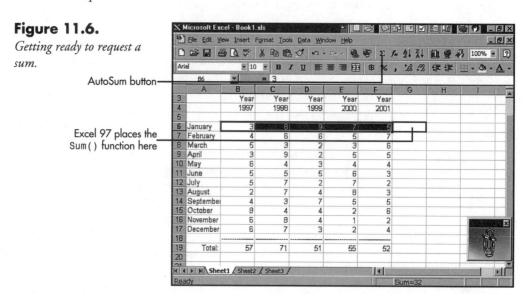

After Excel 97 generates the Sum() function, you can copy the cell down the rest of the column to add the monthly totals. However, can you see another way to perform the same monthly totals with one selection? Select the *entire set* of monthly values with one extra blank column at the right (the range B6:G17). Excel 97 sees the blank column and fills it in with each row's sum when you click AutoSum. You now can select the new column of totals and let AutoSum compute them. Figure 11.7 shows the result of the new sums after you add underlines and a title.

Common Functions

Functions improve your accuracy. For example, if you want to average three cell values, you might type something like this:

```
=C2 + C4 + C6 / 3
```

This formula does not compute an average! Remember that the operator hierarchy forces the division calculation first. If you use the Average() function, as shown next, you don't have to worry as much about the calculation's hierarchy.

```
=Average(C2, C4, C6)
```

Figure 11.7.

AutoSum in action.

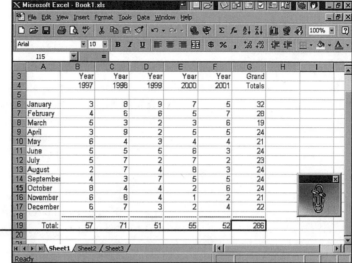

AutoSum summed
this entire column

Another advantage of using functions is that you can modify them more easily than you can long calculations. For example, if you want to throw another cell value into the previous average, you only need to add the extra cell to Average(); if you use a formula, you must remember to change the 3 to 4.

Table 11.2 describes common Excel 97 built-in functions that you find lots of uses for as you create worksheets. Remember to start every formula with an equal sign and to add your cell addresses to the parentheses, and you are set!

Table 11.2. Common Excel 97 functions.

Function Name	Description
Abs()	Computes the absolute value of its cell argument. (Good for distance- and age-difference calculations.)
Average()	Computes the average of its arguments.
Count()	Returns the number of numerical arguments in the argument list. (Useful if you use a range name for the argument list.)
Counta()	Returns the number of all arguments in the argument list. (Useful if you use a range name for the argument list.)

continues

Table 11.2. continued

Function Name	Description
CountBlank()	Returns the number of blank cells, if any exist, in the argument range. (Useful if you use a range name for the argument list.)
Max()	Returns the highest (maximum) value in the argument list. (Useful if you use a range name for the argument list and you need to pick out the highest value.)
Min()	Returns the lowest (minimum) value in the argument list. (Useful if you use a range name for the argument list and you need to pick out the lowest value.)
Pi()	Computes the value of mathematical pi (requires no arguments) for use in math calculations.
Product()	Computes the product (multiplicative result) of the argument range.
Roman()	Converts its cell value to a Roman numeral.
Sqrt()	Computes the square root of the cell argument.
Stddev()	Computes the argument list's standard deviation.
Sum()	Computes the sum of its arguments.
Today()	Returns today's date (requires no arguments).
Var()	Computes the argument list's sample variance.

 Excel 97 supports many more functions than Table 11.2 lists. Excel 97 even supports complex mathematical, date, time, financial, and engineering functions. As you learn more about Excel 97 and create more complex worksheets, you'll run across these functions as you read through the online help.

Advanced Functions

Some of the functions require more arguments than a simple cell or range. For example, Excel 97 contains many financial functions that compute loan values and investment rates of return. If you want to use one of the more advanced functions, click the Paste Function toolbar button to display the Paste Function dialog box (shown in Figure 11.8).

Figure 11.8.

Let Excel 97's Paste Function dialog box type complex functions for you.

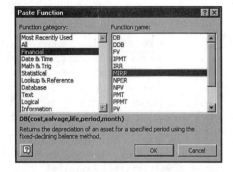

When you select the category in the left column, the Paste Function displays a list of functions within that category. When you click one of the functions, the Paste Function dialog box gives you a helpful mini description. When you find the function you need, double-click it; Excel 97 displays an additional dialog box that requests each of the function arguments, such as the one shown in Figure 11.9. As you continue with the Paste Function dialog box, Excel 97 builds the function in the cell for you. As you get more proficient, you no longer need the help of the Paste Function dialog box.

Figure 11.9.

The Paste Function dialog box walks you through each function argument.

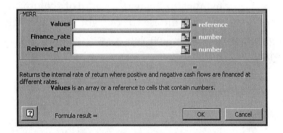

Introduction to Worksheet Formatting

Until now, you've seen no fancy worksheets. I kept the fancy stuff out of the way so that you could concentrate on the work at hand. It's now time to show you how to pretty things up. This hour is about to come to a close, but you still have time to learn some cell-formatting basics and you can continue with Excel 97's more advanced formatting features in the next hour's session.

Justification

Excel 97 right-justifies numbers (and formulas that result in numbers) and left-justifies text labels. You don't have to accept Excel 97's default justification, however. To left-, center-, or right-justify the contents of any cell (or range), select the cell (or range) and click the Align Left, Center, or Align Right toolbar buttons. Center titles above columns and adjust your numbers to look just right.

11

Excel 97 offers a trick that even some Excel 97 gurus forget: if you want to center a title above several columns of data, type the title in a cell above the data. If you cannot center the title over the values by clicking the Center toolbar button, select all the cells around the title so that you've selected as many columns as there is data. Click the Merge and Center toolbar button. Excel 97 centers the title, even though the title resides in a single cell, across the entire column selection.

Row and Column Height and Width

As you learn more formatting tricks, you'll need to adjust certain row and column widths and heights to hold the newly formatted values. To adjust a row's height, point to the line that separates the row number from previous or subsequent rows. When the mouse pointer changes to a double-pointing arrow, drag the row's top or bottom edge up or down. Excel 97 adjusts the entire row height as you drag your mouse. Sometimes large titles need the larger row heights. When you release the mouse, Excel 97 anchors the new row height where you left it.

In the same manner, to change the width of a column, point to the column name's left or right edge and drag your mouse left or right. Excel 97 adjusts the column width to follow your mouse movement. When you release the mouse, Excel 97 anchors the new column width where you left it.

If you shrink a column width so that the column can no longer display all the data, Excel 97 displays pound signs (#####) to warn you that you need to widen the column. Your data is still stored in the cell—it simply cannot be displayed.

To adjust the column width so that the column (or range of columns) is exactly large enough to hold the largest data value in the column, select the column (or columns) and double-click the right edge of the column name. Excel 97 adjusts the column to hold the widest data value in the column.

Font Changes

Feel free to change the worksheet's font to add appeal. Simple font changes, such as boldfacing, italicizing, and underlining, greatly improve the look of titles. The Bold, Italic, and Underline toolbar buttons add the proper formatting to your selected cell or range. If you select Format|Cells and click the Font tab, Excel 97 displays the Font dialog box (virtually identical to that of Word 97), in which you can select a new font name and size. As Figure 11.10 shows, simple font changes can make a big improvement on otherwise dull worksheets.

Figure 11.10.

Already this worksheet looks better.

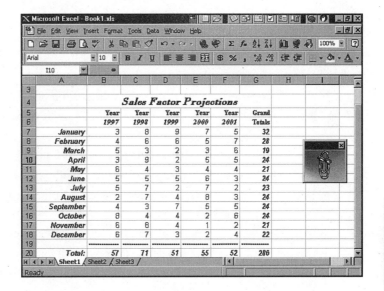

 If you format a row with a font that's larger than the current row size, Excel 97 adjusts the row height to make room for the new font.

Of course, you can use the Font and Font Size toolbar buttons to change a font name or size without displaying the Font dialog box.

Making Format Changes

Now that you've mastered Excel 97 basics, it's time to learn the general format categories Excel 97 uses for worksheet data. Table 11.3 describes each of the format categories. Unless you change the default, Excel 97 uses the General format for data of all kinds.

Table 11.3. Excel 97's fundamental formats.

Format Name	Description
General	The numeric data has no special formatting and generally appears exactly the way you enter the data.

continues

Table 11.3. continued

Format Name	Description
Number	You can set the number of decimal places Excel 97 displays for all numerical values.
Currency	Displays a dollar sign and two decimal places for dollar amounts.
Accounting	Aligns currency and decimal points in a column.
Date	Displays date and time values as values whose formats you can change.
Time	Displays only the time portion of a date and time value.
Percentage	Displays a percent sign. If you type **50** into the cell, Excel 97 changes your value to **50%**.
Fraction	Displays numbers as fractions (great for stock quotes).
Scientific	Uses scientific notation for all numerical values.
Text	Formats *all* data as text. Great for zip codes that are all numbers but that you never use for calculations.
Special	Formats zip codes, phone numbers, and Social Security numbers.
Custom	Lets you define your own cell format. You can decide if you want to see the plus or minus sign, and you can control the number of decimal places.

Format a selection by selecting Format | Cells and clicking the Number tab to display a scrolling list of formats (shown in Table 11.3). If you select the Time format from that list, you must select one of the Time format display variations so that Excel 97 knows how you want the time displayed.

You can also right-click the selection and select the Format Cells command from the pop-up menu. When you do, you see a dialog box that enables you to assign the formats directly to your data.

You can also use Excel's autoformatting capabilities to easily add style to your worksheet. (AutoFormats are covered in the next hour.)

Several formatting toolbar buttons exist that enable quick formatting of cells using the most common format styles. If you select a cell or a range of cells, you can change the selection's format more quickly with a toolbar button than with the Format | Cells dialog box. Not all Excel's formats are available through the toolbar, but these are: Currency Style, Percent Style,

Comma Style, Increase Decimal (to increase the number of decimal places), and Decrease
Decimal (to decrease the number of decimal places).

Summary

This hour extended your worksheet knowledge by giving you more editing tools with which
to insert and delete columns, rows, and cells. After you name important worksheet ranges,
you won't have to track specific addresses in your worksheet; the name is easier to remember,
and Excel 97 changes the range if you insert data in or delete it from the range.

One of the most powerful aspects of worksheets is their recalculation capability. If you change
data or a formula, Excel 97 recalculates the entire worksheet as soon as you make the change.
You're always looking at the computed worksheet with up-to-date formulas no matter what
kind of data changes you make. When you add formulas to cell calculations, you not only
improve your worksheet accuracy, but you finish your worksheets faster.

The next hour picks up where this one leaves off, going into formatting in more detail.
Additionally, you see that graphics spruce up your worksheet and are easy to produce.

Q&A

Q What is the difference between a selection and a range?

A Selections cannot be named, and can be comprised of several disjointed areas of
your worksheet. A range, on the other hand, can be named, and can be any
contiguous rectangular collection of cells, including a single cell or your entire
worksheet data area. Often, you select an entire range, but all selections are not
ranges.

Q Why would I ever use absolute addressing?

A Relative addressing seems to make the most sense for most worksheets. If you have
to rearrange your worksheet, all your relative addresses update as well. Absolute
addresses are great when a formula references a single cell, such as an age or pay
value, that rarely changes. You could use dollar signs to anchor the single cell in the
formula that uses that cell, but keep the other addresses relative in case you need to
copy the formula around the worksheet.

**Q What's the difference between the formatting you get by clicking the Center
toolbar button and the formatting you get by clicking the Merge and Center
button?**

A If you need to center the contents of one cell, both centering formats perform the
same task. If, however, you want to center data (such as a title) above a range of cell
columns, select the range the centered cell is to go over and click Merge and
Center; Excel 97 completes the centering across the multiple columns.

11

Hour 12

Formatting Worksheets to Look Great

This hour concludes your Excel 97 tutorial by explaining how to format your worksheet with professional styles. The AutoFormat feature in Excel 97 quickly formats your worksheet within the boundaries you select. If you want to format your worksheet by hand, the formatting commands you learn in this hour enable you to pinpoint important data and highlight that data so that others who look at and use your worksheets find your highlighted information.

After you create and format your worksheets, use the Chart Wizard in Excel 97 to produce colorful graphs. Often, a worksheet's trends and comparisons get lost in the numeric details. The graphs that the Chart Wizard generates look great, and Excel 97 does all the drawing work for you.

The highlights of this hour include

- ☐ What AutoFormat can do with your worksheets
- ☐ How to apply custom formats to selected cells
- ☐ When special orientation and wrapped text improve your worksheet appearance

☐ How to use the Chart Wizard to produce graphs that show data trends and comparisons

☐ How to modify your charts so that they look the way you want them to

AutoFormatting Worksheets

Before diving into additional formatting commands, you should know that the AutoFormat feature in Excel 97 converts an otherwise dull worksheet into a nice-looking professional one. A worksheet's presentation is almost as important as the data within the worksheet. If your worksheet needs sprucing up, try AutoFormat after you've formatted individual cells because AutoFormat gives a good-looking, consistent dimension to your entire worksheet. After AutoFormat finishes, you can add finishing touches to the worksheet by adding more specific formats to highlight important cell information, such as special totals that you want to make stand out.

To use AutoFormat, press Ctrl+A to select the entire worksheet. Select Format | AutoFormat to display the AutoFormat dialog box (shown in Figure 12.1).

Figure 12.1.

Let AutoFormat improve your worksheet.

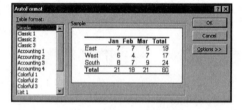

Scroll through the AutoFormat samples until you find an interesting name. Single-click the name to see the style's sample in the Sample window. When you click OK, Excel 97 applies the format to your selected worksheet cells. Figure 12.2 shows that AutoFormat knows to highlight totals and also knows to separate headings from the data detail.

To omit certain AutoFormat format styles, click the Options button in AutoFormat to check or uncheck styles. For example, you can keep AutoFormat from changing your worksheet's font by unchecking the Font option.

Making Your Own Default Format

Suppose that you often print worksheets to fax to others, and your fax requires boldfaced worksheets so that the recipients can read the numbers. Instead of changing your worksheet text to boldface before faxing the worksheet, you can make boldface the default font style.

Excel 97 enables you to change several of the font defaults, so if you find yourself applying the same font style over and over, consider making that style part of Excel 97's default style.

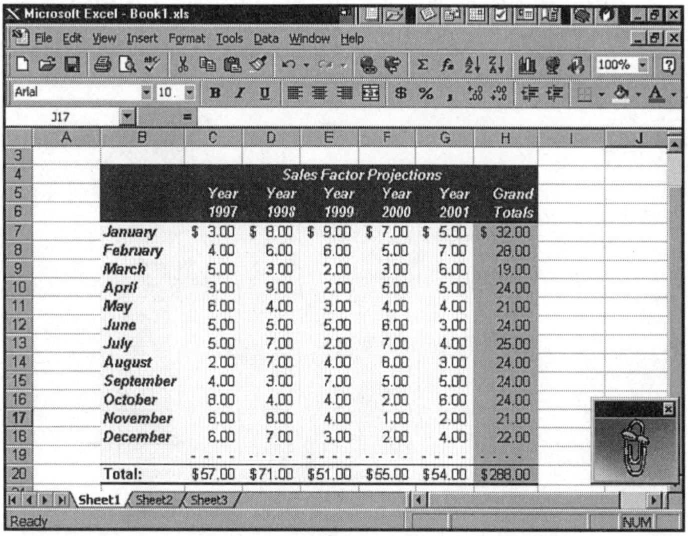

Figure 12.2.

AutoFormat improved the appearance of this worksheet.

To modify the default style, follow these steps:

1. Select Format | Style to display the Style dialog box (shown in Figure 12.3).

Figure 12.3.

You can change any named style.

12

2. Select the default style, Normal, from the Style Name drop-down list box. (The *Normal* style is probably already the style you see when you open the dialog box.) Like Word 97, Excel 97 enables you to modify styles and even create customized styles of your own. When you apply the style changes you added by selecting Format | Style, Excel 97 applies the style set by the Style dialog box to the selected cells.

NEW TERM *Normal style* is the default style Excel 97 normally uses for all your worksheet cells.

3. To change the Normal style, click the Modify button. Excel 97 displays the Format Cells dialog box (shown in Figure 12.4), from which you can modify the named style.

Figure 12.4.

The Format Cells dialog box modifies any format currently set.

4. Click OK to close the Format Cells dialog box.
5. Click OK to close the Style dialog box. Excel 97 applies your style to the selected cells. If you made changes to the Normal style, Excel 97 automatically uses that format on future worksheets unless you modify the format or style.

> If you plan to create additional worksheets that are similar to the one you just created, consider saving the worksheet as a template with File I Save As and then selecting the template type. When you're ready to create the next similar worksheet, load the template and your formats will already be in place.

Additional Formatting Options

Many of Excel 97's formatting features are identical to Word 97's, such as the boldface, italics, underline, font color, and fill color (the cell's background color) features. In addition, you now know how to change a selection's alignment. Excel 97 supports several special formats that go further to improve the look of your worksheets. AutoFormat uses some of these special formats, and you can create your own styles that use these formats as well.

The following sections briefly introduce you to these Excel 97 formatting options, which provide you with additional ways to add impact to your worksheets. You can change any of these formats from the Format Cells dialog box. Open the Format Cells dialog box by selecting Format | Cells, by changing one of the stored styles as you learned in the previous section, or by right-clicking a selection and choosing Format Cells.

Special Alignment

Not only can you left-justify, center-justify, and right-justify, as well as justify across selected cells, you can also orient text vertically or to whatever slant you prefer. When you click the Format | Cells Alignment tab, Excel 97 displays the Alignment dialog box (shown in Figure 12.5), in which you can adjust text orientation.

Figure 12.5.

Align text with the Format Cells dialog box Alignment page.

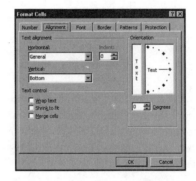

12

Step-Up

The vertical text orientation in Excel 97 is easier to adjust than in previous versions because Excel 97 draws a line to show the text rotation angle as you change the angle.

When you click the Alignment dialog box's first orientation text box (the text box with the word Text dropping down the screen), Excel 97 changes all selected cells to vertical orientation. If you want to slant text, such as titles, select a different Degree value or click the rotating text pointer to the slant you desire. When you click OK, Excel 97 rotates the selected text to your chosen angle. Figure 12.6 shows an example of slanted titles produced by selecting a 45-degree angle in the Alignment dialog box. The text prints at an angle as well.

Figure 12.6.

You can change the vertical alignment of selected text.

Slanted text alignment

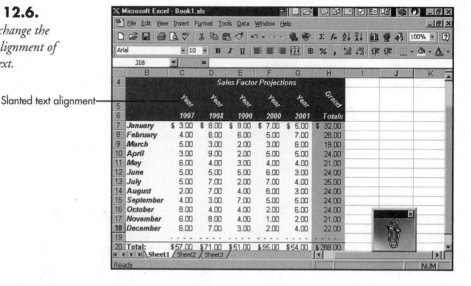

If you need to include a lot of text in one or more cells, you already know (from Hour 9, "Excel 97 Workbooks") that Excel 97 either truncates the cell or pours the cell's contents into the next cell to the right. Excel 97 offers several other options, as well. When a cell requires a lot of text, select the Wrap Text option from the Alignment dialog box. Excel 97 wraps the text within the cell's width, increasing the cell (and, therefore, row) height to display all the wrapped text. If you click the Shrink to Fit option, Excel 97 decreases the cell's font size (as much as feasible) to display the entire cell contents within the cell's current width and height. If you click Merge Cells, Excel 97 combines adjacent cells into a single wide cell.

Special Cell Borders

With the Format | Cells Border dialog box (shown in Figure 12.7), you can apply an outline, or border, around selected cells.

 A *border* is a cell outline that you can apply to enclose selected cells.

The Border dialog box enables you to add a border to any side of the selected cells as well as diagonal lines inside the cells so that you can show a cell X'd out or otherwise cross off a cell's contents for a printed report. As you select among the Outline and Inside options, the preview area shows what the resulting border looks like.

The Borders toolbar button is quicker to use than the Border dialog box, but you cannot control as many border details.

Figure 12.7.

Add borders around cells to highlight key data.

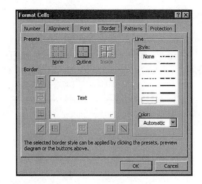

Select Line Style options from the Border dialog box to change the pattern of the border that you choose. If you want to remove any selected cell's border, click None.

Special Cell Shades

The Format | Cells Pattern dialog box enables you to add color or a shading pattern to selected cells. Although the Fill Color toolbar button colors cell backgrounds more quickly than the Pattern dialog box, the Pattern dialog box enables you to add a shading pattern to the background.

When you click the Pattern drop-down box from the Pattern dialog box, Excel 97 displays pattern options (shown in Figure 12.8).

Figure 12.8.

Choose a pattern for the selected cell.

Available patterns

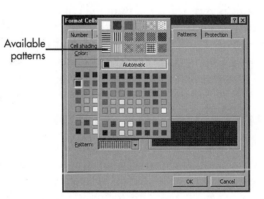

12

Locked and Hidden Cells

When you create worksheets for others, you want to *lock* titles and formulas so that users can enter and change the data areas without harming the worksheet's format. A *hidden* cell is useful when you want to block a cell's value from showing temporarily.

> The locked and hidden cell status activates only when you activate worksheet protection by selecting Tools | Protection and selecting one of the protection options.

NEW TERM A *locked cell* is one whose contents you cannot change if the worksheet is protected.

NEW TERM A *hidden cell* is one whose contents you cannot see if the worksheet is protected.

The Format | Cells Protection dialog box controls the locked and hidden status of selected cells. You can enable and disable locking as well as control the hidden status by clicking the appropriate Protection dialog box options. Excel 97 does not ensure that your users won't deactivate the protection and modify the worksheet. The protection helps protect the worksheet from accidental damage, but anyone can modify the protection status and change locked cells.

Cell locking is great when you want to keep accidental worksheet changes from occurring. If the protection needs to go further than simple safety, add a password when you protect the selection. Only someone with the worksheet's (or workbook's) password will be able to unlock locked cells or show hidden cells. To add a password, select Tools | Protection. You can add a password to the worksheet or to the entire workbook.

Creating Custom Graphs

A picture is worth a thousand words and *numbers*, and Excel 97 produces professional-looking graphs from *your* worksheet data. You don't need to know a lot about graphing and charting unless you want to create extremely sophisticated Excel 97 graphs. You can use Excel 97's *Chart Wizard* in most cases to produce great-looking graphs quickly and easily. When you click the Chart Wizard toolbar button, Excel 97 displays the opening screen of the Chart Wizard dialog box (shown in Figure 12.9).

NEW TERM The *Chart Wizard* is an Excel 97 wizard that displays your worksheet data as a colorful graph.

Figure 12.9.
Excel 97's Chart Wizard
creates graphs for you.

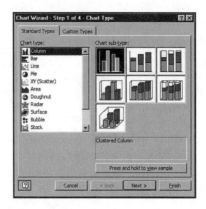

Choosing the Chart Type

Table 12.1 describes each of the chart types that Excel 97 creates. You can select an appropriate chart type from the Chart Wizard's opening screen. To preview your worksheet when formatted with any chart, select a chart type, and then a chart subtype, and click the button labeled Press and Hold to View Sample. Excel 97 analyzes your worksheet data and displays a small sketch of the chart you selected.

Table 12.1. Excel 97 chart options.

Chart type	Description
Column	Shows changes over time and compares values.
Bar	Compares data items.
Line	Shows trends and projections.
Pie	Illustrates the proportional size of items in the same series.
XY (scatter)	Shows relationships of several values in a series.
Area	Emphasizes the magnitude of changes over time.
Doughnut	Illustrates the proportional size of items in multiple series.
Radar	Each category contains an *axis* that radiates from the center of the graph (useful for finding the data series with the most penetration, as needed in market research statistical studies).
Surface	Locates optimum combinations between two data series.

continues

12

Table 12.1. continued

Chart type	Description
Bubble	Shows relationships between several series values, but also (with circles, or bubbles of varying sizes) shows the magnitude of data intersections.
Stock	Illustrates a stock's (or other investment's) high, low, and closing prices.
Cone, Cylinder, Pyramid	Indicates trends and comparisons with special 3D cone, cylinder, and pyramid symbols.

NEW TERM An *axis* is a graph edge that bisects the chart at right angles and indicates the data values in the chart, such as time or dollar amounts.

> If you are new to graphing, you may not know which graph works best for a particular worksheet. Try one! If you see that a bar graph does not show a trend that you want to demonstrate, generate a line graph. Excel 97 makes it easy to select from among several graphs to find the best graph for your needs.

Selecting Data for Your Graph

A *data series* is a single group of data that you might select from a column or row to graph. Unlike a range, a data series must be contiguous in the row or column with no cells in between. Often, a series is comprised of a time period, such as a week, month, or year. One person's weekly sales totals (from a group of several salespeople's weekly totals) would also form a series. Some graphs, such as pie charts, graph only a single series, whereas other graphs show comparisons between two or more data series.

NEW TERM A *data series* is a single column, row, or set of cell values that you group together, such as a given region's sales for a week, month, year, or a single salesperson.

As you look through the graph samples, if one of the series looks extremely large in comparison to the others, Excel 97 is probably including a total column or row in the graph results. Generally, you want to graph a single series (such as monthly costs) or several series, but not the totals—the totals throw off the data comparisons. Therefore, if you see extreme ranges at the beginning or end of your graph, select only the data areas (not the total cells) from the Chart Wizard's second dialog box (shown in Figure 12.10).

You need to tell the Chart Wizard which direction the data series flows by clicking either Rows or Columns from the Chart Wizard's second dialog box.

Figure 12.10.

Be sure to select only data areas for your graph.

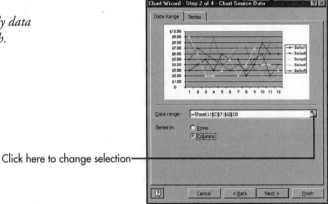

Click here to change selection

When you click the Next button to see the third Chart Wizard dialog box (shown in Figure 12.11), Excel 97 enables you to enter a chart title that appears at the top of the resulting chart as well as axis titles that appear on each edge of your chart.

Figure 12.11.

Enter titles that you want to see on the chart.

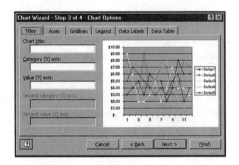

12

You find other tabs in the Chart Wizard's third dialog box that enable you to control the placement of the *legend* and a *data table* .

NEW TERM A *legend* describes how the chart's patterns and colors represent the information in the graph.

NEW TERM A *data table* is a miniature summarized worksheet that appears beneath the graph. The table shows numerically what the graph represents graphically.

Click Next to see the final Chart Wizard dialog box, in which you determine exactly where and how to place the generated graph. Excel 97 can create a new worksheet for the graph or embed the graph inside the current worksheet as an embedded object. You can, in turn, embed the object in other Office 97 products, as you learn in Part VII, "Combining the Office 97 Products and the Internet."

Modifying the Graph

Click the Finish button to see your resulting graph. If you've chosen to embed the graph inside your current worksheet, you may have to drag the graph's *sizing handles* to expand or shrink the graph. In addition, you can drag the graph anywhere you want it to appear on your worksheet. Excel 97 displays the floating Graph toolbar right below the graph in case you want to change it.

NEW TERM *Sizing handles* are eight black handles that appear around certain objects, such as graphs, with which you can resize the object by dragging.

If your graph does not display data the way you prefer, you can click the Graph toolbar buttons to change the graph's properties. You can even change the graph type (from a line chart to a bar graph, for instance) from the Graph toolbar without rerunning the Chart Wizard. The Graph toolbar ensures that all data selections and titles remain in place when you change your graph. If you need to make more extensive graph changes, rerun the Chart Wizard.

In addition to using the Graph toolbar, you can often change specific parts of your graph by right-clicking the graph. For example, if you point to your chart's title and right-click your mouse, Excel 97 displays a pop-up menu from which you can choose the title's pattern, font, and alignment.

When you single-click a graph's element, such as the legend or a charted data series, Excel 97 displays sizing handles so that you can resize the element. If you double-click an element, Excel 97 displays a dialog box with the element's properties, such as color and shape, so that you can modify the way the element appears on the graph.

Summary

This hour completed your Excel 97 tutorial! You can now format your worksheets to look any way you want. If you want to let Excel 97 give formatting a try, select your worksheet data and start Excel 97's AutoFormat feature. Add color, patterns, shading, and borders to your worksheets.

The Excel 97 Chart Wizard turns your data into great-looking graphical charts. By working through the Chart Wizard's dialog boxes, you give Excel 97 all the information needed to generate custom graphs. Graphs can be used to analyze data, compare values, and often show trends faster than the worksheet's details can show.

Now that you've learned how to create great looking worksheets, you'll want to show those worksheets to someone. Why not use PowerPoint 97? The next hour introduces PowerPoint 97, Office 97's colorful presentation creator and editor.

Q&A

Q When would I want to create a style?

A If you find yourself applying the same kinds of format commands on cells quite often, consider giving that set of format commands a style name by using the Format|Style dialog box. After you create a style, you can apply that style by selecting it from the Style dialog box's list.

Q How can I change a locked cell?

A If you lock a cell, your intent is to not allow changes. Locked cells are especially useful when you create worksheets for others to use. By locking the titles and formulas, you ensure that the user can only change data areas. Nevertheless, if you need to edit a locked cell, deactivate the worksheet's protected status. After you edit the cell, activate the protection so that the worksheet is safe from inadvertent changes.

Q I get confused with all the graph terms; how do I know which chart works best for my worksheet?

A Often the best way to find the right chart type is to try a few. Excel 97's Chart Wizard is so simple and fast that you can generate several chart types before you find just the right one. As you produce more and more charts, you begin to judge better which graphs work best for certain kinds of worksheets.

12

PART IV
Presenting with PowerPoint 97

Hour

Hour 13

PowerPoint 97 Presentations

This hour introduces you to PowerPoint 97 and shows you how to get off to a good start. By using the predefined presentation tools of PowerPoint 97, you generate good-looking presentations without needing to worry about design, format, and color specifics. After PowerPoint 97 generates a sample presentation, you need only follow a few simple procedures to turn the sample presentation into your own.

The highlights of this hour include

- ☐ How to start PowerPoint 97
- ☐ What the AutoContent Wizard does for you
- ☐ When to use the design templates
- ☐ What a blank presentation requires
- ☐ How to exit PowerPoint 97

Starting PowerPoint 97

To start PowerPoint 97, perform one of the following:

☐ Click the Office 97 Shortcut bar's New Office Document button and double-click the Blank Presentation icon to create a new PowerPoint 97 document. (Click the General tab if it is not already selected to see the Blank Presentation icon.)

☐ Click the Office 97 Shortcut bar's Open Office Document button and from its directory select an existing PowerPoint 97 presentation that you want to edit.

☐ Use the Windows Start menu to start PowerPoint 97 by selecting Microsoft PowerPoint from the Programs menu.

☐ Select a PowerPoint 97 document from the Windows Start menu's Documents option. Windows recognizes that PowerPoint 97 created the presentation document, starts PowerPoint 97, and loads the presentation file automatically. (The Start menu's Documents option holds a list of your most recent work.)

☐ Click the Office 97 Shortcut bar's PowerPoint 97 button to create a blank presentation. Depending on your Office 97 Shortcut bar's setup, you might not see the PowerPoint 97 button.

Unlike the other Office 97 products, PowerPoint 97 begins by starting a wizard-like template query that prompts you for the type of presentation you want to create. Press Esc to get rid of the opening dialog box that teaches you about the PowerPoint 97 screen.

Figure 13.1 shows the opening PowerPoint 97 screen. Your screen might differ slightly depending on the options that you chose during installation.

Understanding Presentations and Slides

The primary purpose of PowerPoint 97 is to help you design, create, and edit presentations. A *presentation* is a set of screens (slides) that you present to people in a group or workbook tutorial. You don't have to be a design specialist to create good-looking presentations because of the wide variety of predefined PowerPoint 97 templates available.

NEW TERM A *presentation* is a set of screens that you share with a group of people as a slide show.

> Throughout this book, the term *presentation* refers to the entire PowerPoint 97 collection of slides, whereas the term *slide* refers to an individual screen within a presentation.

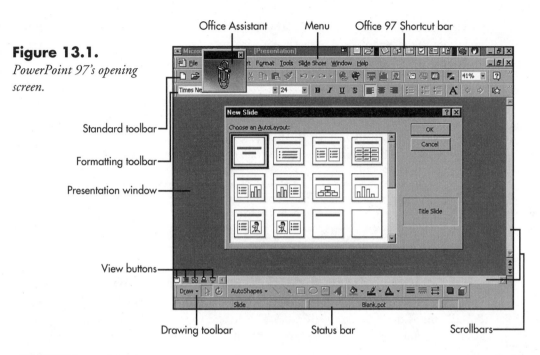

Figure 13.1.
PowerPoint 97's opening screen.

Office Assistant   Menu   Office 97 Shortcut bar

Standard toolbar
Formatting toolbar
Presentation window

View buttons

Drawing toolbar   Status bar   Scrollbars

NEW TERM A *slide show* is a preview of your presentation slides, one at a time, controlled manually or viewed in a timed presentation.

PowerPoint 97 slides can contain information from

☐ Data you type into PowerPoint 97, including text, charts, graphs, and graphics
☐ Word 97 documents
☐ Word 97 document outlines
☐ Excel 97 worksheets
☐ Excel 97 graphs and charts
☐ Access 97 databases
☐ Graphics programs that you use to create and edit graphics
☐ Other software programs, such as desktop publishing programs, whose data you import into PowerPoint 97

Creating a New Presentation

Figure 13.1 shows the opening window that you see when you start PowerPoint 97 and begin a new presentation. The figure shows several design templates that contain layouts you can use (templates are stored in files that contain the .pot extension). The design template works

13

well for creating a PowerPoint 97 presentation one slide at a time, but the design template might not be the best place to begin in many instances. The AutoContent Wizard, covered in the next section, is sometimes a better place to start.

> Plan your presentations! Think about your target audience. Presenting identical information to two different audiences might require two completely different approaches. For example, the same company's annual status presentation would be different for a stockholder's meeting than for the board of director's meeting. After you determine your target audience, think about the content of the presentation. Create an outline before you begin. In the next hour, "Editing and Arranging Your Presentation," you learn about PowerPoint 97's outlining feature, which you can use to outline a presentation before you create the presentation slides.

AutoContent Wizard and Presentation Design

Perhaps the best place to begin creating a new presentation, particularly if you are new to PowerPoint, is the *AutoContent Wizard*. This wizard contains a sample presentation with sample text and a selected design. Use the wizard's dialog boxes to select a design that best suits your needs.

 The *AutoContent Wizard* is a presentation design wizard that contains sample data from which you can select and edit to create your customized presentation.

To use AutoContent Wizard to create your presentation, follow these steps:

1. Start PowerPoint 97.
2. Cancel the design template screen (the one you see in Figure 13.1).
3. Select File | New to display the New Presentation dialog box.
4. Click the Presentations tab to display several sample presentations.
5. Double-click the icon labeled AutoContent Wizard to start the AutoContent Wizard's question-and-answer session.
6. Answer the AutoContent Wizard's questions to design a presentation shell that best fits your application's requirements.

The AutoContent Wizard helps you to create a blank presentation in a design format that best matches the goals of your presentation. As you follow the AutoContent Wizard, you have to determine the answers to these questions: Who is your audience? What message do you want to convey? Are you selling or offering something? The best approach might be to run through the wizard once as practice to see the kinds of questions you are asked.

The AutoContent Wizard selects the best choice from among these 20 template styles after you complete the wizard:

- ☐ Brainstorming
- ☐ Business Plan
- ☐ Achieve Certificate
- ☐ Communicating Bad News
- ☐ Company Meeting
- ☐ Corporate Financial Overview
- ☐ Corporate Home Page
- ☐ Corporate Locations Directory
- ☐ Facilities Assistant
- ☐ Employee Orientation
- ☐ Flyer
- ☐ Human Resources Kiosk
- ☐ Marketing Plan
- ☐ Organization Overview
- ☐ Personal Home Page
- ☐ Recommending a Strategy
- ☐ Reporting Progress
- ☐ Selling a Product, Service, or Idea
- ☐ Training
- ☐ Who's Who

All these AutoContent Wizard templates are available to you if you don't want to run the wizard first. PowerPoint 97 supplies two styles for each template: one for an online intranet or Internet PowerPoint 97 presentation, and one a standalone PowerPoint 97 presentation known as a *standard* presentation.

13

 You can select from a list of icons that represent these presentations from the New Presentations dialog box instead of selecting the AutoContent Wizard.

After PowerPoint 97 creates the presentation outline, you have to fill in the details. Click any slide's icon in the left column of the presentation outline that the AutoContent Wizard produces to edit that specific slide.

Creating Presentations Using Design Templates

As you saw in Figure 13.1, PowerPoint 97 presents you with the New Slide dialog box when you open a new presentation. If you start PowerPoint 97 and select File | New, PowerPoint 97 presents you with the New Slide dialog box. The New Slide dialog box contains several templates that you can use to start your presentation's first slide.

> If you click the toolbar's New button, PowerPoint 97 does not open the New Slide dialog box. Therefore, despite the similar icons, the File | New command does not perform the same command as the New toolbar button.

Display the New Slide dialog box whenever you need to create a new slide for a presentation. A presentation contains one or more slides, so you need to display the New Slide dialog box every time you are ready to add the next slide to the presentation. To display the New Slide dialog box at any time, click the New Slide option in the Common Tasks floating menu.

> If you do not see the Common Tasks menu, select View | Toolbars | Common Tasks.

As you click through the templates, the New Slide dialog box displays a description in the lower-right corner, such as Chart & Text, that describes the template's most common use. Note that the AutoContent Wizard uses several of the templates for its individual slides.

When you double-click the template that best describes the slide you want to create, PowerPoint 97 creates a new slide based on that template (as shown in Figure 13.2).

The instructions on the template's generated slide indicate what to do next. In most cases, you edit the text, possibly change colors, and perhaps add a graphics image to the slide. After you complete the slide, click the New Slide entry from the Common Tasks menu to display the New Slide dialog box and create your presentation's next slide. When you've created your final slide, you can save your presentation.

Opening a New and Blank Presentation

When you create a new presentation from scratch, you can still take advantage of the design templates. One of the design templates in the New Slide dialog box selection list is the Blank template, shown in Figure 13.3.

Figure 13.2.
A template's generated slide.

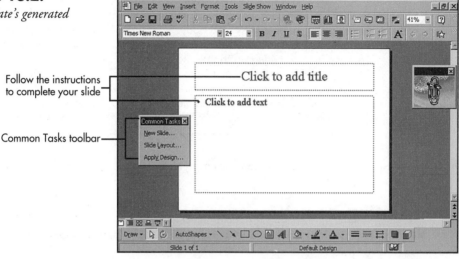

Follow the instructions to complete your slide

Common Tasks toolbar

If you design your own slide from a blank template, you can later apply one of the template styles to the slide! Therefore, if you don't like what you generate from scratch, PowerPoint 97 lets you redesign the slide without requiring you to reenter the slide's text. If you save a presentation as a template file, you can use that presentation's format for subsequent presentations.

Figure 13.3.
Use the Blank template to create your own slide layout.

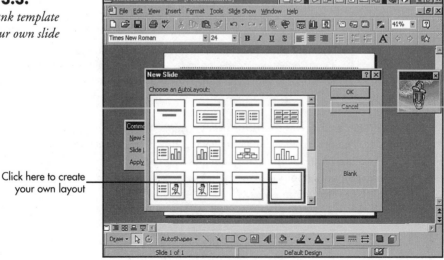

Click here to create your own layout

13

Blank presentations require that you manually create every slide element, including the text, titles, and body. Most slides have a title, text, and an optional graphic image. Why not let the AutoContent Wizard or the templates start things off right? The predefined slides work for so many purposes. Resist the temptation to create your slides from scratch until you acquaint yourself with the predefined slides. In most cases, the AutoContent Wizard and templates provide exactly what your presentation needs.

After PowerPoint 97 displays the new and empty slide, you must add text, graphics, and styles to complete the slide.

Presenting Your Work

After you create your presentation, you can present it to an audience as one or more of the following:

- ☐ Transparency overheads
- ☐ Computer screens
- ☐ Internet web page presentations
- ☐ Audience handouts
- ☐ Workbook contents
- ☐ 35mm slides
- ☐ Color printer documents
- ☐ Reference notes for a speaker

Not only does PowerPoint enable you to create and edit presentations, but it can show your presentation as well. PowerPoint 97 can move from screen to screen, as a slide show does, at whatever pace you request.

If you do not have access to a color printer, many of today's retail office product stores and retail copy centers let you take your PowerPoint 97 presentations, on disk, to their stores where you can request color transparencies and copies of your presentations. In addition, several major photography development businesses can turn your disk-based PowerPoint 97 presentations into 35mm slides.

Quitting PowerPoint 97

When you're finished with PowerPoint 97, quit by performing any of the following:

☐ Select File|Exit.

☐ Press Alt+F4.

☐ Double-click the Control icon.

☐ Click PowerPoint 97's Close button.

 Always quit PowerPoint 97 and shut down Windows (by selecting Start | Shut Down) before turning off your computer so that you won't lose your work.

Summary

This hour introduced you to PowerPoint 97 by showing you how to start PowerPoint 97, how to prepare for your initial slide presentation, and how to quit. PowerPoint 97 prepares all kinds of presentations, all of which have one or more slides (screens). Use PowerPoint 97 to create, edit, and even present your presentations in a slide-projector format.

The AutoContent Wizard is perhaps the best way to start using PowerPoint 97. By answering a few simple questions, AutoContent Wizard creates a presentation with sample text and formatting. To turn the generated presentation into your own, simply change the text and, optionally, change the slides' design elements.

The design templates also provide help when you want to add a new slide to a presentation. When you need to create a new slide, select the closest match from the list of design templates. After the design template creates a sample slide, simply edit and modify the text.

If you have a good eye for design, you can create a blank presentation from scratch. Blank presentations require the most work.

The next hour shows you how easy it is to turn the AutoContent Wizard or template-designed slides into your own.

13

Q&A

Q Do I begin with a PowerPoint 97 template, the AutoContent Wizard, or a blank presentation when I want to create a presentation?

A Unlike the other Office 97 products, you almost always create a presentation using the AutoContent Wizard or a template. A blank presentation requires you to lay out all your slide titles and text, which is too much work for most presentations. Unless your presentation requires unusual features, the AutoContent Wizard and templates produce presentations that will be close to your desired presentation.

The AutoContent Wizard is perhaps the best for PowerPoint 97 newcomers because it presents a series of specific style choices and lays out sample text that you can easily change to fit your presentation needs.

Basically, all three presentation-generation techniques end up producing a new slide on which you must add text, modify colors, change formatting, and add optional graphics. You learn how to apply these slide edits and make improvements in the next hour.

Q I'm still confused. What is the difference between the AutoContent Wizard and the design templates?

A The AutoContent Wizard uses the design templates for its slides. The biggest difference between the two presentation-design tools is that the AutoContent Wizard creates an entire sample presentation, whereas the design templates create individual slide samples.

If you want to add a new slide to a presentation, you may want to use a design template for that individual slide. If you want PowerPoint 97 to generate an entire set of general slides for a specific presentation, such as a corporate business meeting, you can let the AutoContent Wizard generate the entire presentation and then you can fill in the details that your presentation requires.

Hour 14

Editing and Arranging Your Presentation

This hour shows you what to do after you generate a sample slide or presentation. PowerPoint 97's AutoContent Wizard and template samples generate good-looking presentations, but it's up to you to add the specific details that you need.

First, you need to change the sample's text. In the process, you might change or add slide titles and formatting, or maybe a graphic image for more impact. This hour teaches you a few shortcuts to turn the sample presentations into the presentation you need.

The highlights of this hour include

- [ ] When to use the various views that help streamline your PowerPoint 97 work
- [ ] Why you work most often with the Outline view
- [ ] What editing tools PowerPoint 97 supplies for your slide's text
- [ ] How the Slide Sorter view arranges your slide show
- [ ] How to select the presentation printing option you need

Getting Acquainted with PowerPoint's Views

PowerPoint 97 requires you to change views perhaps more than any of the other Office 97 products. Therefore, you will produce presentations more quickly if you master views now and learn the advantages and disadvantages of each view.

> The following list not only describes PowerPoint 97's views, but also explains how to use them to convert the template and AutoContent Wizard text to a specific presentation. As you read this section, pay attention to the information that teaches how and when to edit text from the AutoContent Wizard and design templates.

PowerPoint 97 supports the following views:

- [ ] **Outline view:** Enables you to edit and display all your presentation text in one location instead of one slide at a time. Figure 14.1 shows the Outline view of a presentation. The large titles start new slides, and the details below the titles provide bulleted text for each slide.

- [ ] **Slide view:** Enables you to see each slide, one at a time, and edit each slide's format, color, graphics, style, or text.

- [ ] **Slide Sorter view:** Displays your entire presentation so that you can add, delete, and move slides. The Slide Sorter view acts like a preview tool. You can review your presentation and use the Slide Sorter as an engine that presents your slides at a preset timing, using a specific transitional effect when one slide changes to another.

- [ ] **Notes Pages view:** Enables you to create and edit notes for the presentation's speaker.

Change views by clicking one of the view buttons to the left of the horizontal scroll bar or by selecting the view from the View menu. You work in the Outline view most often when creating and editing the text of your presentation, and you work in the Slide view most often when formatting individual slides.

> As Figure 14.1 shows, PowerPoint 97 contains four buttons that you can click to change any of the four views quickly.

 The *Outline view* shows the table of contents and slide order of your presentation.

Figure 14.1.

The Outline view shows the presentation's overall table of contents.

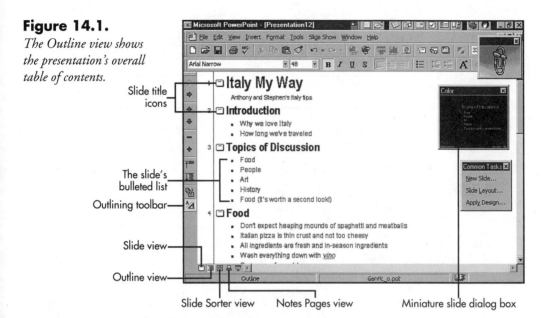

Slide title icons

The slide's bulleted list

Outlining toolbar

Slide view

Outline view

Slide Sorter view Notes Pages view Miniature slide dialog box

Using the Outline View

An outline helps you organize your presentation and sequence the slides properly. Although PowerPoint 97 makes it easy for you to create the presentation slides themselves, the outline is easier to work with than the full slides, especially when you are still in the process of gathering your thoughts on the presentation's design and content. If you get in the habit of first creating an outline, you have less editing and slide rearranging to do later in the development of your presentation.

After you generate a sample presentation by using the AutoContent Wizard or by creating slides from the design templates, go to the Outline view to work on your outline. You can reorganize your slides and edit text in this mode. Click the topic or detail you want to change and edit the text. As you enter and change Outline-view text, PowerPoint 97 updates the *miniature slide* dialog box with your new text so that you can get a preview of your finished slide.

NEW TERM The *miniature slide* is the small slide preview window that shows, when you work in Outline view, what each individual slide currently looks like. As you change the Outline-view text, PowerPoint 97 updates the miniature slide dialog box window to show your edits.

14

All the familiar copy, cut, and paste features work in the Outline view. For example, if you drag a title's icon or a bulleted list's item down or up the screen while in Outline view, PowerPoint 97 moves that item to its new location. When you drag a title, all the points under the title move with it. This is a good way to reorganize slides. When you drag a bulleted item, PowerPoint 97 moves only that item.

Unlike other Office 97 products, PowerPoint 97 does not copy an item if you press Ctrl before dragging the item elsewhere.

Click the up and down Outlining toolbar arrows to move an item up or down in the outline.

Adding and Importing New Items

To add items to the text in the Outline view, click at the end or beginning of a bulleted item to insert a new entry. If you want to insert a completely new slide, click the New Slide item in the Common Tasks dialog box, and PowerPoint 97 displays the New Slide dialog box from which you can select a design and then enter the text. You can also click at the end of an item and press Enter to enter a blank slide.

One of PowerPoint 97's most beneficial text features is its capability to read documents from other Office 97 products. If you create a Word 97 document that you want to include on a slide (or series of slides), select Insert | Slides from the File menu and select the Office 97 file that you want to import to your presentation. It is best to do this in Outline view because this enables you to insert the information in the correct order and see the overall effects. The document's Heading 1 style text becomes slide titles, and the subsequent heading styles become text under the title.

While in Word 97, click the Present It toolbar button to turn your document into a PowerPoint 97-ready presentation.

Promoting and Demoting Elements

The Outlining toolbar appears to the left of the Outline view (refer to Figure 14.1). The Outlining toolbar's most important feature may be its *promotion arrows*. If you type a detail item that you want to become a new slide's title, click the left arrow of the Outline toolbar (the *promote button*). To convert a title to a bulleted item, click the right arrow of the Outline toolbar (the *demote button*).

Promotion arrows are Outlining toolbar arrow buttons that promote Outline view items to slide titles or demote slide titles to Outline view bulleted detail items.

The *promote button* is the Outlining toolbar button that converts detail text to title text. The *demote button* is the Outlining toolbar button that converts title text to detail text.

Using the Slide View

While in Outline view, you can look at the *Slide view* of any item by double-clicking any slide title's icon, which appears to the left of each Outline view slide title (refer to Figure 14.1). As Figure 14.2 shows, the Slide view displays the same slide as your Miniature Slides dialog box, except that you see the slide in a full-screen view. You can make edits to your slide text and see the results of those edits as they affect the slide.

 NEW TERM   The *Slide view* displays each of the presentation's slides one at a time for easier editing and formatting.

Figure 14.2.

The Slide view shows the layout of one of the presentation's slides.

Next slide's vertical scrollbar

Previous slide button
Next slide button

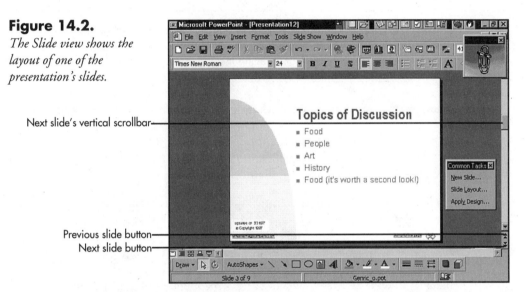

To move from slide to slide while in the Slide view, perform any of the following:

- ☐ Click the vertical scrollbar.
- ☐ Press the PageUp or PageDown keys.
- ☐ Click either the Next or Previous slide button on the vertical scrollbar.

When you want to edit a text (or graphic) object from the Slide view, click the object. PowerPoint 97 displays a sizing box surrounded by sizing handles. PowerPoint 97 treats a slide's title as a single object and the slide's bulleted set of items as another object.

To edit text, perform these steps:

1. Click the text you want to edit to display the sizing box.
2. To move the text, drag one edge of the text's resizing box in the direction you want to move the text.

14

3. To shrink or enlarge the selected text object, drag one of the sizing handles in or out to adjust the object's size. (PowerPoint 97 does not shrink or enlarge text inside the sizing box as you resize the sizing box.)

4. After you display the sizing box, click inside the box at the point where you want to edit text. PowerPoint 97 inserts the text cursor at the location of your desired edit. At that location, you can insert and delete text as well as change the font, color, and style of any text that you select using the toolbar or the Format | Font menu option. To increase or decrease the size of text, use the Format | Font dialog box.

> Select any text, and then click the Increase Font Size toolbar button to quickly increase the font size of the selected text. The Increase Font Size button works faster than opening the Font dialog box.

If graphics appear on the slide, double-click them to edit the images with the graphic-editing tools.

Step-Up

Although the Internet-connection feature can be somewhat advanced, if you right-click an object (such as a graphic object) while editing a slide and select the Action Settings option, PowerPoint 97 displays the Action Settings dialog box (shown in Figure 14.3). By assigning an Internet hyperlink address, a Windows program, or a sound wave file to a mouse click or movement, PowerPoint 97 connects to that hyperlink location, runs the program, or plays the sound during the presentation. You can provide push-button access to programs and Internet web pages while presenting your presentation!

Using the Slide Sorter View

Use the Slide Sorter view to rearrange slides, not to edit text or graphics on the slides. When you display the *Slide Sorter view*, PowerPoint 97 presents several of your presentation slides (as shown in Figure 14.4). The Slide Sorter view lets you quickly and easily drag and drop slides to reorder your presentation. Although you can rearrange slides from the Outline view, the Slide Sorter view lets you see the overall visual results of your slide movements.

NEW TERM   The *Slide Sorter view* displays your slides as though they are in a projector so that you can easily rearrange them.

Figure 14.3.

Assign events to mouse clicks and movements.

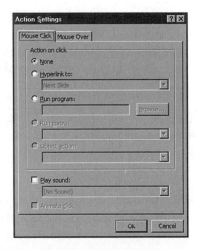

Figure 14.4.

Rearrange slides in the Slide Sorter view.

Click here to view slide transition

Slide Sorter toolbar

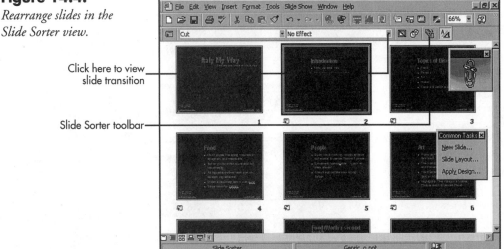

Use your mouse to drag slides from one location to another in the presentation. Remember that the Undo command (Ctrl+Z) reverses any action that you accidentally make. You also can use the Windows Clipboard to copy, cut, and paste, although dragging with your mouse is easier. To delete a slide, click the slide once and press the Delete key.

One of the more advanced (but useful) Slide Sorter features involves the Slide Sorter toolbar, which appears at the top of the Slide Sorter view (refer to Figure 14.4). The toolbar's Slide Transition Effects drop-down list determines how the Slide Show feature *transitions* (dissolves) from one slide to the next when you display your presentation. The next hour,

14

"PowerPoint 97 Advanced Features," discusses PowerPoint 97's Slide Show in more detail. For now, click the Slide Transition Effects drop-down list to see how PowerPoint 97 can move from one slide to the next. The Text Preset Animation button determines how the slide's transitional text appears during the slide show.

NEW TERM The term *transition* refers to the replacement of one slide with the next, often with a special effect that causes the second slide to cover the first in a unique way.

To set up slide-transition and text-animation effects, click a slide and select the desired effects from the Slide Sorter toolbar. Click the icon below each slide to see how the set transition effect will look during the slide show.

Using the Notes Pages View

When you click the *Notes Pages view*, PowerPoint 97 displays your first slide (as Figure 14.5 shows). The Notes Pages view contains a small version of the slide and, below it, a location for a text description of the slide. Therefore, the speaker's notes contain the slides that the audience sees as well as notes the speaker wrote to tell the audience about each slide. Your audience does not see the speaker's notes.

NEW TERM Use the *Notes Pages view* to create and keep the notes you use when presenting your slide show.

Figure 14.5.

Prepare speaker's notes using the Notes Pages view.

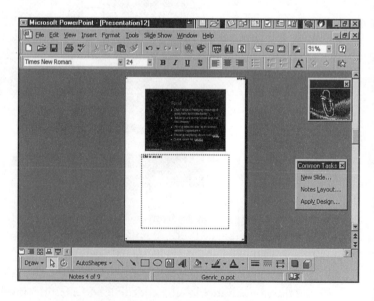

The Notes Pages are designed to be printed for the speaker. However, the speaker can also display the Notes Pages view during a presentation to eliminate paper shuffling. If the speaker's computer has two video cards and two monitors, PowerPoint 97 can send the slides to one monitor and the speaker's slides and note pages to the other. When the speaker moves to the next slide, the speaker's notes change as well.

> Use the PageUp and PageDown keys to scroll through the slides and see the speaker's notes at the bottom of each slide. If the text area is not large enough to read the notes, expand the viewing area by using the Zoom command in the Edit menu.

Saving and Printing Your Work

Be sure to save your presentation after creating and finalizing it. PowerPoint 97 saves your presentation with the .ppt document filename extension.

Of course, you also need to print your presentation, either to paper, to a color printer, or to a printer that supports transparencies. The File|Print dialog box works differently in PowerPoint 97 than in Word 97 and Excel 97. Instead of globally printing the presentation, you must indicate in PowerPoint 97 exactly how and what you want to print.

When you display the Print dialog box (shown in Figure 14.6), open the Print What drop-down list to view the selection list.

Figure 14.6.

Decide exactly what you want to print.

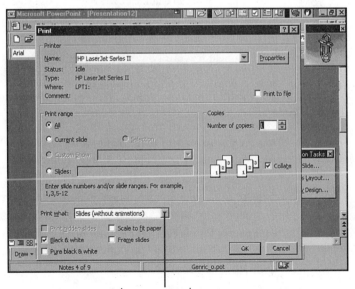

Select your printed output

14

PowerPoint prints your presentation in a black-and-white format. You need to deselect the option entitled Black & White if you print to a color printer. Use the Print What drop-down list box to print your presentation in any of these styles:

- ☐ Slides only for the presentation
- ☐ Handouts (which can hold from two to six slides per page) so that you can give comprehensive notes to the audience
- ☐ Notes for the speaker
- ☐ The outline for proofreading purposes

If you want to print the entire presentation, you have to select File | Print multiple times and print a different component each time.

Summary

This hour furthered your PowerPoint 97 knowledge by showing you how to turn a sample presentation into the presentation you want. The views are more critical in PowerPoint 97 presentation development than in Word 97 or Excel 97. The views give you a completely new perspective of the presentation. In addition, you use the different views for different functions, such as editing, rearranging slides, and previewing your presentation. Whereas one view is for the audience, another view exists for the speaker.

As you might expect, you can change PowerPoint 97 slide text easily by using the basic editing skills you've already mastered. The views enable you to view your slides, outline, and speaker's notes in their most usable form.

The next hour concludes your PowerPoint 97 tutorial by showing how to format your slides with more detail, how to test and start the PowerPoint 97 Slide Show, and how to spruce up your slides with graphics.

Q&A

Q What are the primary PowerPoint views and what does each view do?

A The two primary working views are the Outline view and the Slide view. The Slide view is great for working on the color and format of each slide. Use the Outline view to keep an overall presentation goal in mind as well as to edit all your presentation's text in one location.

Q I want to use PowerPoint 97 to present my slides, but I don't want it controlling the transition and timing of the Slide Show. Can I use PowerPoint 97 to display my slides manually?

A You learn about the details of the PowerPoint 97 Slide Show in the next hour, but rest assured that it supports manual slide shows in which you control the appearance of the next slide. Actually, *most* presenters want complete control over the timing of the slide presentations, and PowerPoint 97 supports such manual transitions. As a matter of fact, you'll probably *never* let it perform a completely hands-off presentation unless you use PowerPoint 97 for a kiosk store display to promote a product as customers walk by.

Q Can I print everything (all views) with a single File│Print command?

A No, you can only print individual slide-show components, such as the speaker's notes, audience handouts, or slides from the File│Print menu. If you want to print everything and every view, select File│Print multiple times and print a different component each time.

Q I'm using a service to turn my presentation into individual color slides. Do I need the PowerPoint 97 Slide Show?

A You learn about the Slide Show in the next hour's session. PowerPoint 97 creates individual slides that you can print or display inside PowerPoint 97, over a web page, or from any other source that displays PowerPoint 97 presentations. The Slide show does *not* have anything to do with the medium on which you present your final presentation, however, so you can turn your presentation into slides without using the Slide Show.

14

Hour 15

PowerPoint 97 Advanced Features

This hour wraps up your PowerPoint 97 tutorial by explaining how to better format your presentations. You can format your entire presentation at one time or apply styles one slide at a time.

In addition to applying global presentation and slide styles, you can edit text and other objects on specific slides. Generally, the AutoContent Wizard and the design templates create presentations that require little editing; however, if you want to touch up specific parts of your slides, PowerPoint 97 provides the tools you need.

After you complete your presentation, use the Slide Show view to watch the presentation one screen at a time. PowerPoint 97 follows your slide-show instructions and moves the slides forward at the pace and in the style you request.

The highlights of this hour include

☐ How to modify your entire presentation's style

☐ Why you sometimes need to make minor edits to individual slides

☐ How to insert art and text from other programs into a slide

☐ When to go to the Clip Gallery for the object you need

☐ What PowerPoint 97 tools you can use to work with text objects

☐ How to set up the Slide Show view to produce special effects

☐ How to prepare your slide-show presentation

Changing Your Entire Presentation's Design

PowerPoint 97 enables you to apply a design template to your entire presentation. If you develop a presentation with the AutoContent Wizard, with individual design templates, or from scratch, you easily can change the format and look of your entire presentation.

> You might want to change your presentation's design if your target audience changes. Suppose that you give a seminar to your employees on ethics and morals in the workplace, and then learn that your local Chamber of Commerce wants to see your presentation. You should formalize the style when you present to strangers, which might require that you change your presentation's tone.

Master layout is the term applied to a presentation's overall design. Use the following process to change the entire presentation's master layout:

1. Click the Apply Design option on the Common Tasks floating toolbar to display the Apply Design dialog box (shown in Figure 15.1).

2. Search the Templates folder in the Apply Design dialog box for a design you like. Double-click the design's folder to open it. PowerPoint 97 shows a preview of that template in the Apply Design dialog box as you select different designs.

3. When you find and select the design template you want, click the Apply button. After PowerPoint 97 finishes changing your presentation, page through the slides to see whether you chose a good design. You can always go back through the process to change the design again, or undo the change.

Changing a Single Slide's Design

In the Slide view, you can change the design of an individual slide (called the *slide layout*) by selecting the Slide Layout option on the Common Tasks floating toolbar. PowerPoint 97 displays Figure 15.2's Slide Layout dialog box, which is the same dialog box that PowerPoint 97 displays when you create a new slide.

NEW TERM The term *slide layout* refers to a single slide's format and design.

Figure 15.1.

Use the Apply Design dialog box to change the entire presentation's design.

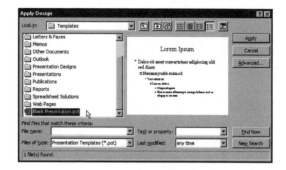

 The Apply button in the Slide Layout dialog box changes to Reapply (shown in Figure 15.2) if you click the slide's current layout.

Figure 15.2.

Use the Slide Layout dialog box to change a single slide's design.

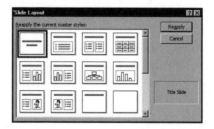

The previous section explained how to change the master layout of your overall presentation. If you use the Slide Layout dialog box to change an individual slide but apply a different master layout, the master layout takes precedence and changes your individual slide (if the master layout differs from the slide).

Editing Individual Slides

In most instances, the master layout and the individual slide layouts provide ample variability and style. Rarely do you have to make substantial edits to your presentation slides. Unlike most PowerPoint 97 tutorials, this book does not go into great detail about slide editing. You don't need to edit individual slides in most cases because of the layouts that PowerPoint 97 provides.

About the only major change you must make is to add text to the slides. All the spell-checking and AutoCorrect features that were so important in Word 97 and Excel 97 also work for text you place in a presentation; a red wavy line beneath a word indicates that Office 97's spell checker does not recognize the word. Correct the word, or add it to PowerPoint 97's dictionary by right-clicking the word.

If you're importing a Word 97 document that uses the standard styles (such as Heading 1 and Heading 2), the document automatically inserts into PowerPoint 97 as a presentation. You can then select styles that you want to change to add flair to the presentation.

Word 97 documents aren't the only documents you can import into a presentation. You can import an Excel 97 worksheet or chart into a presentation, select Insert | Object, click the Create from file option, and click Browse to locate the document you want to import.

Nevertheless, the following section describes the kinds of edits that you might want to make on individual slides when you need to hone a presentation.

Adding Text and Text Boxes

To add text to a slide, such as text that describes clip-art details, add a text box. A *text box* holds text that you can format. To add a text box, follow these steps:

1. Click the Text Box button on the Drawing toolbar.
2. Drag your mouse from the text box's upper-left corner to the text box's lower-right corner. When you release the mouse, PowerPoint 97 draws the text box (as shown in Figure 15.3).
3. Type your text.
4. Use the Formatting toolbar and the Format | Font command to modify the text style and format.
5. Click anywhere on the slide to deselect the text box and return to the rest of your editing chores.

NEW TERM   A *text box* is a box that holds slide text.

Modifying and Rotating Text

You can resize the text box, change the justification and font formatting, move the text box, add a border, and change the font and background colors by right-clicking the text box or by selecting the appropriate Formatting toolbar and Drawing toolbar buttons.

15

Figure 15.3.

Type and format text inside a text box.

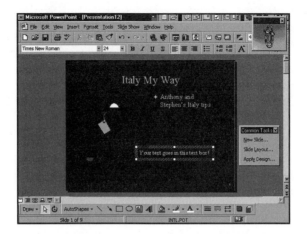

To change the text throughout your entire presentation, select View | Master | Slide Master to change the master layout. PowerPoint 97 displays the Master Layout style slide (shown in Figure 15.4), which you can change to update every slide in your presentation. For example, if you want to format a copyright message at the bottom of every slide, click the slide master's Footer area (to turn the footer area into a text box) and edit the text there (or delete the text to get rid of the footer throughout your presentation).

Figure 15.4.

Change the slide master to update every slide's text properties.

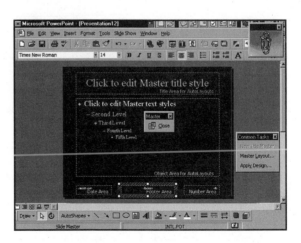

One of the neatest text-editing features is the *Free Rotate* tool. The Free Rotate tool enables you to rotate text to any angle. For example, you might want to slant a title toward or away from text that falls below the title to add a special effect or to call out a cautionary note on a slide.

 The *Free Rotate* tool, on the Drawing toolbar, rotates text, graphics, and any selected slide object in the degree and direction you want to rotate the object. The Free Rotate tool makes the creation of slanting titles and text as simple as dragging your mouse.

To rotate text, click the text to display the text box. Remember that a text box appears around any text, including bulleted lists and titles, when you click those objects. After you display the text box, click the toolbar's Free Rotate tool. The mouse pointer changes to a spiral-shaped pointer. Drag any of the four corners of the text box to rotate the text along an axis. (Figure 15.5 shows a rotated text box.) When you press Escape or click anywhere on the slide, the text box outline disappears and you see the rotated text.

 The Free Rotate tool rotates selected bulleted lists and graphics, as well as text boxes.

Figure 15.5.

Use the Free Rotate tool to rotate any slide's object.

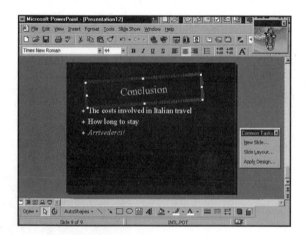

Adding Art

Suppose that you select a slide layout that contains a placeholder for art. Presumably, you have an art image to place on the slide or you would have chosen a different slide layout. When you select a slide layout that includes a placeholder for art, PowerPoint 97 indicates exactly where the art is to go. For example, Figure 15.6 shows an applied slide layout that includes

15

a placeholder for artwork. PowerPoint 97 makes it easy to add the art. Follow the slide's instructions, and double-click the area to add the art.

Figure 15.6.

PowerPoint 97 indicates exactly where the art is to go on the slide.

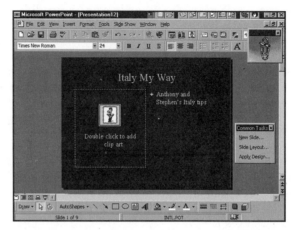

When you double-click the art area, PowerPoint 97 displays the Microsoft *Clip Gallery* dialog box shown in Figure 15.7. A clip (an abbreviation for *clip art*) is a graphic image, and the *Clip Gallery* is a collection of clip-art images. Microsoft arranges the Clip Gallery by subject, and you can see a preview of the selected image on your screen as you look through the Clip Gallery.

NEW TERM   The term *clip art* refers to a stored graphic image you can place on a slide. Sometimes a clip refers to other kinds of files as well, such as a sound or video file.

NEW TERM   A *Clip Gallery* is a collection of clip-art images arranged by subject.

Figure 15.7.

Select art to place in your slide from Microsoft's Clip Gallery.

Microsoft Clip Gallery's Connect to the Web button

As you can see, the Microsoft Clip Gallery dialog box also enables you to include picture, video, and sound clip files. PowerPoint 97 supports the insertion of these other kinds of objects, so if you want a sound to play when a slide appears, you can insert the sound file.

> If you click the button labeled Microsoft Clip Gallery's Connect to the Web for additional clips, PowerPoint 97 accesses the web (logging you on if necessary) and offers thousands of additional clip files you can use in your presentation.

If you want to change the slide's clip art, double-click the art, and PowerPoint 97 displays the Microsoft Clip Gallery dialog box once again.

Your slide does not need to contain a placeholder for you to insert art. The placeholder, however, enables you to more easily manage the artwork and keep the art separated from the rest of the slide's text and art. If you work with a slide layout that contains a placeholder, you can move and resize the placeholder while you add the rest of the slide's elements. When you're ready for the art, double-click the placeholder to insert the art inside the placeholder's border. Without a placeholder, your artwork overwrites existing text and graphics that already appear on the slide. You have to move and resize the inserted art manually to make it fit with the rest of the slide.

> Your art does not have to reside in the Microsoft Clip Gallery for you to insert it. You can insert your own art files, such as logos and pictures, by selecting Insert | Picture | From File and then selecting your file from its directory location.

> If you want to import a scanned image into a slide, you don't have to leave PowerPoint 97 to scan the image. Select Insert | Picture | From Scanner and PowerPoint 97 starts your scanner software. Wait while you scan the image and then insert the scanned image into your slide.

Using PowerPoint 97's Slide Show

One of the best ways to see the overall effect of your presentation is to run *Slide Show*. Slide Show displays your slides in sequence, moving from one slide to another, *transitioning* (changing) with special effects that you have set up, and moving at a preset timing that you can control.

NEW TERM *Slide Show* is the PowerPoint 97 slide projector that displays your presentation slides in sequence, with optional transitions between the slides.

Follow these steps to start Slide Show:

1. Finish editing your presentation and save it.
2. Select the Slide view.
3. Display the first slide in the presentation. (The Home key always takes you to the first slide, and the End key takes you to the last.)
4. Click the Slide Show view button. PowerPoint 97 prepares the slides and displays each slide, full screen, one at a time, as you click the mouse or press PageUp and PageDown. PowerPoint 97 halts at the last slide in the presentation.
5. Press Escape to return to the Slide view.

As you watch the slide show, pay attention to the transition and timing between slides. Remember from last hour's session, "Editing and Arranging Your Presentation," that you can control the way PowerPoint 97 transitions between each slide from within the Slide Sorter view.

Editing Transitions

If you want more control over the slide's transition, select the first slide (from within Slide view) whose transition you want to change and select Slide Show | Slide Transition to display the Slide Transition dialog box (shown in Figure 15.8). From the dialog box, you can control the nature of the transition (choose a transition and watch the Effect window demonstrate the transition), the timing, and the action required to change to the next slide (such as a mouse click).

Figure 15.8.

Select the transition effect and timing.

To make sure the audience notices a new slide, add a sound effect to the transition. That way, when you move to the next slide, PowerPoint 97 plays the sound you associate with the transition.

If you want to use a uniform transition for all slides, click the Apply to All button. If you want the transition to affect only the current slide, click the Apply button to close the Slide Transition dialog box.

> Run through your presentation, using all transitions, before you make your presentation to your audience. Too many transitions can be distracting and can often slow down a presentation and reduce its effectiveness.

Automating the Presentation

Of course, you want to automate your show as much as possible. If a speaker will control the presentation, he will want to use the mouse to move from slide to slide. Otherwise, you might want to run the slide show continuously as a demo or informational display, as you might do at a trade-show booth.

To automate your slide show, select Slide Show | Set Up Show to display the Set Up Show dialog box (shown in Figure 15.9).

Figure 15.9.

Fully automate your slide show with the Set Up Show dialog box.

Select the option that your presentation requires. For example, if the speaker will control the show, click the first option. If you want the show to run continuously, click the Browsed at a kiosk option. In addition, you can elect to show only certain slides for a particular event.

When you subsequently click the Slide Show view button, PowerPoint 97 follows your Set Up Show dialog box instructions and displays the slides as you requested.

Using Speaker Notes

Your slides can have space for speaker notes that you can print and use during your presentation. If you print handouts for your audience, PowerPoint 97 gives you the choice of printing just the slides themselves, or the slides along with your speaker notes.

15

> Print from the Notes Pages view if you want your audience to have both the slides and the speaker notes that go along with each slide.

You can add to your speaker's notes during a presentation or take notes that you can incorporate later for the next presentation. The audience does not see the notes that you add as long as you use a separate monitor for the presentation. To take notes during a slide show presentation, right-click the current slide and select Speaker Notes. A dialog box opens to which you can add notes that PowerPoint 97 saves as that slide's speaker notes. If you give a presentation often and think of additions during one of the presentations, you can use the speaker note dialog box to remind you of additions you want to make before the next presentation.

Letting Others View Your Presentations

You can share your PowerPoint 97 presentations with others who do not have PowerPoint 97 or Office 97 on their systems. Microsoft offers a free PowerPoint 97 file viewer that you can copy and distribute free of charge as often as you want. You can give the file viewer and your presentation to another user in your office and that user can view your presentation, a slide at a time, using the PowerPoint 97 viewer. This is a good feature if you want to review your presentation on a laptop.

You can download the PowerPoint 97 viewer from the following Microsoft web address: http://www.microsoft.com/powerpoint/Internet/Viewer/default.htm.

Summary

This hour concluded the tutorial on PowerPoint 97. You can now make presentations look professional, and you can modify individual slides when needed. In addition to mastering PowerPoint 97's design and editing tools, you also understand how to set up and run the slide-show viewer.

When you use PowerPoint 97 to show your presentations, PowerPoint acts like an intelligent slide projector and displays slides at the pace you select using the transition you choose.

The next hour, "Outlook 97 Basics," introduces you to Office 97's new organizing product called *Outlook 97*.

Q&A

Q Why would I add a text box instead of using Outline view to add the text?

A The text on the Outline view is either a title or a bulleted item. If you want to place text outside these areas, you must draw a text box. You can draw a text box anywhere on a slide, and can even overwrite parts of a clip-art image with a text box. Text boxes are useful for describing figures and for placing extraneous notes on your slides.

Q What if I don't have extensive clip art to embed on my presentations?

A PowerPoint 97 comes armed with many images, so you may not need external graphics-art packages. In addition, PowerPoint 97 includes an Internet link, which enables you to search the Internet for clip-art (as well as picture, video, and sound) files.

If you do not see the Clip Gallery when you request it, run the Office 97 setup program again, select the Clip Gallery, and rerun the install. (Your other files, including data and PowerPoint 97 programs already on your disk, will not be affected.)

PART V
Organizing with Outlook 97

Hour

Hour 16

Outlook 97 Basics

This hour introduces Outlook 97, a program that could change the way you organize your life! For several years, software developers have attempted to produce an all-in-one organizing and planning program; however, these programs were separate from other programs. If you used your word processor and needed an address, you had to open a separate organization program, look up the address, and type it into the word processor.

Be careful—Outlook 97 is addictive! Not only is it a true interactive planning and scheduling program, but it's also fun to use.

The highlights of this hour include

- [ ] What Outlook 97 is all about
- [ ] How Outlook 97 differs from Outlook Express
- [ ] Why Schedule+ users will feel right at home
- [ ] What screen elements Outlook 97 has
- [ ] How to navigate through the calendar views
- [ ] How to schedule meetings
- [ ] When to schedule events
- [ ] Which tools help you manage tasks
- [ ] How to keep notes

An Outlook 97 Overview

You can use Outlook 97 to do the following:

- ☐ Organize your calendar.
- ☐ Schedule meetings.
- ☐ Keep an appointment book.
- ☐ Track a prioritized to-do list.
- ☐ Record your business and personal contacts.
- ☐ Keep a journal.
- ☐ Write notes to yourself that act like yellow sticky notes when you view them (similar to the Excel 97 comments you learned about during Hour 10, "Using Excel 97").
- ☐ Receive all your email, faxes, and network documents in one location.

Step-Up

Previous versions of Office included the Schedule+ organizing program, but that program lacked common features, such as an integrated directory for email and fax connections. Microsoft changed all that when they put Outlook 97 in Office 97. Your planning, scheduling, task lists, and mailing information are now in one location. Outlook 97 improves on all the features of Microsoft Schedule+.

Microsoft first introduced Outlook 97 in Office 97. For its first version, Outlook 97 contains a rich feature set. Although it has some problems common with most first software versions, such as its slow startup and program termination speed, many users are converting to Outlook 97.

One reason for the early popularity of Outlook 97, in addition to a great set of features, is its inclusion in every copy of Office 97 sold. So many people now have and use Outlook 97 that the software industry is recognizing it as the de facto contact and personal information manager. Other software products, such as the popular faxing software called *WinFax Pro*, are supporting Outlook 97 contact databases due to the large acceptance of Outlook 97 for a message and contact manager.

New Term   A *database* is a collection of related information, such as the name and address information that you can store in Outlook 97.

Do not confuse Outlook 97 with Outlook Express. Outlook Express is an add-on program that comes with Internet Explorer 4. If you've upgraded to Internet Explorer 4 (see the appendix, "Internet Explorer 4 and Outlook Express"), you also have Outlook Express. Outlook Express works and looks a lot like Outlook 97. Outlook Express is more limited than Outlook 97, however, and supports only email, a more limited contact database called the *Windows Address Book,* and some special Internet features that you learn about in Hour 24, "Creating Web Pages with Office 97." Outlook Express does not replace Outlook 97, so feel free to use Outlook 97 instead of Outlook Express for your contact information.

16

If you use the Microsoft Network (MSN) online service, you must use version 1 or 2.5 or later to use Outlook 97 as your email program. Outlook 97 does not send or receive email consistently well with MSN version 2. You can still use Outlook 97 as well as MSN 2, but you should use Windows Messaging (Windows Messaging used to be called *Microsoft Exchange* in the first release of Windows 95) available from your desktop Inbox to send and receive email until you upgrade to MSN 2.5. The upgrade is free to all MSN users, so plan to upgrade soon.

Starting Outlook 97

Start Outlook 97 by performing one of the following:

- ☐ Click any Outlook 97-related button on the Office 97 Shortcut bar. The New Message button sends email, the New Appointment button creates a new appointment, the New Task button enters a new task in the scheduled task area, the New Contact button creates a new contact in your contact database, the New Journal Entry button opens the Outlook 97 journal for an entry, and the New Note button opens a new note to which you can add text.

- ☐ Use the Windows Start menu to start Outlook 97 by selecting Microsoft Outlook from the Programs menu.

- ☐ Click the Office 97 Shortcut bar's Microsoft Outlook button to start Outlook 97. (Depending on your Office 97 Shortcut bar's setup, you may not see the Microsoft Outlook button.)

Figure 16.1 shows the opening Outlook 97 screen. Your screen might differ slightly depending on the options that you chose during installation.

Figure 16.1.
Outlook 97's opening screen.

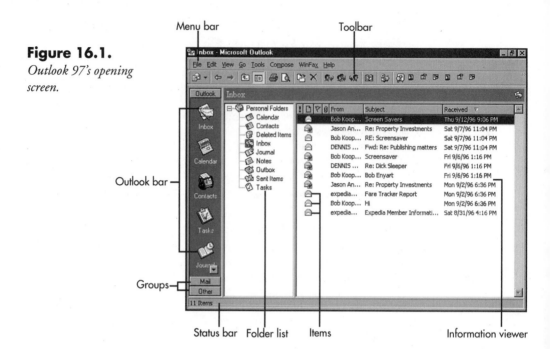

The Outlook 97 screen's format differs quite a bit from that of other Office 97 products. You won't see the typical standard and formatting toolbars. And although Outlook 97's menu bar is similar to that of the other products, the rest of the screen is different because of the different nature of Outlook 97. Therefore, take a moment to familiarize yourself with the following descriptions of Outlook 97's screen elements:

☐ **Outlook bar:** Contains shortcuts to some of the Outlook 97 features. You can rearrange the Outlook bar contents and resize its icons. The Outlook bar lets you access all of Outlook 97's most frequently used areas called *groups*. Click the group names, such as Mail, to view additional groups.

NEW TERM A *group* is an area on the Outlook bar that separates one set of related folders from others.

☐ **Folder list:** Displays your Outlook 97 work folders. As you use Outlook 97, you subdivide your work into folder directories. For example, your Inbox and Outbox mail appear in folders within the Folder list. If a number appears in parentheses after a folder name, the number represents the number of unread items in that folder. For example, if you receive three new email messages, (3) appears after the Inbox folder name.

If you don't see the Folder list, click the Folder List button on the toolbar. You can click the button to hide the Folder list if you decide you want more room for the items within the Information viewer window.

☐ **Information viewer:** Displays items from the selected folder. As you work with items, both the Information viewer's format and content changes. For example, when you look over your daily incoming mail, the Information viewer displays summaries of your mail. When you want to read something specific, you can display the entire item in the Information viewer and hide the summaries.

☐ **Items:** Contains the folder items such as contacts, appointments, and email.

16

> Hour 17, "Communicating with Outlook 97" explains how to add another window so that you can preview selected messages.

Using the Calendar to Schedule in Outlook 97

Outlook 97 includes a calendar that not only enables you to organize and track dates, but also enables you to track birthdays and anniversaries (and gives you automatic time-for-gift-buying reminders), find open dates, keep a task list, schedule meetings, and remind you of appointments. The following sections show you how to use the Outlook 97 calendar to organize your life.

> Not only does Outlook 97 remind you of specific appointments with an audible and visible reminder, but Outlook 97 easily sets up recurring appointments, such as weekly sales meetings or birthday reminders.

When you're ready to work with Outlook 97's calendar, display it by clicking the Calendar icon on the Outlook bar, selecting Calendar from the Folder list, or by selecting Go | Calendar. To display more of your calendar, you can decrease the amount of screen space devoted to the Outlook bar and Folder list by dragging their edges toward the left side of the screen.

> You can adjust the screen columns to show more of any Outlook 97 feature. Most Outlook 97 users prefer to hide the Folder list, displaying it only when needed by selecting View | Folder List. (Figure 16.2 shows the Outlook 97 screen with the calendar feature activated. Notice the Folder list is gone.) To display a drop-down Folder list temporarily, click the active folder name (shown in Figure 16.2).

Figure 16.2.

Working with the calendar.

Click here to see the
drop-down Folder list

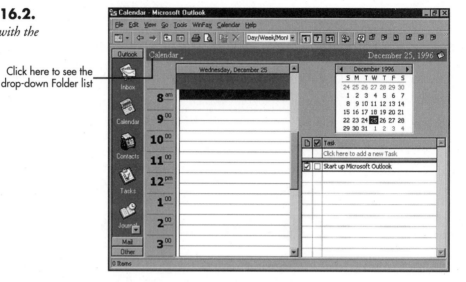

Navigating Times and Dates

Notice that the calendar appears with these major sections:

- [ ] Monthly calendar
- [ ] Daily time planner
- [ ] Task list

The monthly calendar always highlights the current date (getting its information from the computer's internal clock and calendar). The monthly calendar shows the current date by enclosing the day number in a box and the current day's appointments display if you've entered any. The calendar might show two months, depending on your screen settings. You can navigate the calendar through days and months by following these simple guides:

- [ ] Change days by pressing the left- or right-arrow keys or by clicking a date with your mouse.
- [ ] Change months by clicking to the left or right of the calendar's month name or by clicking the calendar's month name and selecting from the pop-up month list that appears.

Click through the calendar's days and notice that the daily time planner changes days accordingly. Although you may not have any appointments set yet, you quickly see how you can look at any day's appointments by clicking that day's date. The weekend day appointment pages are grayed to remind you that you're looking at Saturday or Sunday. In addition, Outlook 97 grays all weekday times before 8:00 a.m. and after 5:00 p.m. The grayed areas are typical nonbusiness hours. Of course, you can enter new appointments into the grayed areas. The gray highlight is just Outlook 97's way of letting you know the times are not normal business hours.

16

> You can change the hours that Outlook 97 designates as business hours by selecting Tools | Options and clicking the Calendar tab. The Start time and End time list boxes hold the business hours that Outlook 97 maintains. In addition, you can select other days to appear as workweek days in case you normally work on Saturday or Sunday.

The calendar also provides a month-at-a-glance format when you click any of the seven day abbreviations above the calendar's day numbers. (Figure 16.3 shows the month-at-a-glance calendar that appears when you select the entire month.)

Figure 16.3.

Looking at the month-at-a-glance.

You can select the entire month

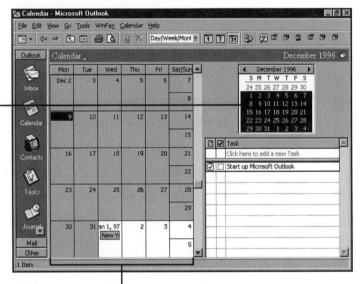

The entire month's appointments appear here

> If you select two or more days, Outlook 97 displays your selection's at-a-glance planning calendar.

As you acquaint yourself with Outlook 97's calendar, select from the View menu to customize the screen for your particular needs. In addition, you can drag any bar separating the window panes to provide more or less room to any portion of the Outlook 97 screen that you need.

Setting Appointments

To schedule an appointment, perform these steps:

1. In Day view, select the day on which you want to schedule the appointment by clicking it.
2. Select the appointment time. You might have to click the time planner's scrollbar or use your up- and down-arrow keys to see the time you want.
3. Double-click the appointment time to display the Appointment dialog box (shown in Figure 16.4).

Figure 16.4.

Scheduling an appointment is easy.

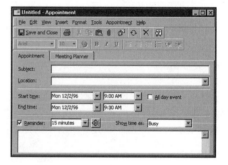

4. Enter the appointment's subject and location. Outlook 97 keeps track of your locations as you add them, so you don't have to retype them for subsequent appointments but only select them from the drop-down list.
5. Set the start and stop times (use Tools|Options to change the default of 30-minute appointments if you often have different appointment lengths) or click the All Day Event option if necessary.
6. Set your reminder time if you want a reminder. Outlook 97 audibly and visibly reminds you of the appointment at the time you request.
7. Click the Recurrence toolbar button if the appointment occurs regularly. Outlook 97 displays the Appointment Recurrence dialog box (shown in Figure 16.5). Set the recurrence options to enable Outlook 97 to schedule your recurring appointment.

You can select Calendar I New Recurring Appointment to go directly to the Appointment Recurrence dialog box when you set up recurring appointments.

Figure 16.5.

Some appointments occur regularly.

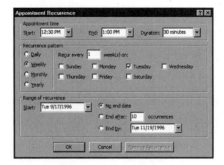

16

8. Click OK to close the Appointment Recurrence dialog box.
9. Click the Save and Close button. Outlook 97 displays your appointment in the time planner.

 An *appointment* is an activity for which you reserve time but which does not require other people or resources.

 If you don't run Outlook 97 at all times in the background, it cannot remind you of pending appointments. Therefore, you should add Outlook 97 to the Windows startup area so that it starts automatically every time you start up your computer.

If you need to change a set appointment, double-click the appointment to display the Appointment dialog box, in which you can change the appointment details. Drag the appointment's top or bottom edges from the time planner to increase or decrease the appointment's duration. Drag the appointment's side edges to change the appointment's start time.

 Click the New Appointment button on the toolbar to schedule a new appointment without first selecting the appointment's date and time.

You can remove an appointment at any time by right-clicking over the appointment to display a pop-up menu and then selecting Delete.

Instead of using the Appointment dialog box to schedule an appointment, you can enter an appointment quickly by clicking the appointment time once to highlight it and entering the text for the appointment directly on the daily planner. When you press Enter, Outlook 97 adds the appointment to the daily planner.

Outlook 97 reminds you of the appointment with an audible alarm 15 minutes before the
appointment. If you want to adjust the alarm lead time or make the alarm recurring, double-
click the appointment entry to display the Appointment dialog box.

> You may not want an audible alarm on all appointments. For example, if
> you use your laptop in meetings and do not want audible alarms interrupt-
> ing conversations, you can remove any appointment's audible alarm by
> right-clicking the appointment and selecting Reminder from the pop-up
> menu. You can select Reminder again from the right-click pop-up menu to
> set the audible alarm once again.

Scheduling Meetings

In Outlook 97 terminology, a meeting differs somewhat from an *appointment*. An appointment is for you; it does not involve other resources (such as people and equipment). A *meeting*,
however, requires that you schedule more people than yourself, and perhaps requires that you
reserve other resources (such as audio-visual equipment and a room in which to hold the
meeting).

NEW TERM A *meeting* is an appointment that involves other people and resources.

To schedule a meeting, create an appointment for that day and time. Click the Meeting
Planner tab in the Appointment dialog box (shown in Figure 16.6). Click the Invite Others
button and type (or select from the name list) the names of those attending. The list might
include people or resources, such as podiums. Outlook 97 gets the names from your contact
manager's database, but you can enter new names as needed. Use the scrollbars to view the
free and busy times for the people you invite. You must also select the meeting time. Outlook
97 shows you the attendees' available free time when you click AutoPick, or you can use your
mouse to schedule the attendees even if their free times all conflict. (Outlook 97 adjusts for
time zones if you invite someone from another time zone.)

Figure 16.6.

*Schedule meetings, invite
people, and reserve
resources.*

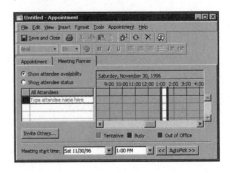

> Obviously, you must be organized and know the attendees quite well to have access to their schedules. Outlook 97 will search your network for the contacts and their free times. If you're not on a network, you do not have access to the free times of the people you invite.

Click the Appointment tab to complete the dialog box. When you click Send, all recipients (if networked or available by email) get invited to your meeting using the notes you entered on the Meeting Planner page.

Scheduling Events

An *event* is an activity not specifically tied to a time frame, such as a holiday or birthday. When you want to record an event, such as your boss's birthday, select Calendar | New Event. Schedule the event as you do an appointment, but click the All Day Event button to show that the event lasts the entire day (otherwise, the event automatically turns into an appointment). Select the Show Time As option if you want your calendar to show the time as Busy or Out of Office time. Select an appropriate reminder time from the Reminder list, such as 2 days, to receive an audible alarm and note reminding you of the event so that you can purchase gifts or prepare for the event in some other way.

New Term   An *event* is a 24-hour activity, such as a birthday or holiday.

When you view the event, Outlook 97 shows it in a *banner*, or a highlighted heading for that day in the day planner's views.

New Term   A *banner* is a highlighted title that signals and describes a day's event.

Managing a Task List

A *task* is any job that you need to track, perform, and monitor to completion. Outlook 97 tasks (like appointments and meetings) might be recurring, or they might happen only once. You can manage your Outlook 97 task list either from the Tasks folder in the Folder list or from the Calendar folder.

New Term   A *task* is any job that you need to track, perform, and monitor to completion.

> Unlike appointments, meetings, and events, tasks don't belong to any specific date or time. Tasks are jobs you need to finish but are not linked to a date or time.

To create a one-time task, perform these steps:

1. Click the New Task toolbar button or select File|New|Task. You can create a task even faster by clicking the task list's entry labeled Click Here to Add a Task.

2. Enter a task description.

3. Type the due date (the date you must complete the task but not necessarily the day you perform the task). If you click the Due Date drop-down list, you can select from a calendar that Outlook 97 displays. You can enter virtually any date in virtually any format, including Next Wednesday. Outlook 97 converts your format to a supported date format.

4. Further refine your task (if you need to) by double-clicking the task to display the Task dialog box (shown in Figure 16.7). You can specify recurring tasks and assign priority. Click the Status tab to update the status of the task as you work on it. The Status page even tracks such task-related information as mileage, time involved, and billing information.

Figure 16.7.

*Modify the task's specifics
and status.*

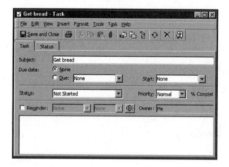

5. Click Save and Close to finalize the task.

When you complete a task, click the task's check box to cross the task from the list. Delete a task by selecting it and clicking the toolbar's Delete button.

If you want to remind yourself of a task's deadline, make an appointment for the deadline on the task's due date. Set the alarm for 24-hours or 2 days. When the deadline draws near, you then are reminded that the task is wrapping up fast.

Writing Yourself Notes

Outlook 97 notes are equivalent to sticky yellow paper notes. You can post a note inside Outlook 97 and retrieve, edit, or delete the note later.

To see your notes, click the Notes icon on the Outlook bar or display the Notes item from the Folder list. Double-click any note to see its contents.

To create a new note, click the New Note toolbar button to display a yellow note (shown in Figure 16.8). Type your note and click the note's Close button to close the note. Resize the note by dragging its lower-right corner. Outlook 97 tracks the note's date and time. Change the note's font by selecting a new font from the Tools | Options | Tasks/Notes tab. Select a different note color by right-clicking the note's icon.

Turn notes into appointments and tasks! Drag a note from the Notes work area to the Calendar or Tasks Outlook bar icons, and Outlook 97 opens an appropriate dialog box with the note's contents filling in the task or appointment's description. In the next hour, "Communicating with Outlook 97," you learn how to work with Outlook 97's email and journal components, and you can drag notes to those Outlook 97 programs as well.

Figure 16.8.

Enter a note to yourself.

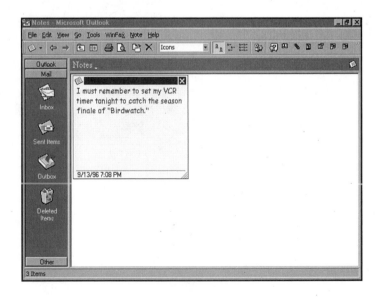

Using Outlook 97 to Explore Your Computer

Although Outlook 97 is not a replacement for Windows Explorer, it can function somewhat like Explorer to help you locate files and hardware. If you click the Other button on the Outlook bar, the My Computer icon and two disk folders (you can change the folders displayed and add folders to the list) are displayed. When you double-click the My Computer icon, Outlook 97 opens the familiar (to Windows 95 and NT 4.0 users) My Computer details.

By double-clicking one of the disk folders, you can display your disk contents (shown in Figure 16.9). If you drag your favorite folder to the Outlook bar, Outlook 97 adds that folder to the Outlook bar permanently. You can drag the folder to any group within the Outlook bar. For example, you might create three new folders to hold incoming email from three larger clients. You put those folders in the Outlook bar group named Mail. Your new folders are then only a click or two away when you want to search through the document files inside the folders. Add new groups by right-clicking over the Outlook bar area and selecting Add New Group. Change your View menu options if you want to change the details that you see in the window.

Microsoft did not replace the Windows Explorer with Outlook 97, but the Explorer-like access lets you quickly find files that you want to send as email attachments or include in notes that you write. This means that you don't have to open both Explorer and Outlook 97 when you need to search your disk for information.

Figure 16.9.

Explore your computer with Outlook 97.

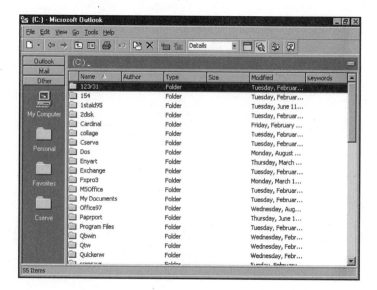

To launch a program from Outlook 97, double-click the program (or a document tied to an application, such as a Word 97 document) in the Outlook 97 listing, and Windows keeps Outlook 97 open while your selected program is opened. The right-click pop-up menu offers the same right-click functionality as you find in Explorer. Therefore, if you use Windows quick viewers, you find the familiar Quick View option on Outlook 97's right-click menus.

16

Quitting Outlook 97

You can quit Outlook 97 by performing any of the following:

- ☐ Selecting File | Exit.
- ☐ Pressing Alt+F4.
- ☐ Double-clicking the Control icon.
- ☐ Clicking Outlook 97's Close button.

Always quit Outlook 97 and shut down Windows before turning off your computer, or you might lose your work. For example, if an email message is in the middle of a transfer and you don't properly exit Outlook 97, you could lose some or all of that message.

Summary

This hour introduced Outlook 97 and explained some of the ways you can use Outlook 97 to check your calendar; manage appointments, meetings, and events; track tasks; keep notes; and explore your computer. If you've used any other personal information management program, you'll really like the integration of Outlook 97 into the Office 97 and Windows environment.

The next hour shows you how to use the contact list to find your associates quickly and easily. Additionally, the journal tracks events as they happen, including incoming mail and faxes that you receive inside the Inbox.

Q&A

Q How can I assign a task to a specific day?

A You cannot assign tasks to days. Tasks transcend days because tasks are one-time or recurring items that you must accomplish within a certain time frame, but not on a particular day. Perhaps you are only confusing Outlook 97 terminology. If you want to assign a particular event to a time and day, assign an appointment or meeting. Tasks are items that you must accomplish and that you can track and assign to other people, but tasks are not tied to a specific time and date.

Q After I set a reminder, how does Outlook 97 inform me of the appointment, meeting, or event?

A You must continually run Outlook 97 during your computing sessions for Outlook 97 to monitor and remind you of things you have to do. Outlook 97 is one program that you probably want to add to your Windows Start-Up group so that it always starts when you start Windows. Outlook 97 cannot remind you of pending appointments if you're not running it.

Outlook 97 tracks incoming and outgoing events. Also, as you learn in the next hour, Outlook 97 monitors your electronic mail, faxes, and network transfers, and keeps an eye on your reminders to let you know when something is due. The only way Outlook 97 can perform these tasks is to keep it running during your work sessions.

Hour 17

Communicating with Outlook 97

This hour concludes coverage of Outlook 97 by showing you how to use the journal, contacts list, Inbox, and Outbox. The Inbox and Outbox components are central to using Outlook 97 as a repository for all your data throughput; these mail boxes constitute your computer's Grand Central Station.

Part of the effectiveness of Outlook 97 hinges on how well you keep your contact lists organized. Use Outlook 97 to keep track of clients, friends, employees, and anyone else you contact. Outlook 97 tracks not only routine name and address information but email addresses as well. After you set up your contacts list, other Outlook 97 programs (such as the Inbox) refer to the list when an address is needed. As you learned in the previous hour, you can even use Outlook 97 to schedule meetings with your contacts.

The highlights of this hour include

- ☐ What a contact is
- ☐ Why Outlook 97 works like a web-page organizer
- ☐ When a journal tracks items automatically

☐ How to enter items manually into the journal

☐ How to send and receive messages

☐ When to use the Outlook 97 Deleted Items folder

☐ How to read and reply to messages

Keeping Contacts

The Outlook 97 contact database keeps track of your contacts so that Outlook 97 has a central, uniform repository of information to use when you send email, hold meetings, and record calls. You can add new contacts, delete old ones you no longer need, and change information of a contact from the Contacts folder. The Contacts folder maintains name, title, address, phone, and email information on your contacts, and it offers fields that you can use for additional information such as notes, family information, and more.

 A *contact* is a person or organization that you correspond with, either by mail, email, phone, or in person.

Recording Contacts

When you first use Outlook 97, you have no contacts entered in the Contacts folder. To record a new contact, perform these steps:

1. Click Contacts on the Outlook bar or select Contacts from the Folder list.

2. Click the New Contact toolbar button on the Contacts screen to open the Contact dialog box (shown in Figure 17.1).

3. Type the contact's full name. If you click the Full Name button, Outlook 97 displays separate fields for the parts of the name (such as title, first name, and last name), so you can keep the parts properly separated when needed. The time you take to separate part names pays off if you use your contact information in form letters and database work.

4. Enter the rest of the contact's information. Click the Address button to track separate parts of the contact's address. Open the drop-down lists to record separate pieces of related data. For example, you can record a business, a home, or another address by clicking the appropriate drop-down address type before entering the address. Open the phone-number drop-down lists as well to store different kinds of phone numbers for your contacts. You might find it useful to increase the size of the dialog box to full screen to see all the fields.

 Notice how many phone number fields Outlook 97 gives you to use. Although you see only four on the form, a phone number field for

Business, Home, Business Fax, and Mobile, you can click the down arrow inside each of these fields to display a list box full of additional numbers such as Business 2 and Pager. Today's communication needs require several phone numbers, and Outlook 97 provides all you need. Any of the list boxes on the Contact form drops down to provide additional choices. For example, you can enter multiple addresses and email accounts for each contact, although only one address and one email shows at any one time.

5. Click the Save and Close buttons to save the contact information and display a blank dialog box for your next contact.

Figure 17.1.
Outlook 97 gives you a lot of contact data fields.

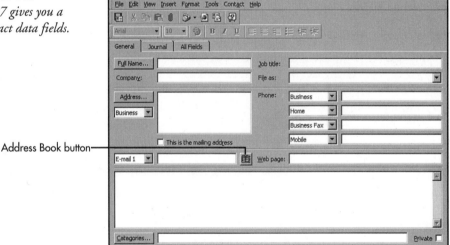

Address Book button

The contact's data page acts like an Internet web-page browser as well as a repository for contact data. If a contact has a web page, enter that web page's address in the Web Page field. When you return to the contact information and click the toolbar's Explore Web Page button, Outlook 97 locates and displays the contact's web page using whatever web browser (such as Internet Explorer) is installed on your system.

If you use Microsoft Exchange or Windows Messaging to track names and email addresses, click the Address Book button (refer to Figure 17.1) to import an email address from your current address book.

 Be on the lookout for shortcuts as you work with Outlook 97. Generally, you can drag and drop information instead of reentering data when you need to transport information from one Outlook 97 area to another. You don't even have to type in all of a client's contact information if you have that information elsewhere in Outlook 97. For example, suppose that you wrote yourself a quick note with a new client's name and phone number using Outlook 97's notes (you learned how to take notes with Outlook 97 in the previous hour). You can transfer the client's information from the note to your contact list by dragging the note to the Contacts icon on the Outlook bar. Outlook 97 sets up the initial client name and number information, to which you then can add. Conversely, you can drag a contact to a note to place that contact information on the note.

When you close the Contact dialog box, your first contact appears in the address book (shown in Figure 17.2). After you enter several contacts, click the alphabetic tabs to the right of the address book to locate specific contacts.

Figure 17.2.

Your contact appears in Outlook 97's address book.

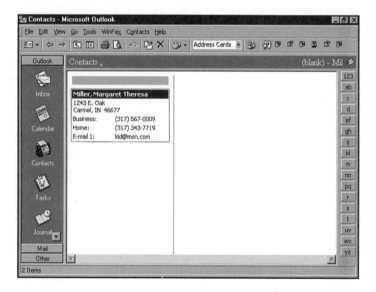

Selecting Contacts

To select a contact, display the contact name in the address book. A few things you can do after you select a contact are

- [ ] Directly edit the addresses, phone numbers, and email addresses displayed on the page by clicking the appropriate fields.

- [ ] Double-click the name to open the Contact dialog box, which displays the contact information, enabling you to edit or view more detail.

- [ ] Right-click the contact name, select AutoDialer, and dial the contact's phone number from the New Call dialog box (shown in Figure 17.3). If you click the Journal Entry option, Outlook 97 adds the call to this contact's journal; the journal records the call! Use the journal to track calls such as payment requests so that you have a record of who you called and when you placed the call. The next section explains all about the journal feature.

- [ ] Right-click the contact name and click the Explore Web Page button to see the contact's web page from within your web browser.

- [ ] Drag the column separators right or left to see more or less of each column. If you prefer to view narrow columns in the Contact folder, you see more contacts but not the full phone number and address field. If you widen the columns, you see more detail for the contacts but see fewer of them at a time.

- [ ] Right-click the contact name and select the New Contact from Same Company option. Outlook 97 creates a new contact entry and transfers all the business-related addresses and phone numbers to the new contact. You only need to fill in the new contact's name and other specifics. Likewise, Outlook 97 enables you to create an employee contact list easily by transferring similar company data to each new employee you enter.

Figure 17.3.

Outlook 97 automatically dials your contact.

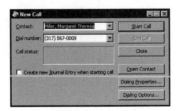

Keeping a Journal

The Outlook 97 *journal* keeps track of all your interactions with contacts, Outlook 97 items, and activities. Although you can make manual journal entries, the real power of the journal appears when you automate Outlook 97 to record the following types of journal entries:

- [ ] Track and record all items (such as email) that you send to and receive from contacts. Depending on the option you selected when you set up a contact, the journal can automatically record all interactions with that contact, or you can record interactions selectively.

- [ ] Keep track of all Office 97 documents that you create or edit. Browse the journal to find a summary of the documents you created and the order in which you created (and edited) them.

- [ ] Track all meetings automatically.

- [ ] Track all appointments and tasks manually. (Outlook 97 does not track appointments and tasks automatically; you must enter them yourself every time you add an appointment or task.)

- [ ] Manually record *any* activity in your Outlook 97 journal, including conversations around the water cooler.

 The Outlook 97 *journal* keeps track of all your interactions with contacts, Outlook 97 items, and activities.

Setting Automatic Journal Entry

Have you ever wished that you had recorded a complaint call you made when you got a bad product or service? Let Outlook 97 track *all* your calls automatically! The journal records times, dates, and people you called. As you use Outlook 97 to make calls, record notes about the calls and track those notes in your Outlook 97 journal. When you open the journal by clicking the Journal icon on the Outlook bar or selecting Journal from the Folder list, you see a blank journal entry (shown in Figure 17.4.)

Figure 17.4.

Your journal starts out blank.

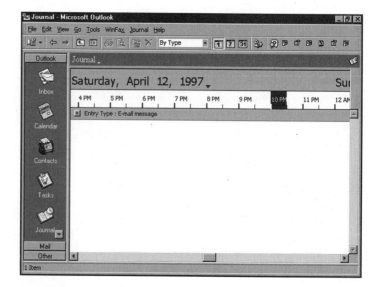

The first thing you want to do with your journal is to designate all items that you want the journal to track. Select Tools|Options and click the Journal tab. Select each item from the list that you want Outlook 97 to track. For example, select Email Message, Fax, Meeting Request, and Meeting Response if those are the items you want the journal to track automatically. In addition, select one or more contacts from the contact list, and Outlook 97 records all activity for those specific contacts.

If you want Outlook 97 to track document files from another program, such as Word 97, simply select that program from the list. Outlook 97 tracks all Office 97 document activity (if you select this option) as well as other Office 97–aware software documents and data files. (Note that not all Windows programs are Office 97–aware.)

Adding Journal Entries Manually

As mentioned earlier in this section, the journal cannot automatically record all activity in your life; however, you can add manual entries for any activities you want recorded. If you want to record an appointment, open that appointment (from within the calendar). If you want to record an item not related to Outlook 97, such as a conversation, create a note for that item (see Hour 16, "Outlook 97 Basics," for help with the note feature) and transport the information from the note to the journal.

To record a manual journal entry from an existing item (such as notes of a conversation), perform these steps:

1. Double-click the item you want to record to display the Edit dialog box for the item.

2. Select the item's Tools menu, and then select the Record in Journal option. The journal now contains an icon that represents the item. Double-click the journal's icon to display the item's details.

Suppose that you wrote a letter to your phone company, for example, and you want to record the complete document in your journal. If you've set up your journal to track all Word 97 documents automatically, the document appears in your journal. If, however, you have not set up the journal to track Word 97 documents automatically, simply display the document's icon in the My Computer window on the Outlook bar and drag the document to the journal icon on the Outlook bar.

You also can add a new journal entry of any item type before you create the item. Display your journal and select File|New. Select Journal Entry to display the Journal Entry dialog box (shown in Figure 17.5). Type a subject and select the type of journal entry. When you click the Save and Close button, Outlook 97 saves your entry in the journal.

17

Figure 17.5.

*Manually enter a new
journal entry.*

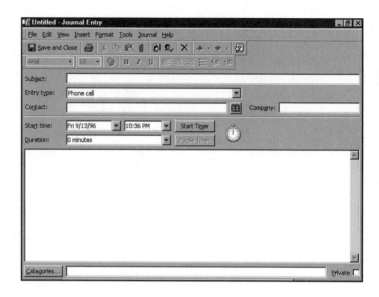

Reviewing Journal Entries

After you set up the automatic recording, Outlook 97 begins logging those activities. When you open the journal for days during which some activity occurred (automatically or manually recorded), you see the journal entry. Suppose that you want to work on files you created a few weeks ago during an end-of-month accounting close period. Open your journal and scroll back to the date of the close. You see a list of all files that you worked on, whether those files are email messages you sent or received, notes, Word 97 documents, or Excel 97 worksheets.

Outlook 97 compacts entries within the same application. For example, instead of seeing every Word 97 document that you worked on this week, you see a band labeled, `Entry Type:` `Microsoft Word`. Click the plus sign on the band to expand the entries and see the individual journal entries recorded for each Word 97 file you worked on. Double-click any of the files you see to open that file. If you double-click a Word 97 document, Word 97 is activated and loads that document. If you double-click a contact you entered, Outlook 97 displays that contact information.

> Periodically, delete older entries from your journal that you no longer need. The journal entries add up quickly. When you delete a journal entry, the files the journal entry describes are not deleted, only their entries in the journal are.

Mastering Outlook 97 Mail

When you click the Mail button on the Outlook bar, the Outlook bar displays the following labeled icons:

- ☐ **Inbox:** Holds your incoming email and faxes.
- ☐ **Sent Items:** Displays mail items you've sent to others.
- ☐ **Outbox:** Holds items you've queued up to send.
- ☐ **Deleted Items:** Holds items, such as email messages, that you've deleted but not removed from Outlook 97. Select Tools|Empty Deleted Items Folder to remove the Deleted Items folder contents.

> When you remove an item from the Deleted Items folder, Outlook 97 does *not* send the item to the Windows recycle bin; Outlook 97 deletes the item completely from your system.

NEW TERM The *Inbox folder* holds messages you've received.

NEW TERM The *Outbox folder* holds all your outgoing messages until you send them.

NEW TERM The *Deleted Items folder* holds items you've deleted from Outlook 97 but not completely erased from the disk. The Deleted Items folder is to Outlook 97 what the Recycle Bin is to Windows 95.

If you want to save messages from your Inbox, move them to a different location. You can select and drag any message from the Inbox to another folder on the Outlook bar. If you change your mind about getting rid of a message stored in your Deleted Items folder, you can move that message to a different folder. Only when you delete a message from within the Deleted Items folder is that message completely deleted.

Creating and Sending Messages

One task you perform quite often is sending a message to a recipient across the Internet. To create a message, perform these steps:

1. Click the Mail button on the Outlook bar.
2. Select File|New|Mail Message to display the Message dialog box (shown in Figure 17.6). (You can also click the New Mail Message toolbar button to open the Message dialog box more quickly than selecting from the File menu.)

3. Enter the recipient's name in the To (your primary recipient) field. If you enter a name in the Cc (carbon copy) field, Outlook Express sends a copy to that recipient and places a Cc before the name. Click these buttons if you want to select a contact in your contacts list (highly recommended because your contacts list holds email addresses). If you have not entered the recipient in your contacts list, add the information now, and then close the contacts list to return to the mail message.

   If you want to send the same message to multiple recipients, select multiple recipients from the Select Names dialog box when you click the To button to see a list of contacts. If you want to enter email addresses directly in the To field, you can separate multiple addresses with a semicolon (;).

4. Enter the message subject. Your recipient sees the subject in the list of messages that he receives.

 Always enter a subject for your email messages so that your recipient knows at a glance what your message is about. This also makes it easier for you to track sent messages.

5. Type your message in the large message area at the bottom of the Message dialog box. To spell check your message, type your message, click your cursor at the beginning of the message, and then select Tools|Spelling. You can activate automatic spell-checking (so that Outlook 97 checks your spelling as you type) by selecting the appropriate option in the Tools|Options dialog box. If you find that Outlook 97 still does not check your spelling as you type your message, make sure that you've checked the option labeled Use Microsoft Word as the Email Editor in the Tools|Options|E-mail dialog box.

6. Click the Options tab to select certain message options (such as the message importance level and a delivery date). The recipient, like you, is able to order received mail by importance level when reading through the messages.

7. Click the Send button. Outlook 97 sends the message to your folder named Outbox. If you are logged into the Internet, Outlook 97 sends your message immediately.

8. Select Tools|Check for New Mail to send your Outbox messages. If you are logged on to the Internet when you click the Send button in step 7, Outlook finishes sending your mail and also collects any incoming messages waiting for you. If you are not logged in to the Internet, Outlook displays the Login dialog box. Always check your Inbox for mail after sending mail from the Outbox using Tools|Check for New Mail in case new mail was delivered to you.

Figure 17.6.

Enter the message you want to send.

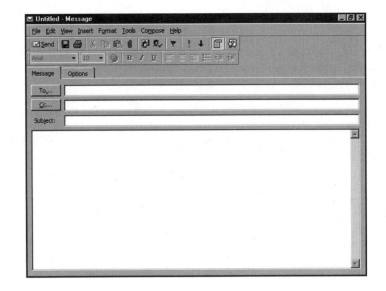

Not all messages are text-only, and Outlook 97 works with all file types. To attach another document file to your message, such as a Word 97 or Excel 97 document, click the Insert File toolbar button and select a document file from the Open dialog box that appears. Any text that you typed is followed by the file that you attach.

Checking Mail

Regularly, you need to check your Inbox folder to see what items await you. As mentioned in Step 8 of the previous section, you must select Tools | Check for New Mail to send Outbox items and receive Inbox folder items. Outlook 97 logs you on to your Internet provider if needed. Your Inbox folder on the Outlook bar displays a number if you have unread messages that require your attention.

If you use multiple email services, select the Tools I Check for New Mail On option and select the email service that you want to check. For example, you might use Microsoft Network at home and a local Internet provider at work. You can set up both services on your home and office computer and select which service's email to retrieve when you select the Tools I Check for New Mail On option. To add a new email service to Outlook 97, select Tools I Services I Add and select the appropriate service. You may need to contact your Internet service provider to set up the appropriate properties to work with Outlook 97 after you add a service.

If you find that Outlook 97 logs you off your Internet provider after you retrieve your email but you often want to remain logged on to check the web, you can request that Outlook 97 stay logged on. Select Tools | Services and select your Internet service. Click the Properties button and uncheck the option labeled Disconnect after Transferring Mail from Remote Mail.

When you display your Inbox folder (by clicking the Inbox icon on the Outlook bar), you see a list of incoming message headers like the ones shown in Figure 17.7.

If you only see headers (with no text), select View | Current view | Messages with *AutoPreview*. The AutoPreview lets you read the first few lines of each message in addition to showing the message header. The next section explains how you can open a new preview pane for selected messages so that you can read the entire message body without opening the message.

NEW TERM *AutoPreview* is the Inbox folder's mode that displays each message's subject as well as three lines from each message.

Figure 17.7.

Use the AutoPreview feature to get a glimpse of each message.

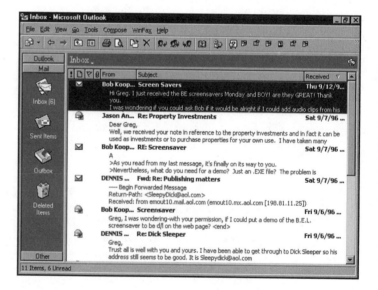

Outlook 97 utilizes icons to let you know what is happening. As you read each message, the message icon changes to show that the message has been read. Revert the read message flag back to an unread state by

> right-clicking the message and selecting Mark as Unread from the pop-up menu. A paper clip icon appears next to each message that contains an attached file. When you open a message with an attached file, Outlook 97 shows the attachment as an icon that you can right-click to save or open it.

To read a message, simply double-click it. To reply to the sender (in effect, sending a new message to your Outbox folder), click the toolbar's Reply button and enter a reply. You can reply to the sender and all Cc recipients of the sender's message by clicking the Reply All toolbar button.

Making a Phone Call from Outlook

You can place a phone call from Outlook 97 if you have a modem connected to your computer. To make a call from anywhere inside Outlook 97, display the Tools menu and select Dial. If you select New Call, Outlook 97 displays the New Call dialog box, from which you can select a contact to dial or manually enter a number. If you have not set up automatic journal recording for the call's recipient, click the option labeled Create New Journal Entry When Starting Call. If you recently called the recipient, click Tools | Dial | Redial and select from the list of recently called numbers.

Figure 17.8.

You can place a call from Outlook 97 at any time.

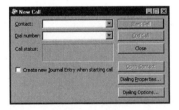

Obtaining Internet Updates for Outlook

If you have access to the Internet, as you probably do if you use Outlook 97 for email, consider going to the Microsoft web site to get Outlook 97 updates and sample files. The web address is http://www.microsoft.com/officefreestuff/outlook/ and the site includes several add-ons for Outlook 97 such as Draw 97, a drawing system that lets you add lines and shapes to your messages (Hour 22, "Office 97's Synergy," explains how to use Draw 97).

One of the most helpful updates you can get is the three-pane extension patch that enables you to display a preview window to read the bodies of a selected email message without first opening the message. Figure 17.9 shows the preview pane.

17

Figure 17.9.

*Read the message from
the preview pane.*

Message
being
previewed

The preview pane

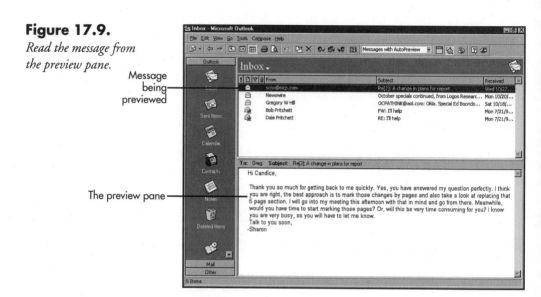

You might also want to download the Outlook Inbox icon patch. After you apply the downloaded patch, your Windows desktop Inbox is labeled `Microsoft Outlook` and starts Outlook 97 when you click the icon from your desktop.

Summary

This hour explained the remaining Outlook 97 features. You now understand contacts and the importance of entering as much information as you can about them into Outlook 97. All Office 97 products use the contacts list for names and addresses. When you automate your journal, the journal contains all contacts you've elected to track.

One of the busiest Outlook 97 areas is the messaging Inbox and Outbox folders. Outlook 97 organizes incoming and outgoing messages and makes it easy for you to respond to messages that you receive.

The next hour, "Access 97 Basics," begins exploring Access 97, the Office 97 database that is arguably the most useful and powerful personal-computer database available today.

Q&A

Q What if I don't have a web browser?

A You do have a web browser because Office 97 comes with one. You might not have Internet access, however. You must sign up with an Internet provider to use any Internet-based features. Hour 23, "Office 97 and the Internet" discusses the Internet in more detail if you are a newcomer.

Q How does a message reply differ from a forwarded message?

A When you reply to a message, you create a brand new message that contains new information about the recipient's original message. If you forward a recipient's message, you send the message exactly as you first read it to another recipient (or to a list of recipients).

Q Why does Outlook 97 not send my messages as soon as I complete outgoing messages and send them?

A Outlook 97 does not send messages until you select Tools | Check for New Mail (F5 is the shortcut key) unless you are already logged in to your Internet account. If you use the Internet in an office setting with a T1 or satellite connection, you are probably logged on to the Internet most of the time. If, however, you use a modem to access the Internet, you have to initiate the logon sequence when you want to check for email.

Dialing and logging on takes time. Instead of logging on to your Internet provider every time you create an Outbox folder message, Outlook 97 waits until you request the check for new mail to get your waiting mail and to send your outgoing mail. By waiting, Outlook 97 only has to log on to the Internet one time to send all your messages.

17

Part **VI**

Tracking with Access 97

Hour

Hour 18

Access 97 Basics

Everyone trudges through data at work and at home. A database manager, such as Access 97, lets you organize your data and turn raw facts and figures into meaningful information. Access 97 processes data details, so you can spend your valuable time analyzing results. Suppose that your company keeps thousands of parts in an Access 97 inventory database, and you need to know exactly which part sold the most in Division 7 last April. Access 97 can find the answer for you.

This hour introduces you to the world of databases with Access 97. The nature of databases makes Access 97 one of the more involved programs in the Office 97 suite of programs. Generally, people find that they can master Word 97, Excel 97, PowerPoint 97, and Outlook 97 more quickly than they can Access 97. Access 97 is not difficult to learn and use, but you must understand the structure of database design before you can truly understand Access 97.

The highlights of this hour include

- [ ] What a database is
- [ ] Which database-related objects Access 97 manages
- [ ] Why databases contain tables
- [ ] What fields and records are
- [ ] How to create and modify tables

Database Basics

Whereas previous hours of this book began by showing you how to start the program, this hour begins by explaining the database concept. You need to learn a little about how a database management system organizes data before using Access 97.

A *database* is an organized collection of data. Access 97 is called a *database management system* because it lets you create, organize, and manage data stored in databases.

 A *database* is an organized collection of related data you can easily retrieve and use.

 A *database management* system is a program, like Access 97, that lets you create, organize, and manage your data stored in databases.

> Database experts have written complete books on database theory. This hour won't give you an extremely in-depth appreciation for databases, but you learn enough to get started with Access 97.

A database typically contains related data. In other words, you might create a home office database with your household budget, but keep another database to record your rare-book collection titles and their worth. In your household budget, you might track expenses, income, bills paid, and so forth, but that information does not overlap the book collection database. Of course, if you buy a book, both databases might show the transaction, but the two databases would not overlap.

When you design a database, define its scope before you begin. Does your business need an inventory tracking system? Does your business need an electronic general-ledger system? If so, an Access 97 database works well. Only you and your accountants can decide whether the inventory should be part of the general-ledger system. The database integration of inventory into the general ledger requires much more work to design, but your financial requirements may necessitate the integration.

> Not all database values directly relate to one another. For example, your company's loan records do not relate to your company's payroll, but both probably reside in your company's accounting database. Again, you have to decide on the scope when you design your database. Fortunately, Microsoft made Access 97 extremely flexible, so you can change any database structure when you begin using your database. The better you analyze the design up front, however, the easier your database is to create.

Step-Up

Although you can read Access 95 databases from Access 97, it's best to convert Access 95 databases to Access 97. Do so by selecting Tools | Database Utilities | Convert Database. Access 97 does not enable you to change the structure of an Access 95 database until you convert it to Access 97.

Database Tables

If you threw your family's financial records into a filing cabinet without organizing them, you would have a mess. That's why most people organize their filing cabinets by putting related records into file folders. Your insurance papers go in one folder; your banking records go in another.

Likewise, you cannot throw your data into a database without breaking the data into separate related groups. These groups are called *tables*; a table is analogous to a folder in a filing cabinet.

NEW TERM   A *table* is a collection of data about a specific topic.

18

A database might contain many tables, each being a further refinement of related data. Your financial database might contain tables for accounts payable, customer records, accounts receivable, vendor records, employee records, and payroll details, such as hours worked during a given time period. The separate tables help you eliminate redundant data; when you produce a payroll report, Access 97 retrieves some information from your employee table (such as name and pay rate) and some information from your time tables (such as hours worked).

Access 97 is a *relational database*. That means Access 97 uses data from multiple tables instead of requiring you to duplicate data in two or more places. Therefore, if you increase a customer's discount, you only need to change the discount in one customer table instead of in the customer table, the pricing table, and the sales table.

NEW TERM   A *relational database* relates data from multiple tables instead of requiring you to duplicate data in more than one location.

Access 97 stores all tables for a single database in one file that ends with the .mdb extension. By storing the complete database in one file, Access 97 makes it easier for you to copy and back up your database. You never have to specify the .mdb extension when you create a database. As with all the Office 97 data files, a database is referred to as a *document* when you want to open the database from the Office 97 shortcut bar and menus.

> You can import data from an Access 97 document (database table) into a Word 97 document. This makes creating and reporting data simple.

Records and Fields

To keep track of table data, Access 97 breaks down each table into *records* and *fields*. In a way, the table structure looks a lot like an Excel 97 worksheet. As Figure 18.1 shows, a table's records are the rows, and a table's fields are the columns. Figure 18.1 shows an electronic checkbook register table; you usually organize your real checkbook register just like the computerized table, so you'll have no problem mastering Access 97's records and fields.

NEW TERM A *record* is a row from a table.

NEW TERM A *field* is a column from a table.

Figure 18.1.
Tables have records (rows) and fields (columns).

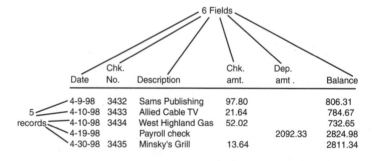

Your table fields contain different data types. As Figure 18.1 shows, one field might hold a text description, while another holds a dollar amount. Every item within the same field must be the same data type, but a table might contain several fields that differ in type. When you design your database, you are responsible for indicating to Access 97 which data type you want for each field in your database tables.

The types of data that you can store in an Access 97 database table are

☐ **Text:** Text data consists of letters, numbers, and special characters. You only report text data; you cannot calculate with it. A balance-due field would never be a text data type, but addresses, names, and Social Security numbers are examples of text fields. Generally, you store short text items (names, addresses, cities, product names, and part codes) in text fields.

- [ ] **Memo:** The memo field can hold an extremely large amount of text, including paragraphs. Memo fields consume a lot of space, and not all tables require memo fields.

- [ ] **Number:** A number field holds numbers. Use this field to calculate values.

- [ ] **Date/Time Fields:** These fields hold date and time values (similar to the date and time format in Excel 97). Access 97 lets you enter data into date and time fields using many formats. Additionally, Access 97 respects your Windows international settings, so you are able to enter a date in your country's format.

- [ ] **Currency:** This field holds dollar amounts. Access 97 keeps the dollar amounts rounded to the proper decimal alignment. Access 97 recognizes your Windows international settings, and uses international money amounts when needed.

- [ ] **AutoNumber:** This field holds sequential numbers, a different number for each record in the table.

NEW TERM *AutoNumber* refers to a field data type that holds sequential numbers, one for each record in the table. Access 97 automatically adds the AutoNumber data to tables as you add records to a table. You can use the AutoNumber field as a special record locating field because of its guaranteed unique value in the table.

- [ ] **Yes/No:** These fields hold Yes and No (or true and false) two-pronged values to indicate the existence or absence of an item or to indicate the answer to an implied question.

- [ ] **OLE object:** This is an embedded object, such as a graph you create in Excel 97. Your Access 97 databases can hold any kind of OLE-compatible embedded object.

NEW TERM *OLE*, which stands for *Object Linking and Embedding*, refers to objects from another program that you can insert into an Access 97 table. When you change the linked object within the Access 97 table, that change is reflected in the original file.

- [ ] **Hyperlink:** This is an Internet web-page site address. Such a field can hold an Internet address for a file as well as a network or an intranet address within your system network. When the database user clicks the hyperlink, Access 97 shows the hyperlink's web page or network file.

 The Internet integration of Office 97 extends to Access 97. When you click a hyperlink Internet web-page address in a table, Access 97 sends you to the web page, logging you on to your Internet provider if necessary.

18

Using a Key Field

Every Access 97 table requires a *primary key field*. The primary key field (often just called a *key*) is a field that contains no duplicate entries. Whereas a table's city field might contain multiple occurrences of the same city name, a key field must be unique for each record. You can designate a field as a key field, or you can use the AutoNumber field that Access 97 adds to all tables as the key field.

> If you access a particular field very often, even if that field is not a key field, designate it as an *index field* in the Design view property settings. Access 97 creates an index for every database and locates the index fields in that index. Just as an index in the back of the book speeds your searches for particular subjects, the index field speeds searches for that field.

If you were creating a table to hold employee records, a good key-field candidate would be the employee's Social Security number because every person's Social Security number is unique. If you're not sure that your data contains unique information in any field, specify the AutoNumber field that Access 97 creates as the key.

Access 97 uses the key field to find records quickly. For example, when you want to locate an employee's record, search by the employee's key field (the Social Security number). If you search based on the employee's name, you might not find the proper record; two or more employees might be named *John Smith*, for example.

> The reason that so many companies assign you a customer number is because the customer number uniquely identifies you in their database. Although today's computerized society sometimes makes one feel like "just another number," such a customer number enables the company to keep your records more accurate and keep costs down.

Starting Access 97

To start Access 97, perform one of the following:

☐ Click the Office 97 New Office Document button on the Shortcut bar and double-click the Blank Database icon to create a new Access 97 database. (If you don't see the Blank Database icon, click the General tab.)

☐ Click the Open Office Document button on the Shortcut bar and select an existing Access 97 database from its directory that you want to edit.

☐ Use the Windows Start menu to start Access 97 by selecting Microsoft Access from the Programs menu.

☐ Select an Access 97 database from the Document option on the Windows Start menu. Windows recognizes that Access 97 created the database, starts Access 97, and loads the database automatically. (The Start menu's Documents option holds a list of your most recent work.)

☐ Click the Access 97 button on the Shortcut bar to create a blank database. (Depending on your Office 97 Shortcut bar's setup, you might not see the Access 97 button.)

Figure 18.2 shows the opening Access 97 screen. Your screen might differ slightly depending on the options that you chose during installation.

Figure 18.2.

The opening screen when you start Access 97 from the Start menu.

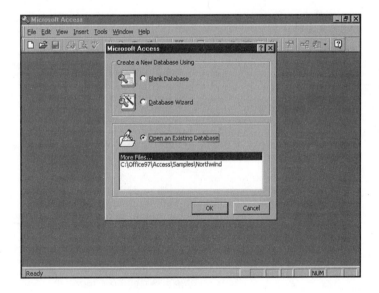

18

The center of the opening screen contains a dialog box that guides you to your first Access 97 operation. The dialog box lets you do one of the following:

☐ Create a blank database, which requires that you manually set up the entire database structure including tables, fields, and other pertinent database-structure information.

☐ Start a database wizard that walks you through the creation of a database using predefined wizard formats.

☐ Open an existing database so that you can modify the database structure or work with the database information.

Creating an Access 97 Database

When you start Access 97 and see the opening dialog box (shown in Figure 18.2), select Blank Database and click OK to create a new database. Access 97 prompts you for a database name using the default name db1 with the filename extension .mdb. You should change the db1 to something more meaningful. Enter a new name and click the Create button to display the *Database window* (shown in Figure 18.3). The Database window title bar includes the name of your database (My First in Figure 18.3) and lists the names of your database *objects*, none of which exist when you create the database.

 The *Database window* lists your database object names and provides the central control panel for your Access 97 work.

 Objects are tables, queries, forms, reports, macros, and modules within your database.

Figure 18.3.

The Database window displays a list of your database objects as you create them.

 A database object is a piece of an Access 97 database. For example, a table is an object. A database report that prints database data is an object. Your data values, however, are not objects.

Adding Objects to Your Database

As you create your database, you add objects to the Database window's six object categories. Any database can contain many objects from each category. The following are brief descriptions of the six kinds of Access 97 objects:

☐ **Tables:** Related data within a database

- [ ] **Queries:** Stored instructions that select data from one or more tables for reporting, analysis, and data-management purposes
- [ ] **Forms:** Onscreen representations of paper forms that you and others use to enter data into tables
- [ ] **Reports:** Printed listings of database data
- [ ] **Macros:** Stored task lists for Access 97 commands
- [ ] **Modules:** Programs written in Visual Basic, a powerful (but advanced for nonprogrammers) programming language with which you can automate any database task

As you create your database, you create one or more instances of the database objects. For example, you might create 25 tables and 50 reports. When you want to create, edit, or work with one of the database objects, return to the Database window (the toolbar always contains a Database Window toolbar button when you're using Access 97 but not working in the Database window) and click the tab of the object with which you need to work.

Generally, you select the object category, and then click New to create a new object in that category. Alternatively, you might select an object and click Open to work with that object.

18

Creating a Table

You must create tables before you can do anything with a database. The tables hold the data on which the other objects operate. As mentioned earlier in this hour, begin creating your tables from scratch until you learn more about Access 97 and can modify tables and other database objects generated by the wizards.

To create a table, follow these steps:

1. In the Database window, with the Tables tab selected, click New. Access 97 displays the New Table dialog box (shown in Figure 18.4).

Figure 18.4.

The New Table dialog box helps you to create tables.

2. Select Design View and click OK to display the *Design view* dialog box (shown in Figure 18.5). Describe your table's fields in the Design view dialog box.

NEW TERM
Design view displays your table's design showing the individual fields and field properties. Other Database window objects also have Design views to show their structures.

3. Type a field name, such as First Name or Quantity, for the first field in your database. The names have nothing to do with the data type that you eventually store in the table's field. The field name lets you refer to the field as you design your table. Only after you completely design the table do you enter data in the table. The order in which you add fields does not affect your database use. Nevertheless, try to add the fields in the general order in which you want to enter the table data.

4. Press Tab and click the drop-down list that appears in the Data Type field to select the field's data type.

5. Press Tab and type a description for the field. Some field names are optional and don't require a description, but the more you document and describe your data, the easier it is to modify your database later.

Figure 18.5.

Define your table's fields in the Design view dialog box.

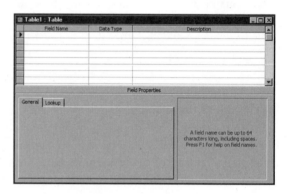

6. After you enter the first field's name, data type, and optional description, describe the field properties in the lower half of the Design view dialog box. Some fields do not require property settings, but most require some type of setting.

The next section describes how to set field property values.

Setting Field Properties

The lower half of the Design view contains settings for your field property values. Each field has a data type, as you already know. In addition to describing the field's data type in the Design view's upper half, you can further refine the field's description and limitations in the Field Properties section.

You can configure a different set of field property values for each data type. For example, text fields contain properties related to text data (such as an address or a name), whereas numeric fields contain properties related to numbers (such as decimal positions).

Open the property value selection list by clicking the property values. A few common field property values that you might want to set as you create your table are

- ☐ **Field Size:** Limits the number of characters the field can hold, thereby limiting subsequent data entry of field data.

- ☐ **Format:** Displays a drop-down list with several formats that the field's data type can take.

- ☐ **Caption:** Holds a text prompt that Access 97 displays when you enter data into this table's field. If you don't specify a caption, Access 97 uses the field name. Access 97 displays the caption in its status bar when you enter data into the table.

- ☐ **Default Value:** Contains the field's default value, which appears when you enter data into this table. The user can enter a value that differs from the default if desired.

- ☐ **Required:** Holds either Yes or No to determine whether Access 97 requires a value in this field before you can save a table's data record. If you specify a field as the key field instead of letting Access 97 add a key field, your key field must contain Yes for the Required property. If you don't want the user leaving a field blank, enter Yes for the Required property.

- ☐ **Decimal Places:** Holds the number of default decimal places shown for numbers entered into this field.

Figure 18.6 shows a completed table's Design view. The selected field's (the field with the arrow, or *field selector* in the left column) property values appear at the bottom of the dialog box. As you enter your own table fields, edit any information that you type incorrectly by clicking the field name, data type, description, or property value, and move the text cursor to the mistake to correct the problem.

18

Figure 18.6.

A more complete table definition.

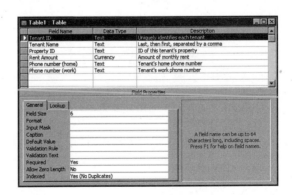

Setting the Key and Saving the Table

After you complete your table's fields, you cannot close the table's Design view without designating a field as the table's primary key field. If you do not designate a key and attempt to close the table, Access 97 warns you that no key exists. Access 97 adds a key field using the AutoNumber format if your data does not contain a key field.

Consider adding your own key field for tables that you access often. The key field enables you to search the table more quickly. The key might be a Social Security number, a phone number, or some other code (such as a unique inventory code or customer number) that is unique for each record in the table.

To specify a key field, select the table Design view's record by clicking to the left of the field name and then clicking the Primary Key toolbar button. Access 97 adds a small key icon to the left of the record, indicating the table's key field.

After you add the key field, save the table by clicking the Save button on the toolbar. (If you close the table before saving it, Access 97 prompts you for a name.) If you don't specify a new name, Access 97 uses `Table1` (and `Table2`, `Table3`, and so on as you create additional tables); however, you should use a more meaningful table name, such as `Tenants`, so that you can easily identify the table.

Modifying Table Structures

The beauty of Access 97 is that, unlike other database programs, you can easily change the structure of your tables even after you've added data. Access 97 makes it easy to add and delete fields, as well as change field properties.

> Some table-structure changes affect table data. For example, after you add data to a table, you lose columns of data if you delete fields, and you lose some data through truncation if you limit a field's size property. If you add fields to an existing table, you have to add the data for the new fields in every existing record in the table.

To modify a table, switch to the table's Design view. If you've closed the table and returned to the Database window, select the table name (which now appears in the Database window) and click Design. After you master table design changes, you are better equipped to use the database wizards to create initial tables that you can change to suit your specific table requirements.

Adding Fields

To add a field at the end of your table, simply click the first empty Field Name box and enter the field information as you did when adding the table's initial fields.

To insert a new field between two other fields, select the field that is to appear *before* your new field by clicking the selection box to the left of the field name. Next, right-click the row and select Insert Rows. Access 97 opens a new field row and enables you to enter the new field information. Figure 18.7 shows a new field being inserted into a table.

Figure 18.7.

The new field will go in the empty space.

Access 97 made room for the new ⟶ view

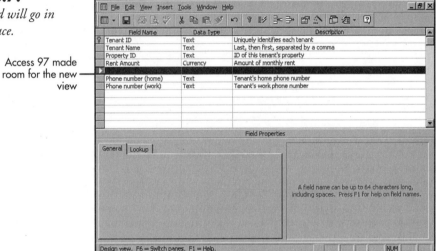

Deleting Fields

To delete a field, select the field from within the Design view and press Delete. You can delete fields from either the Datasheet view or the Design view. You can delete several fields in one operation by selecting multiple sections and dragging your mouse down several fields in the Design view.

 Use Undo (Ctrl+Z) to reverse an accidental field deletion. Access 97 supports multiple levels of undo so that you can reverse several recent actions by issuing undo multiple times.

Resizing and Rearranging Fields

Use your mouse to make minor adjustments to your table (such as the height of each row and the width of columns). Although the Field Size property determines the exact data storage width of each field in your table, the column widths determine how much of a field you can read while entering and editing table data and the table's structure.

At any time during your table design or data entry, you can drag a column divider left or right to increase or decrease the width of a column displayed. You can also drag a record divider up or down to increase or decrease a record height.

To rearrange the location of a field, either in Datasheet view or in the table's Design view, drag a Datasheet view field name or a Design view field selector to its new location in the table and release the mouse. Access 97 moves the field to the location you select.

> The order in which you structure a table's fields has little bearing on the table's use. You can report a table's data in any field order that you want regardless of the physical field order. Order your fields in whatever way makes the most sense to you.

Viewing Table Design and Entering Simple Data

Until now, you've worked exclusively in the Design view of the table, which describes the table's fields, properties, and key. If you open the table and click the *Datasheet view* toolbar button (or select from the View menu), Access 97 changes your table's Design view to the Datasheet view, like the view shown in Figure 18.8. Unlike the Design view, the Datasheet view enables you to enter and edit data in the table. Unlike the Design view, however, you cannot change the table's structure from the Datasheet view apart from changing the field names. The table's Datasheet view remains empty until you type data into your table.

NEW TERM   The *Datasheet view* displays your table and table data (if the table contains data) in a worksheet-like format. The Datasheet view enables you to view and edit multiple records from your table. You can enter data into your tables faster from the Datasheet view than from the other views.

The Datasheet view enables you to work with your table in row and column format, like an Excel 97 worksheet. Until you enter data in the table, the Datasheet view shows only one empty record. Although Access 97 offers several ways to enter data into a table, the Datasheet view is the fastest and simplest if you understand records and fields. The Datasheet view is not fancy, however, and some users need more help when entering data. For example, if you build a database application for a video store's inventory, the clerk should not be adjusting the inventory table directly within the Datasheet view when a customer rents a tape. You learn in the next hour how to design forms for such data-entry that walk the user through the data-entry process for such scenarios so that the user does not inadvertently change information in the wrong record.

Although the Datasheet view is not fancy, it enables you to quickly see your table's design results and enter data. If you cannot read a full field name, drag the field separator left or right to increase or decrease the field width shown on the screen. You learned more about modifying the view in the section titled "Resizing and Rearranging Fields."

Figure 18.8.

Use the Datasheet view to see your table's design results and enter data.

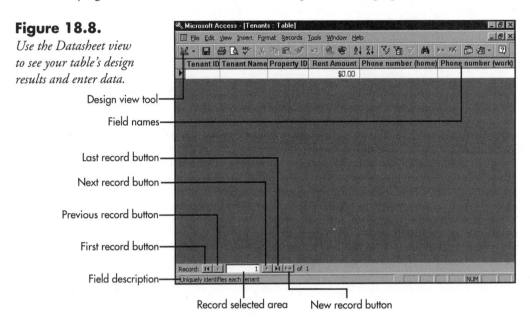

Design view tool

Field names

Last record button

Next record button

Previous record button

First record button

Field description

Record selected area   New record button

18

If you have not saved your table's design from within the Design view, Access 97 prompts you for the table name before showing you the Datasheet view.

Use the toolbar or the View menu to switch back and forth between the two views. As you design a table, the two views help you pinpoint design and data problems.

Most Database window objects offer two views: a Design view and another view that displays the final object, such as the Datasheet view and the form's Form view.

You can even design a table from the Datasheet view, but you make more work for yourself if you do. The default Datasheet view field names are Field1, Field2, and so on until you right-click the names and change them. You cannot set specific field properties from the Datasheet view. Use the Datasheet view for simple data-entry and table-design verification unless you create only an extremely simple table.

Using Wizards to Create Databases

While you are learning Access 97, practice designing your early databases without the help of the Access 97 wizards. In most cases, the wizards do not create *exactly* the kind of database you require, and you have to change the database structure as soon as the wizard completes the database design and creation. Changing an existing database is difficult to do if you've never worked with Access 97. The best way to gain Access 97 mastery is to design and create your own database from scratch so that you better understand the inner workings of data.

After you master Access 97, a wizard saves you a lot of time if you find one that creates a sample database that is close to what you need. After the wizard creates the database, you can modify the database to suit your needs.

Some of the Access 97 database wizards that you can use after you master Access 97's fundamentals are

- **Address book:** This wizard keeps track of names and addresses.
- **Asset tracking:** This wizard manages your company's assets.
- **Book collection:** This wizard lets you record titles and values for your book collection (you can easily convert this database wizard for a coin, baseball card, or virtually any other kind of collection you want to track).
- **Donations:** This wizard manages donations for nonprofit organizations.
- **Household inventory:** This wizard keeps track of your home items for inventory and estate-management purposes.
- **Inventory control:** This wizard tracks and manages your company inventory records.
- **Order entry:** This wizard is a complete order-entry and transaction system.
- **Students and classes:** This wizard is a school or church class planner.
- **Workout:** This wizard is a collection of exercise-tracking tables.

In addition to the wizards, Access 97 comes with a comprehensive database called the *Northwind Traders, Inc., Database*, which you can study to learn about advanced database operations.

Quitting Access 97

When you're finished with Access 97, quit by performing any of the following:

- Select File | Exit.
- Press Alt+F4.
- Double-click the Control icon.
- Click Access 97's Close button.

Always quit Access 97 and shut down Windows before turning off your computer, or you might lose your work.

Summary

This was a theory-based hour because Access 97 requires more preparation than the other Office 97 products. After you learn about the elements that make up a database—tables, records, and fields—the Access 97 mechanics are easy to understand.

To create an Access 97 database, add tables that describe the database data. Each table contains fields and records. When you design a table, you must describe the field names and data types that the table requires.

Now that you know how to create and edit tables, you are ready to enter data and master forms in the next hour, "Entering and Displaying Access 97 Data." By using forms for data entry and editing, you make Access 97 tables easier to manage for you and others who use databases that you create.

Q&A

Q Would I ever want to configure a field with the AutoNumber format?

A Your data might require a unique sequential number for each record, like invoice numbers. Most often, however, Access 97 uses the AutoNumber format for the key field that is added when you don't specify a key field.

Q Can I enter data in the Datasheet view?

A Certainly. As explained in this and the next hour, the Datasheet view is a handy view for entering simple data and for viewing multiple records of data from a table. The Datasheet view offers a worksheet-like view of your data in a row and column format. The Datasheet view gives you quick access to a table's data.

Remember that a Datasheet view shows only a single table's data at one time. It does *not* show the entire database because a database often contains multiple tables of data.

Q Can a key field contain duplicates?

A No. If you have to locate records by field and that field is not unique, you cannot make the field a key. You must decide on another key or let Access 97 add the key field. You can speed up the access on the duplicate field by making it an index field in the field's Design view property settings. Access 97 sets up a special quick-find index for that field.

18

Hour **19**

Entering and Displaying Access 97 Data

This hour explains how to use the Access 97 tables you learned to create in the previous hour, "Access 97 Basics." After you master this lesson, you'll be able to enter and edit table data.

You want to print the data to proofread for accuracy and to keep as a back-up. You don't have to master all of Access 97's reporting tools to print good-looking reports, as you learn in this hour.

Finally, this lesson explains how to use the Form Wizard to generate forms that match your data. Forms offer a different data perspective than datasheets. The Access 97 forms you create look like printed forms on the screen.

The highlights of this hour include

- ☐ How to enter data into tables
- ☐ Which table-editing commands Access 97 supports
- ☐ How to print tables

☐ When to use the Form Wizard to generate forms from tables

☐ How to use forms for data entry and editing

☐ The drawbacks of forms

☐ How to print forms

Entering Table Data

Access 97 gives you two primary means for adding data to tables that you create:

☐ Datasheet view

☐ Forms

The Datasheet view enables you to enter, view, and edit several records at one time, and displays many records on your screen. When you use a form, on the other hand, you typically only work with one record at a time. You learn more about forms later in this hour's section, "Using Forms to Enter and Edit Data." The next section focuses on the Datasheet view.

> You can quickly change from the Form view to the Datasheet view by clicking the down arrow on the View toolbar button and selecting Datasheet View. By switching between the views, you can see multiple records (in the Datasheet view) and single records (in the Form view), depending on your needs.

Using the Datasheet View

In the previous hour, you learned how to display and work with the Datasheet view. The Datasheet view offers one of the simplest ways to enter and edit data in an Access 97 database.

Entering Data

To enter data in the Datasheet view, simply click the Datasheet view's first field and enter the field information. When you enter data into the first field, Access 97 opens an additional blank record below the one you're entering. Access 97 always leaves room for additional records. As you enter data, press Tab, Shift+Tab, or the arrow keys to move from field to field. You can also click any field into which you want to enter data. As you enter data, watch the status bar. If you entered a description for a field, Access 97 displays that description in the status bar when you enter data in that field.

> If you enter data and see a number appear, Access 97 is automatically entering an AutoNumber field (such as a key field).

Figure 19.1 shows a Datasheet view that contains several records. The record pointer always moves as you enter and edit data to show the current record. The asterisk to the left of the empty record indicates a new record into which you can enter data.

Figure 19.1.

A Datasheet view containing several records of data.

Current record selector or pointer

Total number of records

Current record number

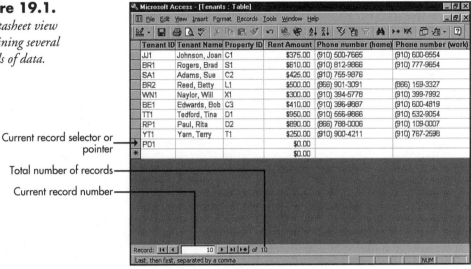

Often, multiple records contain the same data in certain fields (as is the case with city and state names in a table). Press Ctrl+' to copy the previous record's field value into the current field's cell.

As you enter data, take advantage of Office 97's AutoCorrect feature. When you enter AutoCorrect abbreviations and shortcuts, Access 97 substitutes the shortcut with the AutoCorrect correction. Access 97 does not automatically enable the Office 97 automatic spell checker because much of your table data contains formal names that would appear to the spell checker as misspellings.

To change a mistake, such as a transposed number, click the mistake to insert the text cursor in the Datasheet view's field and correct the entry. You can also press the arrow keys to move to any field, and press F2 to edit the field's text.

When you finish entering or editing a table's data, save the table and click its Close button to return to the Database window. If you've not saved the table before attempting to close it, Access 97 prompts you for a name. By default, Access 97 uses the names Table1, Table2, and so on, but you should rename the tables to reflect the data they contain.

19

Formatting Your Data

Access 97 is forgiving when you enter special data such as dates, times, monetary amounts, and memo field values. You can basically enter data in these fields in whatever way seems best to you! For example, you can enter a date in a date field using any of the following formats:

```
5/12/98
05/12/98
5/12/1998
May 12, 1998
May 12 1998
```

Access 97 uses a predefined date format to display dates and times in the Datasheet view, so after you type a date, it can be immediately reformatted to match this view. By default, Access 97 uses the date format mm/dd/yy.

As with dates, you can enter time in several common ways. Add AM or PM or use 24-hour clock time. Access 97, by default, formats your time values to the hh:mm:ss format.

> Press Ctrl+; to enter the current date in a field, and press Ctrl+: to enter the current time. Access 97 gets these values from your computer's clock and calendar setting.

Access 97 currency fields accept a wide variety of formats. You can type a dollar sign (or whatever currency symbol matches your Windows' international country setting), decimals, and even insert commas in currency values. After you enter a currency amount, Access 97 displays the amount with the default format.

Access 97 automatically adjusts to the current Windows International settings. Your Windows Control Panel contains an icon labeled Regional Settings. The language specified in your PC's regional settings determines how Access 97 displays data. Therefore, you can maintain one database for multiple users around the world. The PC running the Access 97 database determines, therefore, how the data appears on the screen and in reports.

> If you need to format a currency amount in a different format from your Windows international settings, you can do so by specifying the format in the Design view's property settings.

If you enter a format that Access 97 does not recognize, such as placing two decimal points inside a single dollar amount, Access 97 displays a dialog box (shown in Figure 19.2), indicating you should correct the value before entering the next field.

Figure 19.2.

*Access 97 lets you know if
you enter a bad format.*

Access 97 does not let you leave a record that contains a bad format. Therefore, when you close your tables, you can be assured that Access 97 saves all the data with the proper data type.

Editing Data

All the editing skills you mastered with the other Office 97 products work with Access 97. You can rearrange the order of fields and records by dragging them with your mouse. You can select more than one field or record at a time by dragging your mouse through the record selectors or field names or by holding Shift while you click record selectors or field names. Press Ctrl+A to select all records in the table.

To delete one or more records or fields, select the records or fields you want to delete and right-click them. Select Delete Column or Delete Record.

> When you right-click the selected records or fields, the pop-up menu provides quick Cut, Copy, and Paste commands as well as Insertion commands for records and fields. Use the Hide command to temporarily hide records and fields (they physically stay in the table) that you want out of the way while you work with other data, and reveal the data when you're ready to work with the entire table again. Additionally, you can *sort* records in *ascending order* or *descending order* with the right-click's pop-up menu options.

19

 To *sort* is to alphabetize or numerically order table records.

 To sort by *ascending order* is to sort from low to high order.

 To sort by *descending order* is to sort from high to low order.

> If you often need to adjust the width or height of records and fields, consider changing your table's font size and style (by selecting Format | Font) to fit more data in a smaller screen area.

Navigating Large Tables

Use the record selector at the bottom of the Datasheet view to move through and jump over large blocks of records that don't interest you at the time. The record selector works somewhat like a VCR, enabling you to move forward and backward through your data.

A few pointers are

☐ Click Next Record to move the record selector to the next record.

☐ Click Previous Record to move the record selector to the previous record.

☐ Click First Record to move to the table's first record.

☐ Click Last Record to move to the table's last record.

☐ Click the Record Number area and type a new record number to jump directly to that record.

Simple Printing

Access 97 includes powerful reporting tools, but they take some time to master. You learn about reporting in Hour 21, "Advanced Access 97," but if you just want to print a listing of your data, you can do so easily from the Datasheet view. Access 97 automatically prints the Datasheet view with field titles.

Perhaps you need to check a table listing for errors, or you want a printed listing (called a *hard copy*) so that you can proofread the data values that you entered. Before printing, display a preview (like the one shown in Figure 19.3) by selecting File|Print Preview. Move the magnifying glass mouse cursor over any portion of the preview and click to see a close-up.

NEW TERM A *hard copy* is a printed listing of your data.

To print a Datasheet view's table, select File|Print (or click the Printer button on the toolbar).

Using Forms to Enter and Edit Data

When you computerize your records, you want to make it as easy as possible for people to enter, edit, and view data in your database. Often, Access 97 reduces paperwork. For example, a credit agency might use Access 97 to keep track of loan applications that borrowers fill out. As borrowers bring in their completed applications, a clerk types the data from the application into an Access 97 table. Although a Datasheet view would work fine for the data entry, a form works even better! The form can, on the screen, mimic the look and feel of paper forms that many people are accustomed to using. You do not have to keep files of paper forms now that you use Access 97.

NEW TERM An Access 97 *form* enables you to enter data into your tables using the familiar format of a paper form.

Figure 19.3.

*Get a preview of printed
datasheet tables.*

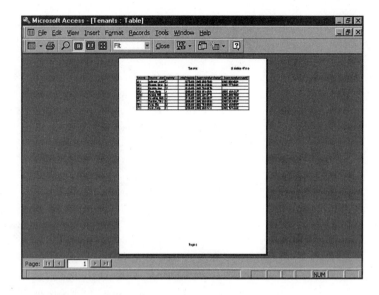

Generating Forms Using the Form Wizard

You probably want to use the Form Wizard to create your first form. The Form Wizard
generates simple forms that work well in most cases.

Follow these steps to start the Form Wizard:

1. Display the Database window.
2. Click the Forms tab to display the Forms page.
3. Click New to display the New Form dialog box (shown in Figure 19.4).

Figure 19.4.

Creating a new form.

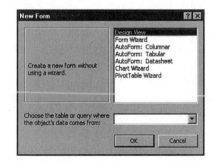

4. Select the Form Wizard option.
5. Select the table in the lower part of the dialog box to use as a basis for the form. If
   your database contains multiple tables, those tables appear in the drop-down list.

6. Click OK to display the opening Form Wizard dialog box (shown in Figure 19.5). This dialog box lists the available fields that you can include for your selected table.

Figure 19.5.

The opening Form Wizard dialog box shows your selected table and its available fields.

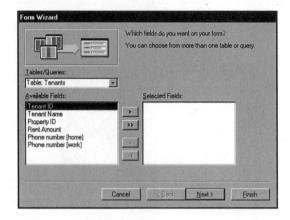

You may or may not want to include every field on every form you create. For example, suppose that you want to create a form for your company's personnel that contains employee names and extension numbers, but not employee pay rates. Therefore, the next step in creating your form is to indicate to Access 97 which fields to include.

To select table fields for the form, select a field and click the button labeled >. Access 97 adds that field to the selected field list. To include all the fields, click the button labeled >>. The Form Wizard sends all the table's fields to the selected field list.

If you send a field to the form accidentally, select that field and click the button labeled < to remove the field from the form. Clicking << removes all the fields, so you can start over if you want to rearrange the fields or copy new ones from scratch.

Click the Next button to display the Form Wizard Layout dialog box (shown in Figure 19.6). Click the different options to see a preview of how that option changes the form's layout.

 The Tabular and Datasheet form layouts are similar to the Datasheet view. The Columnar and Justified layouts look more like typical paper forms.

When you click the Next button, the Form Wizard displays a dialog box (shown in Figure 19.7), from which you can select a form style. Click through the style selections to see a preview of those available. Many styles have unique personalities that can add eye-catching appeal to an otherwise dull form.

Figure 19.6.

Select a layout for your form.

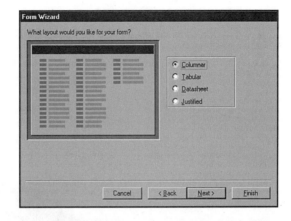

Figure 19.7.

The Form Wizard supports several form styles.

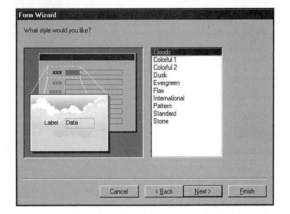

19

When you click the Next button, you see the Form Wizard's closing dialog box, which asks for a form title (the default title is the name of your selected table). Click Finish to generate the form.

When you learn more advanced Access 97 commands (see Hour 21), such as how to use the form-creation and editing tools, you are able to open the generated form's Design view and change specific parts of the form. The Form Wizard generates your form, and you can then modify the form to look exactly the way you want it. For now, the Form Wizard's generated forms work well.

In some cases, generated forms contain problems. For example, Figure 19.8 shows a generated form with a record's data. The Form Wizard automatically uses field names for the form prompts and data descriptions. If your field names are long, the Form Wizard may not display the entire field name for the prompt. Also, some data does not align properly, such as the Rent Amount field shown in Figure 19.8. In addition, if your table does not contain many fields, the form does not take up the full screen and may look too small. You can maximize the form on the screen.

Figure 19.8.

The Form Wizard generates good forms, but they sometimes have problems.

Long field names do not display

Value appears too far to the right

New Record button

Record selection control

Figure 19.8 shows the form in the Form view. The *Form view* displays records in the form-like format. Access 97 also contains a form's Design view (not unlike the table's Design view), in which you can edit the form and change its appearance.

Form view is Access 97's display of forms with record data appearing in the form fields.

When using forms, you must understand how all the data types appear. The Yes/No data-type fields appear with an x to indicate the Yes value. For example, if you name a rental property's tenant field `Pet Deposit?` and assigned the Yes/No data type to the field, those owners who pay a pet deposit have an x for this field value. Memo fields hold a lot of data, so if you use a memo field, keep typing when the text cursor reaches the right side of the field. Access 97 scrolls the field to enable you to continue. Form views display memo fields with scrollbars, so you can look at all the data in the fields.

Navigating Forms

Forms typically show only single records. Unlike the Datasheet view, the form is a much better tool for working with single records. In the Datasheet view, you can often see many records but not all the fields in those records, because the fields rarely fit on the Datasheet view screen. The form shows only a single record, but often manages to include all fields from the records because of the form layout.

Access 97 offers several ways to move through records in the Form view. Press up arrow, down arrow, Tab, and Shift+Tab to move from one field to another. Press PageUp and PageDown to move to the preceding and next table record, respectively. The record number appears at the bottom of the form window's record selection control. As in the Datasheet view, you can click the record selection control to move from record to record.

> To jump to a record quickly, press F5, type a record number, and press Enter. F5 sends the cursor to the record selector so that you can find a different table record.

Editing Forms

As you move through the form records, feel free to change data in the record. The record selector arrow changes to an editing pencil to show that you're editing the record. If you use Tab or Shift+Tab to move from field to field, press F2 when the highlight appears over the field you want to edit. When you change data from within the Form view, Access 97 changes the data in the underlying tables.

19

> To add records from the Form view, click the record selector's New Record button to display a new one that you can fill out.

Printing Forms

If you select File | Print from the Form view, Access 97 prints the forms. Unlike the onscreen Form view, Access 97 prints as many forms on the page as fit (select the File | Print Preview to see what will print, like the preview shown in Figure 19.9).

Figure 19.9.

Access 97 prints multiple records per form.

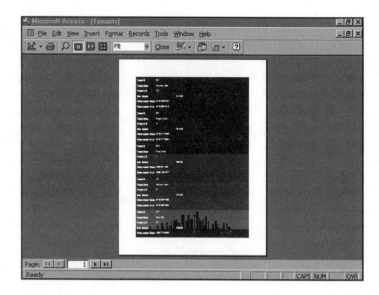

Summary

This hour extended your Access 97 knowledge by showing you how to use the Datasheet view to enter and print data. You also learned how to create and use forms. Access 97 replaces the paper forms you are used to and provides a form-like approach to data-entry and editing.

The Form Wizard quickly generates nice forms for you from your table data. The Form Wizard is a great place to start designing your forms because it analyzes your table and generates a form based on that analysis.

The next hour, "Retrieving Your Data," teaches you how to filter data and use queries so that you can work with subsets of table data.

Q&A

Q When I open a table's Datasheet view, why does the data appear in a different order from the order in which I entered it?

A Access 97 sorts data, in an ascending order, according to the table's selected key field. Your Datasheet views always appear in the order sorted by the key field unless you change the sort order by right-clicking the field that you want to sort by. Access 97 uses the key field to locate records quickly when you search for data.

Q **Why should I use the Form Wizard but not the Table Wizard when I begin learning Access 97?**

A You must understand tables, records, and fields before you use the Table Wizard to generate tables because you almost always have to modify the Table Wizard's generated table to suit your exact needs. Therefore, it helps, when starting out, to create tables from scratch and learn how tables work. After you learn how to use the table's Datasheet and Design views, you are better equipped to edit tables generated with the Table Wizard.

The Form Wizard looks at tables that you generated and creates simple data-entry forms with the format and layout that you request. Forms require less editing when you generate them from the Form Wizard than tables do. You'll be pleased with the Form Wizard from the moment you create your first form.

Q **Can I edit the AutoNumber field?**

A If you enable Access 97 to create and enter your table's key field, let Access 97 maintain the AutoNumber that it enters for you. When you create reports, you're able to hide the AutoNumber field so that the field does not appear with the data that others see. The AutoNumber field is Access 97's bookkeeping field when you fail to designate a key. Access 97 keeps the table sorted in the key order, and you should not bother with this field. If you want, rearrange the table to move the AutoNumber field to the far right side of the Datasheet view. Then you rarely see the field when you work with the data.

19

Hour 20

Retrieving Your Data

This hour teaches you about Access 97 filters and queries. Although your database contains a lot of data, you rarely want to see all that data simultaneously. Generally, you want to see only data subsets. Filters and queries produce those subsets for you.

When you view data subsets, you prevent unwanted data from getting in the way of the information with which you need to work. The power of queries is that you can select records and fields from multiple tables and view that selected data subset from within a single Datasheet or Form view.

The highlights of this hour include

- ☐ What a filter is
- ☐ Why you sometimes use Filter by Selection and sometimes use Filter by Form
- ☐ When a filter limits you
- ☐ Why queries are more robust than filters
- ☐ How to use the query wizards
- ☐ How to use the Query Design view to create and edit queries
- ☐ Where to specify advanced selection criteria

Using Data Filters

A *filter* is a subset of data from a table. Suppose that you want to see only certain records from a table, such as all customers who are past due. Instead of hiding the records that you don't want to see, create a filter. The filter removes unwanted records from view. The records don't go away, and you don't have to unhide the records later (as you do when you actually hide records). A filter works like a short-term record hider, putting certain records out of the way while you work with the filtered data.

 A *filter* temporarily creates a subset of records from a table by screening out unwanted data.

Access 97 supports three filtering approaches:

- ☐ **Filter by Selection:** Filters data based on selected table data
- ☐ **Filter by Form:** Enables you to choose the data fields that you want Access 97 to use for filtering
- ☐ **Advanced Filter/Sort:** Controls advanced filtering options from the Access 97 menu bar

The easiest and most common filter options are Filter by Selection and Filter by Form, which the following two sections describe.

 Access 97 includes an Advanced Filter/Sort option on the Records | Filter menu, but you'll almost always prefer creating a query over using the advanced filter.

Filter by Selection

Filter by Selection works by example. Suppose that you want to display only those table records that contain a specific field value; for example, you need to work only with customer records from Brazil. If your customer table contains a Country field with scattered Brazil entries, you can filter out all those records that do *not* contain Brazil in their Country fields.

Perform the following steps to design such a filter:

1. Display the Datasheet view for the customer table.
2. Locate one record with Brazil in the Country field.
3. Double-click the entire field to select it. If you select only the first part of the field, such as the B, you filter all records that do not start with B.
4. Click Filter by Selection on the toolbar. Access 97 filters out all records that don't match your selected criteria. Figure 20.1 shows a filtered Datasheet view that

displays only records containing a `Brazil` entry in their Country field. Before the filter, this Datasheet view held 91 records.

 NEW TERM The term *criteria* refers to a specific request pattern that you want Access 97 to use to find a value.

5. To return to the full Datasheet view, click the toolbar's Remove Filter button.

As you can see, a filter removes unwanted records; Access 97 filters those unwanted records from view.

> To filter all records that contain your selected values, leaving all those that don't contain the selected value, select Records | Filter | Filter Excluding Selection. The Filter Excluding Selection option works like a reverse filter.

Figure 20.1.

Filter by Selection filters out all unwanted records.

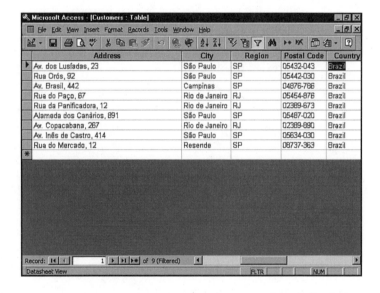

> You do not first have to locate a customer record from Brazil to create the previous list's filter. If you right-click any field value in the table and then type a value in the pop-up menu's Filter For text box, Access 97 applies the Filter by Selection command to your entered filter value. Therefore, you can type Brazil in the Filter For text box, press Enter, and more quickly create the same filter that the previous steps created.

20

Filter by Form

Filter by Form enables you to filter by multiple values instead of by only one value. Filter by Form can be performed from the Datasheet and Form views.

Perform these steps to use Filter by Form:

1. Click the Filter by Form button. Access 97 displays a single blank record.
2. Scroll to the field you want to filter by and select the empty field.
3. Click the field's drop-down arrow that appears. Access 97 displays a scrolling drop-down list of every value (without duplicates) that appears in that field.
4. Select the value by which you want to filter.
5. Optionally, click another empty field value and select from that field's drop-down list of available values. You can select as many filtering field values as you need. Unlike the Filter by Selection, which enables you to filter only by one field value, Filter by Form enables you to filter by several fields.
6. Click the Apply Filter button to display the filtered records.
7. Click the Remove Filter button (this button is called the Apply Filter button before you begin filtering) when you are ready to return to the full-record view.

If you filter by a date field, Access 97 surrounds the filtered value with pound signs (#). You often see pound signs around dates, such as #7/4/1998#; this enables Access 97 to distinguish the date from a formula.

Access 97 can perform an *Or* filter, meaning that Access 97 filters to find all records that include one or more of your selected filter field values. For example, if you want to find all customers who live in New York or who live in Maine, select New York, click the Or tab at the bottom of the Filter by Form window, and select Maine. You can continue adding or conditions to select from one of several fields.

 An *or condition* occurs when Access 97 performs a search or filter on one or more value matches at the same time.

Although Access 97 uses an or condition to select from one of several field values, it uses an *and condition* to select across fields. That means that if you select Brazil for the Country field filter and Rio for the City field filter, Access 97 filters to find all records with both Brazil as a country *and* Rio for the city. If a record contains the country Brazil but San Paulo for the city, such a filter would not keep that record.

An *and condition* occurs when Access 97 performs a search or filter on multiple value matches at the same time.

Using Queries

A *query* is really nothing more than a question you ask Access 97 about your data. Access 97 does not understand questions the way you generally ask them, so you must ask your question with its special query format. A query differs somewhat from a filter. A query is the request that produces a subset of data. A filter, on the other hand, simply hides, temporarily, certain data from your Access 97 views so that you can see only a subset of data from a table.

 A *query* is a stored set of database record selection commands. The query indicates to Access 97 exactly which data you want to edit based on search criteria that you specify.

A query is an object, just like tables and forms are objects. Therefore, you see the Query object page on the Database window and you create, edit, and execute queries from this page. As with other objects, queries have names that you give them. Many queries are nothing more than filters; however, filters go away when you are finished with them, whereas you can recall a query later by its name. If you want to reapply a filter, however, you must reproduce the filter.

 Although you cannot name filters, you can turn a Filter by Form request into a named query. When you enter the Filter by Form request, click the Save as Query toolbar button. Access 97 prompts you for a query name and stores the filter as a query. Often, creating a named query from a Filter by Form is faster than generating a new query from scratch if you only want to create a simple query that filters records.

20

Queries are often much more advanced than filters. A query enables you to specify selected records from a table or from another query. You can create a query that selects records and fields from multiple tables. The data subset that a query generates often becomes a table-like Datasheet view from which you can report. For example, you can build a query that extracts certain records and fields from three tables, and then generate a report from those extracted records and fields.

Not only can you create a query that extracts fields and records, but you can specify the exact order of the resulting data subset, sort the subset, and use powerful extraction criteria to select data based on very specific requirements.

The created data subset is sometimes called a *dynaset*.

Creating a Query with the Query Wizard

Although you can build a query from scratch, the Query Wizard can do the dirty work for you in most cases.

Access 97 includes these four query wizards:

☐ **Simple Query Wizard:** Extracts fields from one or more tables and from other queries

☐ **Crosstab Query Wizard:** Creates a worksheet-like query that summarizes field values and cross-tabulates matching values

☐ **Find Duplicates Query Wizard:** Creates a data subset from two or more tables or queries that contain matching values in one or more fields that you select

☐ **Find Unmatched Query Wizard:** Creates a data subset from two or more tables or queries that contain no duplicate records

You use the Simple Query Wizard most often because of its general-purpose design. When you create a new query by clicking New on the Queries Database window page, Access 97 displays the New Query dialog box (shown in Figure 20.2).

Figure 20.2.

Begin creating your query in the New Query dialog box.

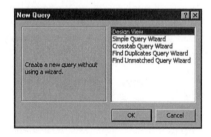

Follow these steps to build your first query using the Simple Query Wizard:

1. Select the Simple Query Wizard from the New Query dialog box. Access 97 starts the wizard and displays the Simple Query Wizard dialog box shown in Figure 20.3.

2. Select a table (or an existing query) to hold the data you want the query to extract. Access 97 displays fields from the selected table (or query) in the Available Fields list.

3. Select one or more fields and click the button labeled >. Access 97 includes these fields in the resulting query data subset. For example, if you want the query to

extract all customer names and balances from a customer table, select those two fields and click > to send them to the Selected Fields list. The Selected Fields list is the query's resulting structure, and holds a description of the data subset that the query eventually produces.

4. Optionally, select another table or query from the Tables/Queries drop-down list and add more fields to the Selected Fields list. If Access 97 prompts you to create a relationship between the tables, click Yes to create the relationship. Access 97 relates the tables automatically if you've created the relationship link elsewhere. You are now building a query that extracts data subsets from multiple sources. If you send the wrong field to the Selected Fields list, select the incorrect field and click < to remove it. To remove all your selected fields and begin again, click the button labeled <<.

5. Click Next to select either a detail or summary query. A detail query includes every field of every record; a summary query does not show duplicate selected records and includes summary statistics if you select them by clicking the Summary Options button.

6. Click Next and select a title for the query. Access 97 bases the default name for the new query on the first selected table or existing query.

7. Click Finish to complete the query. Access 97 builds the query and displays the selected records from the query in the Datasheet view. When you close the Datasheet view, you see the new query listed on the Queries page of the Database window.

Figure 20.3.

Use the Simple Query Wizard to generate your first query.

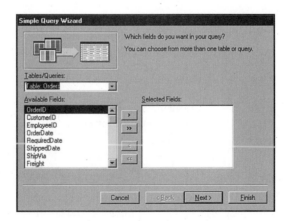

20

Take a moment or two to reflect on what you just did. For the first time, you have the power to extract records from multiple tables to create a new Datasheet view.

You can also create a new form (using one of the form wizards) to display the results of a query. When you created a new form in the previous hour, "Entering and Displaying Access 97 Data," you knew only how to create forms from single tables. If multiple tables contain data you want to display in a form, however, create a query to extract from the two tables and base the form on that query.

To synchronize a multiple-table query, all tables must have a common field (such as a customer number), or you must use advanced Access 97 commands to relate the two tables in some way. Without a relationship, such as a common field, the query cannot combine the fields from the two tables.

Access 97 does not save your query *results*. Therefore, if you want to see a data subset twice, you must open the Database window's Queries page, select the query, and click Open to generate the query extraction once again. Although the extraction requires a little time to generate (usually the speed is negligible unless the tables contain many records), the query is always fresh. If you change one value in any table and open the query again, your most recent table edit appears in the query.

Another advantage of generating the query every time you need to use the data subset is that Access 97 does not have to store the data twice (once in the source tables and again in the query).

If you edit data from the resulting query's Datasheet view (or from the query's Form view), Access 97 updates the data in the original tables! Suppose that you want to edit the pay rate for every employee who works in your company's Northeast division; simply create a query to extract only the Northeast division employees, make the edits, and close the query. Find and edit the Northeast employees' pay rates without the other employee records getting in the way.

Using the Query Design View

When you edit a query or create a query from scratch, you use the Query Design view (shown in Figure 20.4).

Although the Query Design view looks somewhat strange at first, the view's design is logical. The top of the Query Design view contains the source tables and queries, and the bottom of the Query Design view displays the criteria (the query-selection commands).

Figure 20.4.

The Query Design view enables you to create powerful queries.

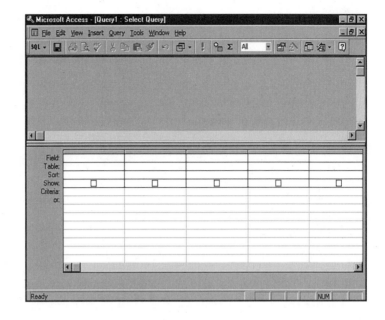

You use the Query Design view when you must

☐ Create an advanced query that the query wizards cannot create

☐ Edit an existing query

When you learn to create a query with the Query Design view, you also understand how to use the Query Design view to edit existing queries.

Creating a Query

To use the Query Design view to create a query, follow these steps:

1. Display the Queries page in the Database window.

2. Click the New button to open the New Query dialog box.

3. Select Design View and click OK to open the Query Design view. Access 97 displays the Show Table dialog box (shown in Figure 20.5).

4. Click tables that you want to add to the query and click Add. As you add tables to the query, Access 97 displays a new table in the Query Design view showing in the background. If you want to base your new query on another query, click the Queries tab to display a list of them from which you can choose, and then add the selected query. If you want to add both tables and queries, click the Both tab to display all your database tables and queries, and then select the ones you need.

5. Click Close to close the Show Table dialog box.

20

Figure 20.5.

Selecting tables and queries for the new query.

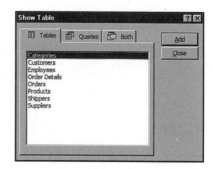

You have yet to build the entire query, but you have selected tables, existing queries, or both, on which to base your new query. Next, enter the query's criteria so that Access 97 knows which records and fields to select from your tables and existing queries.

Figure 20.6 shows the start of a new query. This query extracts from two tables, one named Customers and one named Orders. Access 97 drew the line from the Customers table to the Orders table. The line indicates the table relationship that Access 97 found. The table boxes include all the fields from each table, and the two tables share a common field: Customer ID. You recall from the previous section that Access 97 must base queries on related tables and queries, and the common field relates the two tables.

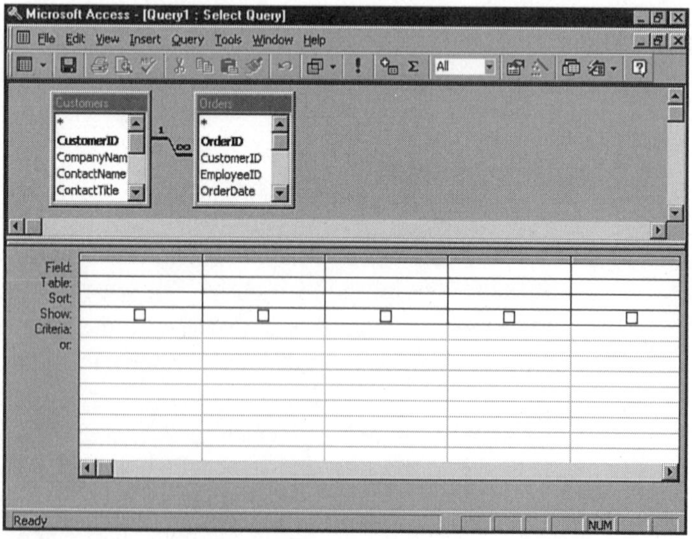

Figure 20.6.

This query extracts from two related tables.

> Think of the top half of the query's design window as starting the request, "given these tables and queries…" and the lower half of the window as finishing that request, "…extract all data that meets these conditions." The Query Design view contains your instructions when you want Access 97 to extract data from one or more tables or queries and display the result in a table subset.

Each column in the Query Design view's lower half contains the resulting query's fields. Therefore, if you want the resulting data subset to contain four fields, you fill in four of the Query Design view's lower columns. These columns contain the instructions that indicate to the query how to extract the data.

Working with Complex Queries

To finish the query, follow these steps:

1. Click the first column's row labeled Table and select the table that contains the resulting query's first field. For example, if you want the query's data subset to start with a field from the Customers table, select Customers from the drop-down list.

2. Click the first column's row labeled Field and select the field that you want to place first in the resulting data subset. For example, you might select Customer ID from the list.

3. If you want to sort the resulting query's subset based on the first field, select either Ascending or Descending from the row labeled Sort. You don't have to sort on the first field that you add to the query; you can sort on any field that you add. The query sorts all the resulting data based on the value of the field by which you sort. If you sort on two or more fields, Access 97 sorts the data in the left-most Sort column first.

4. Leave the Show option checked if you want the field to appear in the resulting query's data subset. Generally, you want the field to appear. If you want to sort the subset on a field but not send that sort field to the resulting extracted subset, uncheck the Show option for that field.

5. Click the first column's row labeled Criteria and enter a criterion. If you type a value, such as 101, Access 97 extracts only those records with a field containing 101. You can continue adding criteria values beneath the first one. For example, you can type the values 102, 103, 104, and 105 for five rows of criteria (still in the first column). This is like asking Access 97 to extract only those customers whose Customer ID is 101 through 105. If the field is a text-data type, Access 97 encloses the criteria in quotes (shown in Figure 20.7). Access 97 encloses dates inside pound signs (#1/6/98#, for example) if you enter dates in the criteria.

20

6. It gets fun here. Instead of selecting the field from the second column's drop-down list labeled `Field`, drag the field name from a table in the upper half of the Query Design view (such as the Order Date field in the Orders table). Access 97 automatically fills in the table and field name in the second column of the query!

7. Enter the selection criteria for the new field. The criteria indicate exactly how you want to pull records from the table. If you want to extract all the records (all that fall within the criteria of the first field that you've entered), leave the second field's criteria blank. You can further limit the extraction by entering an additional criterion for the second field. Suppose that you not only want customers with the IDs listed in the first criteria, but also want to limit the selection to any of those five who have an order date of January 6, 1998. You enter `#1/6/98#` for the criteria.

8. Continue adding fields that you want to appear in the resulting query. When you execute your query, these fields appear in the resulting table.

Figure 20.7.

This query must match several criteria values for Customer ID.

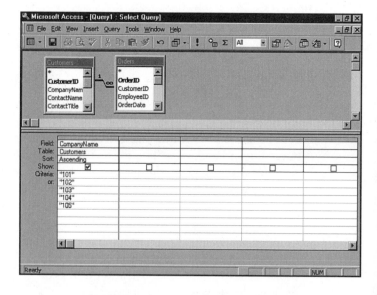

As you work with the query, you might want to add more tables. Add the tables in the Query Design view by selecting Query | Show Table. Add as many tables (or queries) as you like to the query from within the Query Design view, but remember that the tables and queries must relate somehow. Remove a table or query from the Query Design view by right-clicking the table name and selecting Remove Table.

> All the cut, copy, and paste methods that you learned earlier in the book work for the query-extraction fields. For example, you can move a field from one location to another by selecting, cutting, and pasting it. Resize column widths by dragging the field column edges. Change any value by clicking that value in the Query Design view.

If you really want to get fancy, use the relational operators in Table 20.1 to add to your extraction power.

Table 20.1. Access 97's relational operators improve extraction power.

Operator	Description
>	Greater than
<	Less than
>=	Greater than or equal to
<=	Less than or equal to
<>	Not equal to
=	Equal to (not needed for simple matches)

Suppose that you want to include customer-order details in a query, but you only want to include orders with more than 20 units. Enter >20 for the Quantity field's criteria to limit the selection to those records that match the other criteria and that have order quantities of more than 20 units. The relational operators work with numbers, text values that fall within a range of words, and dates.

The Between keyword is useful when you want to extract values that fall between two other values. For example, if you type Between #1/1/97# And #1/31/97# for a date criteria, Access 97 extracts only records whose date falls between 1/1/97 and 1/31/97 (including the days 1/1/97 and 1/31/97).

Access 97 uses an implied Or when you specify multiple criteria. For example, instead of entering the five criteria lines described earlier for Customer IDs (101, 102, 103, 104, and 105), you could enter 101 Or 102 Or 103 Or 104 Or 105. (Of course, entering Between 101 And 105 would even be easier.) (Figure 20.8 shows a completed and fairly complex query.)

20

Figure 20.8.

A completed query that contains a lot of extraction criteria.

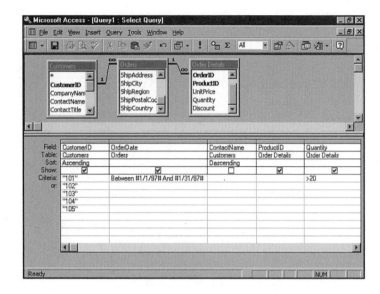

Be sure to save your query when you finish with it. Click the Query Design view's Close Window button and name the query so that you are able to refer to it later. When you select the query and click Open from the Queries page of the Database window, Access 97 runs the query, extracts the data, and displays the result in your Datasheet view.

Summary

This hour showed you how to narrow your data and form subsets. Often, a table contains many more fields and records than you want to work with at any one time. Access 97's filter and query powers enable you to create subsets of data to make your work more manageable.

Filters provide quick subsets, but queries provide much more power. After you run a filter or query to create a subset of your data, you can make changes to the subset and still be changing the underlying tables. Although the Query Design view takes some getting used to, it enables you to specify powerful query extraction criteria so that Access 97 searches for and finds the data with which you need to work.

Now that you can produce subsets of data, you need a way to report that data. The next hour, "Advanced Access 97," explores some of the reporting capabilities. The Report Wizard makes quick work of report generation from your tables and queries.

Q&A

Q Should I use a filter or a query?

A When you quickly want to see a subset of a table, use a filter. However, you sometimes use the subset in another way (as input to a report, for example), so creating a query that you can name and execute makes more sense (except in the case of one-time extractions to a Datasheet view).

Q If I save a filter as a named query, what does the query's Query Design view look like?

A Filters are much less powerful than queries, but they are easier to designate. As you create more queries and get used to your data needs, you find that many of your queries are little more than filters. Instead of messing with the Query Design view to design the query, generate a simpler Filter by Form filter and save it as a query. If you then want to modify the filter-based query or add more complex criteria, open the query's Query Design view and you see that Access 97 selected the proper source table and field names for you. You then can add to the criteria lines and request additional fields if you like.

Q Does the row on which I place criteria make a difference?

A Yes, although you're getting into some confusing logic. The way you specify criteria between two fields often indicates how you want the combined criteria to work. If you place one field's criteria on the same row as another field's, an implied and relation takes place, and Access 97 extracts only those records that contain a match for both criteria values. If you place one field's criteria on a different row from another field's, an implied or relation takes place between them.

Q How can I see my data in two ways, say, with the field names arranged alphabetically and with the fields arranged in the order of my table's design?

A Create a query that extracts all the fields from your table. The query's output, or data subset, will contain all data that the original table contains (the subset will be the same size as the table). Set up the query's output for ordering the fields alphabetically. Queries aren't just for creating smaller subsets of tables; you can create a query to report table data in an order that differs from a table's original design order.

20

Hour 21

Advanced Access 97

This hour shows you how to create custom reports. Access 97 includes several reporting tools, both automatic and manual, that produce complex reports. You can create a simple report by clicking a toolbar button. If you spend a little time developing the report with a report wizard, the report can look extremely nice.

You do not have to master the Report Design view, an extensive report-creating tool, to create most of your reports. Some people have never designed an Access 97 report from scratch because of the report wizards' power. The report wizards give you complete control over a report's design.

The highlights of this hour include

- ☐ How to create report queries
- ☐ How AutoReport creates simple reports
- ☐ Which report wizards Access 97 supports
- ☐ How to use the main Report Wizard to generate virtually any report you need by making a few selections

☐ When to request summary statistics

☐ Why you should preview reports

Introducing Access 97 Reports

You often want printed listings of your data, and the Access 97 reporting tools enable you to produce professional reports with ease. This hour explains how to use the report wizards and discusses the different reporting styles and options available. You learned how to produce printed listings in Hour 19, "Entering and Displaying Access 97 Data"; in this hour you learn how to add flair to your reports.

Unlike forms, a report often displays multiple records in a view that resembles the Datasheet view. The difference between the Datasheet view and a printed report is that the report provides summary statistics, fancy headings, footers, page numbers, and styles that accent your data.

> A *report* is not just a listing of multiple data records. Anytime you need to send Access 97 data to paper, you must create a report. Therefore, a report might be a series of checks or mailing labels that you print.

Before you print any report, use the print preview to see the report on your screen. Often, you notice changes that you need to make, so previewing a report can save you time and paper. Your computer's print *spooler* is too difficult to stop quickly, so you usually end up printing the first few pages of a report even if you attempt to stop the printing.

 The *spooler* is the Windows memory area where Access 97 sends your report before the report goes to paper. The spooler frees up your program while the printing continues.

When you are about to print a report, the Report sheet in the Database window enables you to preview any report by clicking the Preview button. Access 97 can generate fancy reports (see Figure 21.1).

Rarely do you report all the data from a single table. Except for detailed reports, such as inventory listings and master customer listings, you almost always report part of a table or values from more than one table.

Almost all reports that you generate, therefore, get their data from queries that you've created. If you need to report from part of a table's data or from multiple tables, create a query on which to base the report. Your queries can order the data the way you want to see it, and Access 97 can then print your query's results.

Figure 21.1.

*The report preview shows
how Access 97 formats
your report.*

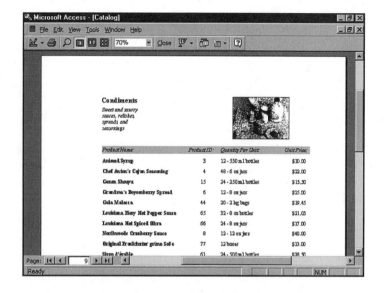

Generating Simple Reports Using AutoReports

Access 97 includes an *AutoReport* feature, which quickly generates reports from your
Datasheet views. As Figure 21.2 shows, the AutoReport feature is simply a listing of field
names and their corresponding field values.

  AutoReport is Access 97's automatic reporting tool that creates simple reports from
your Datasheet views.

Figure 21.2.

*AutoReport generates
simple reports.*

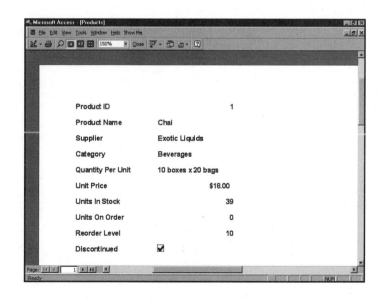

21

Unlike the printed listings you get when you select File | Print, AutoReport formats your data in a readable manner without squeezing too much information on a single page. If you need to run a quick report from a table, follow these steps to enable AutoReport to generate the report:

1. Display your data in a Datasheet view. If you want to report from a subset of data or from a collection of multiple tables, display the query's Datasheet view.

2. Click the down arrow next to the AutoForm button on the toolbar. Some toolbars already show the AutoReport button, depending on your last Access 97 task.

3. Select AutoReport from the button's drop-down list. Access 97 generates a report from the current Datasheet view and shows a preview of the report (shown in Figure 21.2).

4. If the preview shows what you want, click the preview's Print icon to print the report.

5. Click the Close button to close the AutoReport preview. Access 97 displays the Report Design view (shown in Figure 21.3). The Report Design view can be difficult to understand when you first see it. For now, don't worry about the contents. AutoReport created the report's design and saved you from having to use the Report Design view.

6. Close the Report Design view and enter a report name if you want to save the AutoReport's design. If you think you'll edit the AutoReport design later or generate the report often, save the report. Generally, you use AutoReport only to produce quick reports and use the report wizards (described next) to generate more standard reports.

Figure 21.3.

AutoReport enables you to avoid the Report Design view.

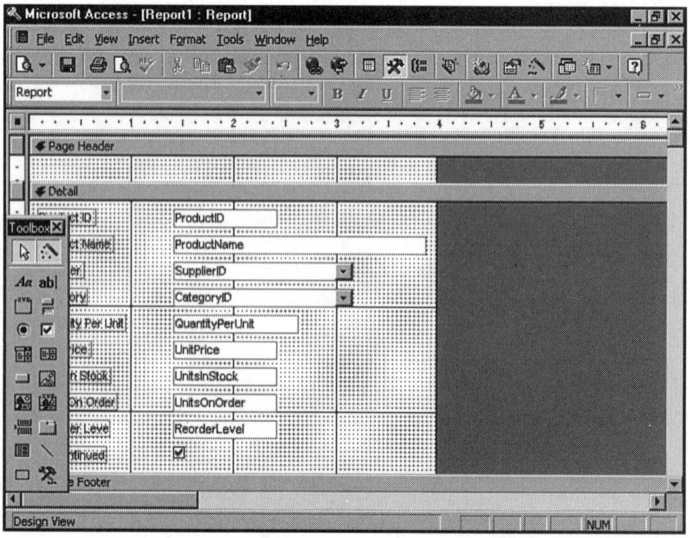

> AutoReport generates reports using Access 97's report-designing tools. After you learn how to modify a Report Design view, you can use AutoReport to generate the foundation of a report, and then change the report to fit your exact needs.

If you like using AutoReport for quick reports, check out the AutoForm feature. AutoForm creates fast and simple forms from your Datasheet views.

Generating Reports Using the Report Wizards

Access 97 includes several report wizards that design reports for you. Select one of the report wizards by opening the Database window, clicking the Reports tab (which displays the database reports), and clicking New to create a new report. The New Report dialog box enables you to access the following reporting components:

- ☐ **Design View:** A blank Report Design view on which you can add a new report's headers, footers, detail, and *summary* requests. When you want to generate a report from scratch, use the Design View in the New Report dialog box.

NEW TERM A *summary* is a subtotal, total, average, minimum-value search, or maximum-value search that Access 97 performs when printing your reports.

- ☐ **Report Wizard:** Walks you through the report-generation process by enabling you to select the source tables and queries as well as the fields that you want in the final report. You run Report Wizard the most often because it generates less specific reports than other reporting wizards. The next section, "Using the Report Wizard," explains how you use Report Wizard to create reports.
- ☐ **AutoReport: Columnar:** Generates a report that contains all the fields from the underlying table or query. The columnar report looks much like the AutoReport, except that the columnar report makes better use of your report's page space and designs a more routine report. As Figure 21.4 shows, a columnar report can include titles and special fonts, and can emphasize field data.
- ☐ **AutoReport: Tabular:** Generates a report that displays on a single line the record of each source table or query by adjusting the font size to fit your report page. The tabular report looks much better than a simple Datasheet view, and is often more useful than the generic AutoReport you learned about in the previous section. (Figure 21.5 shows a sample of the wizard's tabular report.)
- ☐ **Chart Wizard:** Produces graphs from your data. Access 97 graphs resemble Excel 97 graphs, and you can control the format and style as well as the table from which Access 97 graphs.

21

☐ **Label Wizard:** A generic mailing-list report that produces mailing labels for all common labels. The mailing label industry has a standard numbering system (the *Avery numbering system*, after the company that is perhaps best known for computerized mailing labels). Most office-supply stores sell mailing labels with an official Avery number, so you can format a report for your labels.

Figure 21.4.

Columnar reports look much better than AutoReports.

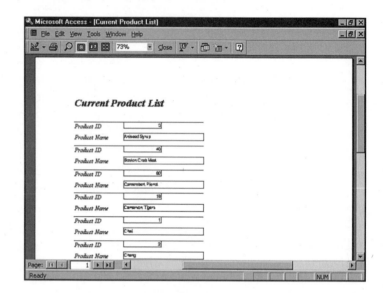

NEW TERM   The *Avery numbering system* is an industry-standard mailing-label numbering system. You can request an Access 97 mailing-list report that works with your labels by matching the Avery numbers.

Step-Up

You'll be surprised at how little the report wizards in Access 97 differ from those in Access 95. Except for some dialog box format changes, you'll be familiar with every report wizard dialog box. If you've mastered the ins and outs of Access 95 reports, you may want to skip to the next hour, "Office 97's Synergy."

Using the Report Wizard

The second New Report dialog box option, Report Wizard, is probably the most common selection you make when you generate customized reports. The Report Wizard walks you through a series of steps to create a custom report from your tables and queries, and it includes many common reporting styles and special features that you need.

Figure 21.5.

Tabular reports produce well-organized listings of your data.

ProductID	Product Name	Supplier	Category	Quantity Pe
1	Chai	Exotic Liquids	Beverages	10 boxes x 20
2	Chang	Exotic Liquids	Beverages	24 - 12 oz botti
3	Aniseed Syrup	Exotic Liquids	Condiments	12 - 550 ml bot
4	Chef Anton's Cajun Seas	New Orleans Cajun	Condiments	48 - 6 oz jars
5	Chef Anton's Gumbo Mix	New Orleans Cajun	Condiments	36 boxes
6	Grandma's Boysenberry	Grandma Kelly's H	Condiments	12 - 8 oz jars
7	Uncle Bob's Organic Drie	Grandma Kelly's H	Produce	12 - 1 lb pkgs.
8	Northwoods Cranberry S	Grandma Kelly's H	Condiments	12 - 12 oz jars
9	Mishi Kobe Niku	Tokyo Traders	Meat/Poultry	18 - 500 g pkg

> You must create a named query before generating a report from that query.

To start the Report Wizard, follow these steps:

1. Display the Database window.
2. Click the Reports tab to display your Database reports.
3. Click the New button to display the New Report dialog box.
4. Select Report Wizard.
5. Open the New Report's drop-down box to select from a list of tables and queries that reside in your database. You're not limited to the data of this single table or query.
6. Click the OK button to display the Report Wizard's field-selection dialog box (shown in Figure 21.6).
7. Select the fields that you want in the final report by highlighting the field in the Available Fields list and clicking > to send the field to the Selected Fields list. As you can see when you open the Tables/Queries drop-down list box, you can select

21

fields from several tables and queries in addition to the primary source you selected in step 5.

8. After you select the fields for the report, click Next.

Figure 21.6.

Select the fields you want for your report.

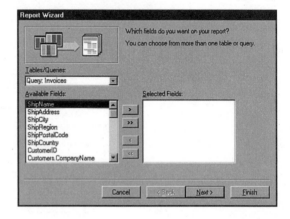

Grouping Report Summaries

Now that you've selected the report fields, you must indicate how the report is to be summarized. Rarely do you want to print a data listing without requesting a summary. Depending on the type of fields you select for your report, the Report Wizard prompts you for subtotal and total summary information or grouping information. If your report contains numeric data, the Report Wizard shows its Summary dialog box (shown in Figure 21.7). Use this dialog box to indicate how you want Access 97 to group your report. If Access 97 does not display the Summary dialog box, the Report Wizard prompts you for grouping information, and you can select the field on which you want your data grouped.

 A report *summary* concludes a report by showing totals and averages from the report detail.

 A report *group* is a collection of records whose designated group field contains the same data values.

> Access 97 can group the report on numeric fields, not text fields. The numeric fields enable the Report Wizard to produce subtotals and total summaries, whereas no such summaries are possible with text fields.

Select only those numeric fields that produce proper subtotals. For example, if you report a division number field and that field is numeric, you wouldn't want Access 97 to subtotal and total the division number. If, however, you print a report with customer past-due balances, you do want to print a subtotal for each customer and an overall grand total of past-due balances.

Figure 21.7.

Indicate how Access 97 is to produce the subtotals and totals.

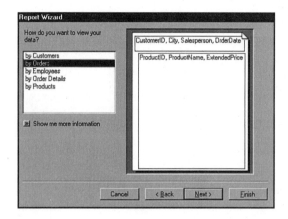

The grouping field should be groups, such as customer IDs, for which you are printing a detailed list. Although the same customer might appear on several report lines, you want Access 97 to subtotal only when the customer ID changes to the next customer in the report. The grouping capability keeps multiple customer IDs from appearing down the column when you print multiple records for the same customer.

As you click each field that you selected, the grouping dialog box displays a preview of your report, showing how the grouping will fall out. Generally, the grouping options and preview give you enough information to decide on a grouping scheme. If you need more control over the grouping, click the cross-reference labeled Show Me More Information, and read the dialog box presented. If you *still* need verification, click the cross-reference labeled Show Me Examples, and Access 97 provides examples of different grouping options using your database's data.

Figure 21.8 shows one such example and gives you visual feedback on how the report will look given the selected grouping options.

Click Close until you return to the grouping dialog box, and then select your grouping preference. Access 97 displays the grouping level dialog box.

If you want to group on multiple fields, the group order you select determines the priority that Access 97 uses to group the data. The highest priority grouping level (if you select multiple groups) appears on the left of the report, the second grouping level appears to the right of the first one, and so on. Generally, multifield grouping gets confusing. If you want to add such grouping levels, click every group level from the series of fields that Access 97 displays. The Report Wizard prioritizes the multifield groups in the order that you select the fields.

21

Figure 21.8.

Preview a sample of one grouping option.

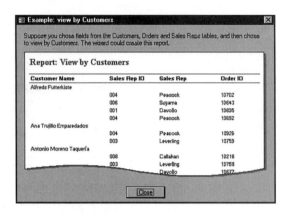

You can group by a maximum of four field-grouping levels. If you need to group by more than four fields, you have to edit the report design or create a report from scratch. Rarely do you need more than four groups.

If the Report Wizard has presented you with the grouping view dialog box instead of the subtotal and total summary dialog boxes described here, you need only click the field by which you want to group the report. For example, if you are producing a customer balance report, the Report Wizard might enable you to group by either the Customer ID field or the Customer Order Number field.

When you've set up the grouping levels that you need, click Next to select a sort and summary order for the report.

The Report's Sort and Summary Order

When you see the sorting and summary dialog box (see Figure 21.9), you're almost done creating your report. Select from one to four fields that you want Access 97 to use for sorting your data. If you're reporting from a query that already contains sorted data, and if you generate the report so that the data groups in the order of those sorted fields, don't select any fields by which to sort. If, however, you want to sort by one or more fields that do not enter the reporting system already sorted, select up to four fields and click the button labeled AZ to sort in ascending order.

The AZ button changes to ZA when you click it, so you can then select a descending sort.

Figure 21.9.

Select from one to four fields by which to sort.

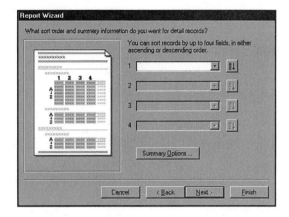

Whether or not you select a sorting option, click the Summary Options button to display the Report Wizard's Summary Options dialog box. Each of your report's numeric fields appears in the box, so you can select any or all these summaries for that field:

☐ **Sum:** Requests a total for the field

☐ **Avg:** Requests an average for the field

☐ **Min:** Requests that Access 97 highlight the minimum value in the field

☐ **Max:** Requests that Access 97 highlight the maximum value in the field

> You cannot display summaries if your report has no numeric fields or if you are grouping by the numeric fields.

Choosing a Report Layout and Style

Click OK to close the summary options dialog box, and then click Next to choose a report layout. Click through the various layouts to select one that fits your needs. As you click layouts, Access 97 displays thumbnail sketches of those layouts. For example, if you click the Block style, you see that Access 97 displays boxes around your report fields.

After you select the layout, click Next to select from the Report Wizard's style dialog box (shown in Figure 21.10). The style dialog box adds the finishing touches to your report.

Click Next, enter a report title if you don't want to use the original source table or query name, and click Finish to generate the completed report. Sometimes Access 97 takes several minutes to generate the report, especially if the source tables and queries contain several records and your report contains several grouping levels. When finished, Access 97 prints a preview of your report so that you can look at your handiwork.

21

Figure 21.10.

The style dialog box determines the overall appearance of your report.

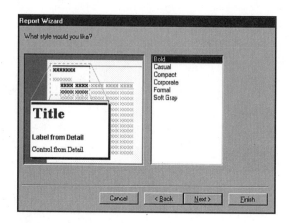

Summary

Access 97 is certainly a powerful program. Despite its ease of use, it does take some getting used to before you fully master all its features. You'll probably use the Access 97 wizards more than any other wizard in any other Office 97 product.

At this point, you are ready to begin generating sample databases and practicing with Access 97. As you create more databases, you learn how to partition your data properly into tables and generate data-entry forms and reports.

The next hour begins the part of the book that explains how the Office 97 programs work together to help you with your data-processing requirements. In addition, you learn more about using Office 97 with the Internet.

Q&A

Q How does the toolbar's AutoReport differ from the AutoReport entries I see on the Report Wizard's opening dialog box?

A The AutoReport entries on the Report Wizard's opening dialog box create more finished reports than the AutoReport toolbar button. Use the AutoReport toolbar button to quickly generate a report from your Datasheet and Form views. Use the Report Wizard AutoReport entries to produce more complete reports without taking the time to set up summary and sorting features. Not all reports require summaries, and the two AutoReport wizards suffice for many reports that you will generate.

Q What is the largest page size that I can produce in an Access 97 report?

A Access 97 report pages can be as large as 22 inches wide by 22 inches long.

Q Do I subtotal on numeric fields or fields that I want to group by, such as Customer ID numbers?

A When you specify grouping instructions, the field that you group by is usually a nonnumeric field, such as a Customer ID field. Access 97 collects all the customer ID records together and reports each customer's information in one group. When Access 97 finishes reporting a customer's records (when the ID changes), Access 97 subtotals the numeric fields in that group before starting the next group.

21

PART VII

Combining the Office 97 Products and the Internet

Hour

Hour 22

Office 97's Synergy

This hour explores how Office 97 products work together and how you can enhance your documents. Office 97 programs integrate so well that it's hard to know where to start describing the possibilities. Generally, if you need to work with two or more Office 97 program documents together, you're able to load or embed one document within the other even though the Office 97 programs that created the two documents are completely different.

From inserting a Bookshelf Basics definition into a Word 97 document to combining an Access 97 table and an Excel 97 worksheet into a PowerPoint 97 presentation, Office 97 supplies the combining tools you need. You can also add your own graphics to your Office 97 documents by using the supplied clip art or by drawing with the Office 97 drawing tools.

The highlights of this hour include

- [ ] How you can grab a definition from Bookshelf Basics while working in the various Office 97 products
- [ ] Why drag-and-drop operations work so well between Office 97 programs
- [ ] How to control a drag-and-drop operation to produce a copy, a move, a link, or a shortcut

☐ How to edit and break links between Office 97 documents

☐ What requirements a Word 97 document must meet to serve as a PowerPoint 97 presentation

☐ Which steps you must take to import Access 97 data into Word 97

☐ How to add your own art (or sound or video) clip files to Office 97's Clip Gallery

☐ When the AutoShapes toolbar comes in handy

☐ How to select WordArt styles when you want to add fancy text titles and banners to your Office 97 documents

Bookshelf Basics and Office 97

In Part I of this book, you learned how to access Bookshelf Basics by itself so that you could look up definitions, synonyms, and quotes. The real power of Bookshelf Basics comes into play when you need a Bookshelf Basics item while writing in Word 97 or using other Office 97 products.

For example, suppose that you're typing a meeting report from your boss's handwritten notes and you run across the word *praenomen*. Because you're unsure of the spelling (and perhaps the meaning), why not use Bookshelf Basics to verify the boss's writing? Type and select the word, and then choose Tools | Look Up Reference. Word 97 displays the Look Up Reference dialog box.

> The Keyword option in the Look Up Reference dialog box limits the search to Bookshelf Basics article titles, whereas the Full Text option searches through the text of all the Bookshelf Basics articles for your term. The full-text search takes longer to complete, and often returns more information than you need.

Click OK to start Bookshelf Basics's search. In a moment, Bookshelf Basics displays a definition for *praenomen* (as shown in Figure 22.1).

> If you select Edit | Copy (or press the Ctrl+C shortcut key) while in Bookshelf Basics, Office 97 copies the complete article (definition, quote, or synonym list) to the Windows clipboard. When you paste the clipboard contents to another Office 97 program (or to any other Windows program that accepts pasted text), Windows pastes the entire article.

Figure 22.1.

Bookshelf Basics displays a definition for praenomen.

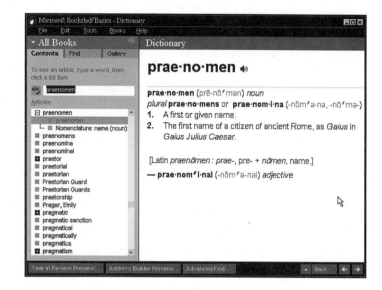

22

Sharing Data Between Applications

Office 97's cornerstone is data sharing among its programs. Office 97 offers several ways to share data among products. The following sections explain the most common methods.

Drag and Drop

Suppose that you want to use part of an Excel 97 worksheet inside a Word 97 document. If you have both Excel 97 (with the relevant data loaded) and Word 97 running at the same time, perform these steps to drag the worksheet to the Word 97 document:

1. Select Window|Arrange All to arrange your program windows so that you can see both the *source document* (the Excel 97 worksheet) and the *destination document* (the Word 97 document).

 The *source document* is the document that holds an item that you want to drag to another location.

 The *destination document* is the document that receives the object that you drag from a source document.

2. In the Excel 97 worksheet, select the cells that you want to copy and transfer to Word 97.

3. Hold the Ctrl key and drag the edge of the highlighted cells to the location in your Word 97 document where you want to place the table.

4. Release the mouse to anchor the table. (Figure 22.2 shows the result of such a copy.)

If you did not first press Ctrl before dragging the cells, Excel 97 would have moved the table from the Excel 97 worksheet to the Word 97 document instead of copying the table.

Depending on the size and style of your Word 97 document, you might want to format the copied table differently from Excel 97's format. Right-click the table and select Format Object to display the Format Object dialog box. You can apply colors, lines, shading, and other formatting attributes to the copied object from the Format Object dialog box.

Figure 22.2.

The Word table came from Excel 97.

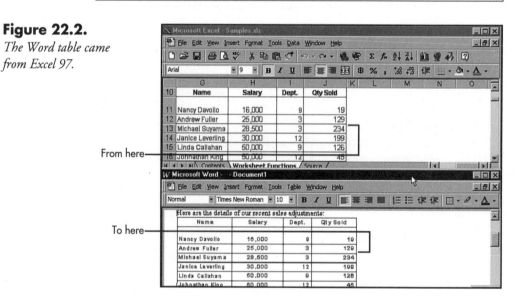

Creating Links

Suppose that you create a monthly sales report using the same Word 97 document and the same Excel 97 worksheet every time. Only the details in the Excel 97 worksheet change (obviously, you've created templates for these files long before now). You don't have to drag the updated Excel 97 table to your Word 97 document before printing the Word 97 document each month. Instead of copying or moving the cells, you can create a *link* to the cells.

NEW TERM A *link* is a cross-reference to another file. Instead of copying or moving the contents of one file to another, the link maintains a live connection to the other file. Therefore, if the source file changes, the destination file always displays those changes. The destination file does not actually hold the source file's data, but displays the data as though it resided in the destination file.

As long as you've inserted a link to the Excel 97 worksheet, you need only change the Excel 97 worksheet each month, start Word 97, load the report document, and print the document. You won't have to copy or move the actual Excel 97 cells into the report. The report always points to the worksheet cells via the link that you inserted when you created the Word 97 document.

To create a link, perform these steps:

1. Select Window|Arrange All to arrange your two program windows so that you can see both the source document (the Excel 97 worksheet) and the destination document (the Word 97 document).

2. Select the cells in the Excel 97 worksheet that you want to link and transfer to Word 97.

3. With the right mouse button, drag the edge of the highlighted cells to the location in your Word 97 document where you want to place the table.

4. Release the right mouse button. Word 97 opens a pop-up menu with these options: Move Here, Copy Here, Insert Excel Object Here, and Create Shortcut Here.

5. Select Insert Excel Object Here to indicate to Word 97 that you want to create an object link (as opposed to a move or a copy of the cells). Although the cells appear as though Office 97 copied them into the Word 97 document, the cells represent only the link that you created between the Excel 97 source and Word 97 destination document.

> The destination document (in this case, the Word 97 document) always reflects the most recent changes to the source document (in this case, the Excel 97 worksheet). Therefore, if you must keep archives of old reports with the previous monthly values, you want to copy the cells instead of creating a link.

To see the interactive nature of the links, change a value in the source Excel 97 worksheet. The Word 97 document immediately reflects your change.

After inserting one or more links, select Edit | Links to display the Links dialog box (shown in Figure 22.3). The Links dialog box contains every link in your document and enables you to change, break, or lock any link. When you break a link, the data becomes embedded in the document and no longer updates when you update the source. When you lock a link, you temporarily prevent the link from being updated when its source is updated.

Figure 22.3.

Use the Links dialog box to manage your document links.

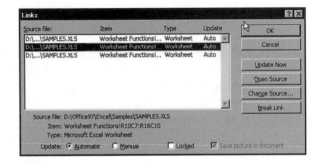

Creating Shortcuts

Instead of inserting a copy or a link, you can insert a *shortcut* in the destination document.

 A *shortcut* is an icon inserted in your document that you can double-click to access data from a document stored elsewhere.

You probably use shortcuts less often than links and embedded copies when producing reports because you usually want the reports to show actual data and not icons. However, if you often work with data from one program while in another program, the shortcuts are nice. The data does not get in your way until you're ready to work with it because you see only icons that represent the shortcut data.

If you create a shortcut from one Office 97 program to another, Office 97 actually displays the data and does not display a shortcut icon. If you double-click the data, Office 97 opens the appropriate program and enables you to edit the original data using the source program that created the data. If, however, you insert a shortcut into a non-Office 97 program, Office 97 inserts a shortcut icon that represents the data. If you double-click the icon from within the other program, the appropriate Office 97 program begins, and you can edit the data.

22

Consider this scenario: You're working in Excel 97, modifying weekly salary figures for a large worksheet that you maintain. Each week you must study the salary amounts and enter a 10-line explanation of the salaries. Instead of typing the definition each week or (worse) using Excel 97 as a limited word processor and editing the text each week, you could embed a shortcut to a Word 97 document that contains a template for the text. When you double-click the shortcut, Excel 97 starts Word 97, which automatically loads the template. You can create the final text in the template, copy the Word 97 text into your salary worksheet (replacing the shortcut), and save the worksheet under a name that designates the current week's work.

To insert a shortcut, perform these steps:

1. Select Window|Arrange All to arrange your program windows so that you can see both the source document (the Word 97 template document) and the destination document (the Excel 97 worksheet).

2. Select the Word 97 template text that you want to use for the shortcut. (Press Ctrl+A if you want to select the entire Word 97 template document.)

3. With the right mouse button, drag the edge of the highlighted template text to the location in your Excel 97 worksheet where you want to place the shortcut.

4. Release the right mouse button.

5. Select Create Shortcut Here from the pop-up menu. Office 97 creates the shortcut. As with a link, the shortcut data does not actually appear in the destination document. Unlike a link, you can drag the shortcut to your Windows desktop, to Explorer, or to another program to create additional copies of the shortcut.

Before inserting an Access 97 table into another Office 97 program, run a query to filter data that doesn't interest you. (Hour 20, "Retrieving Your Data," explains how to form data queries.) In most cases, you want to use Word 97's special Access 97 Database Insert feature to load Access 97 data into a Word 97 document. Later in this hour, the section titled "Using Word 97 and Access 97" describes how to insert Access 97 data into a Word 97 document.

Turning a Word Document into a Presentation

Word 97 and PowerPoint 97 share a special link that enables you to turn a set of notes into a presentation. Before creating your notes, be sure to use the Heading 1 through Heading 5 styles. PowerPoint 97 uses the Heading 1 style for each slide's title and uses the Heading 2 through Heading 5 styles for the slide's subsequently indented text.

If your Word 97 document contains other styles, PowerPoint 97 ignores those paragraphs.

You can easily apply Heading 1 through Heading 5 styles to a Word 97 document that you've already created by clicking a paragraph (or by moving the mouse pointer anywhere within the paragraph), pressing Ctrl+Shift+S, and selecting Heading styles from the drop-down list box. You can also select the style by opening the Style drop-down list box and scrolling to the heading style that you want to select.

After you create the Word 97 document, open it from PowerPoint 97 or click the Present It toolbar button in Word 97 to create the presentation. (Depending on your Word 97 customization, you might not see the Present It toolbar button until you add it by using the Tools | Customize menu.)

Using Word 97 and Access 97

A database can be extremely large with many tables. Often, you want to export a portion of an Access 97 database to a Word 97 document. The drag-and-drop method does not always offer exactly what you need to get the data you want into a Word 97 document.

 If you want to use an Access 97 table in a PowerPoint 97 presentation, load the table into a Word 97 document, and then convert the Word 97 document to a PowerPoint 97 presentation as described in the previous section.

To load Access 97 data into a Word 97 document, perform these steps:

1. Display the Database toolbar in Word 97 (select View | Toolbars and click the Database option).
2. Click the Insert Database toolbar button. Word 97 displays the Database dialog box.
3. Click the Get Data button and locate the database you want to import. Word 97 does not import the data yet, but you must locate the database before specifying the data to be imported. To display Access 97 databases, select MS Access Databases (*.mdb) from the list box labeled Files of Type. Word 97 displays the dialog box shown in Figure 22.4, which contains a list of every table and query from the selected database.

Figure 22.4.

Indicate exactly which table Word 97 is to use.

4. Select the table or query that you want to load into the Word 97 document and click OK to return to the Database dialog box.

5. Click the Query Options button if you want to limit the table's records or fields. (If you don't select the Query Options button, Word 97 imports the entire table.) Word 97 displays an Access 97 query window, from which you can select records and fields using normal Access 97 database-selection criteria. You can add tables if you want Word 97 to import data from multiple tables.

6. Click the Insert Data button to insert your selected data.

7. You now can format the data and use it in your Word 97 document as if you typed the data yourself.

Enhancing Your Office Documents

Office 97 enables you to insert images and other objects into your documents. Graphics spruce up newsletters and other documents that require eye-catching images.

In Hour 15, "PowerPoint 97 Advanced Features," you learned how to use the Clip Gallery to insert images, sounds, and videos into presentations. In addition to producing the Clip Gallery, the Insert | Picture option produces a menu with the following options:

☐ **From File:** Enables you to insert an image from any graphics file. Use this option when you don't want to confine your images to the ones supplied in the Clip Gallery.

☐ **AutoShapes:** Inserts one of Office 97's *AutoShapes*, which you can manipulate.

NEW TERM *AutoShape* is a ready-made shape that you can use in a document. After you insert a shape, you can resize, rotate, flip, color, and combine that shape with other shapes. The Drawing toolbar contains an AutoShape section, which produces the AutoShapes floating toolbar. Use the AutoShapes floating toolbar to insert and edit AutoShapes.

☐ **WordArt:** Displays the *WordArt* Gallery of WordArt styles (shown in Figure 22.5).

WordArt enables you to convert text into shapes. Despite its name, WordArt is available from all Office 97 products, not just Word 97.

☐ **From Scanner:** Enables you to scan an image into the Office 97 document. You must have a TWAIN-compliant scanner attached to scan images into Office 97. (Most scanners follow the PC scanner standard called *TWAIN*; your scanner's documentation should indicate whether your scanner is TWAIN-compliant.)

☐ **Organization Chart:** Starts an Office 97 add-in application that creates organizational charts (available only in Excel 97).

☐ **Chart:** Displays a small Excel 97-like worksheet (called a datasheet) in which you can enter data. The datasheet offers a sample set of cells in which you can enter your own values or import data from Excel 97. When you close the datasheet, the resulting bar chart appears in your document (available only in Word 97).

Figure 22.5.

You can select a WordArt style from the WordArt Gallery.

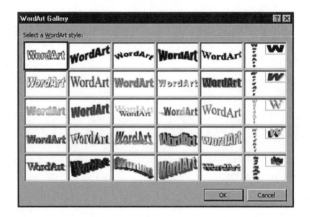

The next three sections describe the most common graphics insertions you can make into your Office 97 documents from the Insert|Picture menu.

Inserting Images from Files

To add an image (or sound or video) clip-art file to a document, select Insert|Picture|From File to display the Insert Picture dialog box. Locate the image on your disk (or on your network, or the Internet by selecting the source from the Look in list box) and click Insert to insert the image.

22

> Uncheck the Float over Text option if you want to place the image on the same layer as the text. Leave the Float over Text option checked if you want to place the image on a special art layer. Use the Draw menu to place text on top of or underneath the art image.

If you often insert the same image, sound, or video clip, consider adding the clip to your Office 97 Clip Gallery. The Clip Gallery makes common clips easy for you to find, thus eliminating the need for you to search your disk drive every time you want to insert a clip file.

To add a clip file to your Clip Gallery, perform these steps:

1. Display the Clip Gallery by selecting Insert | Picture | Clip Art.
2. Click the Import Clips button.
3. Locate the clip-art file that you want to import. When you locate the file and press Enter, Office 97 displays the Clip Properties dialog box (shown in Figure 22.6), which shows a thumbnail sketch of the image along with the image's details.

Figure 22.6.

Enter a frequently used image into the Clip Gallery category so that you can quickly find the image later.

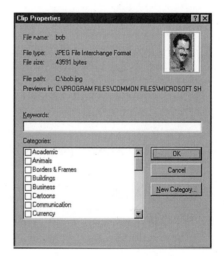

4. Select the category and add a keyword or two (to help with subsequent searches for the image).
5. Press Enter to add the image to the proper Clip Gallery category.

Using OfficeArt Tools

Office 97 introduces a completely revamped set of *OfficeArt* tools. Instead of simply upgrading previous Office drawing tools, Microsoft rewrote them for Office 97 to improve performance.

 OfficeArt is the general term applied to the Office 97 drawing tools such as AutoShape and WordArt.

OfficeArt provides a single drawing interface for all the Office 97 programs. If you learn how to use AutoShape inside PowerPoint 97, you also know how to use AutoShape in Excel 97. Although you might expect such an integrated and consistent drawing system, Office 97 is the *first time* Microsoft successfully integrated one consistent drawing interface into all the Office 97 products.

> Outlook 97 contains no OfficeArt tool support.

> OfficeArt's drawing tools work with all the applicable Office 97 features. Therefore, you can spell check the text in an AutoShape drawing.

Not only did Microsoft help you learn the OfficeArt tools more quickly, but Office 97 includes only one set of OfficeArt code. Therefore, whether you install only Word 97 or the entire set of Office 97 programs, Office 97 installs a single shared copy of the OfficeArt code. As a result, the drawing tools work quickly and efficiently, consuming much less disk space than if each program contained its own drawing code.

Inserting AutoShapes

The AutoShapes toolbar that appears when you insert an AutoShape provides numerous drawing tools for creating line drawings inside Word 97, Excel 97, or PowerPoint 97. When you click one of the toolbar options described next, Office 97 opens a set of drawing tools for that option. For example, if you click the Basic Shapes tool, Office 97 displays a drop-down selection box of about 30 shapes. After you select a shape, you can continue drawing with that shape until you select a different shape or another AutoShape tool. To draw a shape, drag the mouse over the editing area.

The following list describes the AutoShape tools you find on the AutoShapes toolbar:

☐ **Lines:** Provides straight, curved, and free-form lines that you can draw with the mouse

☐ **Basic shapes:** Provides circles, ovals, rectangles, and other shapes that you can select and draw with

☐ **Block arrows** (Word 97 only)**:** Provides several connecting arrows that you can use for pointing parts of a drawing to each other

☐ **Flowchart:** Draws various flowcharting symbols

☐ **Stars and Banners:** Places stars and various banners on the editing area

☐ **Callouts:** Draws spoken and bubble-thought cartoon callouts so that the figures you draw can be made to speak

☐ **Connectors** (Excel 97 only)**:** Draws several kinds of lines from one AutoShape image to another

Figure 22.7 shows how you can have fun by combining AutoShape and OfficeArt images in a Word 97 document.

Figure 22.7.

Combine AutoShape and OfficeArt images to create doodles in Word 97 documents.

AutoShapes toolbar

Drawing toolbar

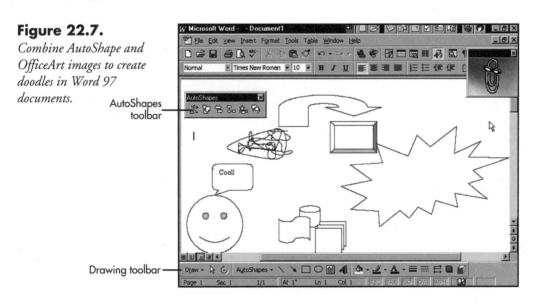

AutoShape offers two ways to add text to your image:

☐ **Placing text in a callout:** As soon as you add an AutoShape callout to your drawing, Office 97 enables you to enter text for that callout.

☐ **Placing text anywhere on the AutoShape image:** Right-click anywhere over the AutoShape area and select Add Text from the pop-up menu to place text on any AutoShape image.

> When you click any AutoShape image that you draw, resizing handles appear so that you can resize the image. In addition, you'll see the image's yellow *adjustment handle*. Drag the *adjustment handle* to change the shape's most prominent feature, such as the smile on the happy face.

When you add an AutoShape to your document, Office 97 displays the Drawing toolbar on your screen. Select from the Drawing toolbar to change the orientation of any selected AutoShape image. For example, you can vertically or horizontally flip an image. Any text you've placed on the image retains its original orientation.

Inserting WordArt

WordArt displays text in several shapes, colors, and styles to add pizzazz to your documents. For example, you can add an eye-catching title at the top of an Excel 97 worksheet to grab the reader's attention.

To add a WordArt image, perform these steps:

1. Select Insert|Picture|WordArt to display the WordArt Gallery dialog box.
2. Select the WordArt style that you want to use by double-clicking the style. Office 97 displays the Edit WordArt Text dialog box (shown in Figure 22.8).

Figure 22.8.

Provide text for WordArt to format.

22

3. Enter the text that you want to format as WordArt and select the proper font and point size. The WordArt style that you select follows your font and size request as closely as possible.

4. Click OK to insert the WordArt text. Office 97 displays resizing handles around the WordArt image, which you can use to resize or move the image. In addition, the WordArt toolbar that appears provides several editing techniques that you can apply to the image, such as rotation and color.

Figure 22.9 shows a sample WordArt image inserted at the top of a small Excel worksheet.

Figure 22.9.

A sample of WordArt's appeal.

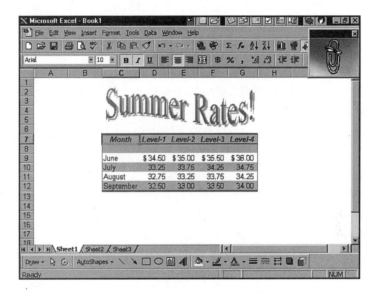

Summary

This hour described how to integrate Office 97 products by sharing data files among the programs. One of the most elegant ways to copy or move data from one Office 97 program to another is to use drag and drop. By holding your right mouse button, you can control how the drag-and-drop operation sends the data from one document to another.

Word 97 and PowerPoint 97 share data files easily as long as you use the proper heading styles. Presenters often use Word 97 documents as a basis for a presentation, and you'll appreciate the automation Office 97 provides. After you convert your Word 97 document to a PowerPoint 97 presentation, you can adjust the presentation's format and add slides if you want.

When importing Access 97 data into Word 97, you must be selective. Databases are often huge, and you usually want to import only a small part of the database into your Word 97 document. First, indicate to Word 97 what data from what table you want to import so that you get only the data you need.

This hour also explained how to use the graphics-related tools to insert art and draw pictures inside your Office 97 documents. As you might expect, the Office 97 tools are easy to use and appear (along with their toolbars) when you request them, but stay out of the way when you don't need to work with art.

The next hour, "Office 97 and the Internet," introduces the Internet and shows you how to access web pages using the Internet Explorer web browser included with Office 97.

Q&A

Q What format does my data take when I drag and drop something from one Office 97 product to another?

A Office 97 provides excellent intuitive conversions when you combine data from more than one Office 97 product. For example, when you drag a worksheet from Excel 97 to Word 97, the worksheet becomes a Word 97 table. You then can use all the standard table-editing tools in Word 97 to modify the appearance of the worksheet. Excel 97 converts Word 97 text to text-cell entries. Excel 97 converts Access 97 table data to worksheet cells, respecting the data types when possible (so the numbers stay numbers and the dates stay dates).

Q What is the advantage of a shortcut over a link?

A If you're sticking with Office 97 products only, you probably want to use links to embed live connections from one document to another. However, if you share Office 97 documents with other programs, those programs probably recognize shortcuts and present your Office 97 document as an icon. For example, if you use a standalone email program (such as Eudora) to send a Word 97 document, the Word 97 document appears in your email note as a Word 97 icon. If you double-click that icon (or if your email recipient double-clicks the icon after receiving the email), Word 97 starts (assuming Word 97 resides on the system), and you (or the recipient) are able to edit the document.

Q Why would you ever want to copy data and not create a link to another document?

A When you copy data, it is copied into the destination document, so the data resides in both the destination document and the source document. If you were to take the destination document to another computer, the document could not access its original link (if you had used a link). In addition, you may not want the destination document's data being hooked "live" to the source data. For example, if you

22

are creating archive files of older data, you want always to copy the data and not form a link or shortcut to the original source data.

Q Why would you not import a complete database into Word 97?

A A complete database contains tables, queries, reports, forms, macros, and modules, and all those items make little sense in a Word 97 document. If you need to report data using the entire Access 97 database, use Access 97 to generate reports. Word 97 is useful for printing database subsets. If you want to include part of an Access 97 database table in a Word 97 report, you can easily send the table's data into Word 97 using the tools described in this lesson.

Q What is the difference between AutoShape, WordArt, and OfficeArt?

A AutoShape is the general term applied to all the drawing tools provided when you insert an AutoShape picture into an Office 97 document. The AutoShapes toolbar appears when you draw AutoShape graphics to help you with free-form drawings and to supply common shapes that you might need. WordArt is a system that manipulates and colors text to turn standard text into various eye-catching 3D colorful styles. The term *OfficeArt* is a general term applied to all the graphics and drawing tools you find in the Office 97 suite of products, including AutoShape and WordArt.

Q What is the difference between an adjustment handle and a resizing handle?

A Adjustment handles change the form of shapes, while resizing handles change the size of shapes.

Hour 23

Office 97 and the Internet

If you are new to Internet technology, this hour introduces you to a whole new world. The Internet is much more a part of computer users' lives than ever before. Microsoft recognizes this and includes Internet access capabilities in Office 97. The individual Office 97 products include Internet connections, and Office 97 also includes *Internet Explorer*, an Internet *browser* that enables you access the Internet from within Windows. Microsoft is committed to integrating Internet access more completely into future Office and Windows releases, and you see that commitment already in Office 97.

If you've used the Internet before, you may want to skim this hour to see how the Office 97 products connect you to the Internet.

The highlights of this hour include

- [ ] Why the Internet and the web are so important
- [ ] How to start and use Internet Explorer
- [ ] How to surf the Internet to find and view multimedia information
- [ ] How to use search engines to locate the exact Internet information you need
- [ ] How to access the Internet from within an Office 97 product
- [ ] How to view Office 97 documents from within Internet Explorer
- [ ] How to include web links in your Office documents

Introducing the Internet

The Internet began as a government- and university-linked system of computers that has since turned into a business and personal system that contains a seemingly infinite amount of information. The Internet is a worldwide system of interconnected computers. Whereas your desktop computer is a standalone machine, and a network of computers is linked together by wires, the Internet is a worldwide online network of computers connected to standalone computers through modems.

 The *Internet* is a worldwide network connection of computers that provides information and offers electronic mail services to the users who access the Internet from their own computers.

The Internet offers the most unique research and information-access tools ever invented. You can get up-to-date news, stock quotes, and sports scores. You can locate product information, purchase everything from cars to airline tickets, play games, listen to music, view videos, and chat with other Internet users around the world via your keyboard or microphone.

That vast amount and format of Internet data requires a standard so that all may share in the Internet's content. Internet technicians began standardizing Internet information when it became apparent that the Internet was growing and becoming a major information provider. The most important standard that's emerged has been *web* pages on which you view Internet content.

Introducing the Web

The *web*, or *World Wide Web (WWW)*, is a collection of Internet pages of information. Web pages can contain text, graphics, sound, and video. Figure 23.1 shows a sample web page. As you can see, the web page's graphics and text organize information into a magazine-like readable and appealing format.

 The term *web*, or *World Wide Web (WWW)*, is given to the interconnected system of Internet information pages that you can access to read specific information. Many of the web pages are connected with hypertext links that enable you to more easily traverse the pages that you view.

Generally, a web site might contain more information than fits easily on a single web page. Therefore, many web pages contain links to several additional extended pages, as well as other linked web pages that may be related to the original topic. The first page you view is called the *home page*, and from the home page you can view other pages of information.

Figure 23.1.

Web pages provide Internet information in a standard format.

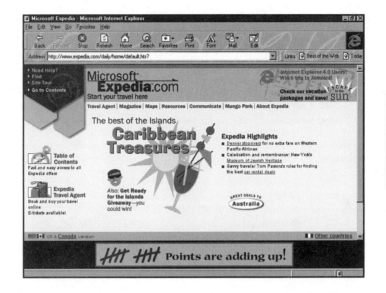

The Internet has standardized web page locations with a series of addresses called *URLs*, or *Uniform Resource Locators*, that are formatted like this: www.microsoft.com. You can view any web page if you know its URL. If you do not know the URL, the Internet provides several *search engines* that find web pages when you search for topics. You learn how to search the Internet later this hour in the "Searching for the Information You Need" section.

Using Internet Explorer

A *web browser*, or just *browser*, is a program that can bring web data to your desktop. Microsoft's web browsing program, *Internet Explorer*, comes with every version of Office 97. Therefore, you already have the tools you need to access the Internet if you have Office 97.

This hour's figures and tasks use Internet Explorer version 3, the version that comes with most Office 97 installations. Microsoft has recently introduced version 4. The appendix, "Internet Explorer 4 and Outlook Express," explains the features of Internet Explorer 4 so that you can decide if you want to update to the newer version.

If your company offers cabled Internet access, you need the interface card in your PC that can accept the cable. If you use the Internet from home, or from an office that does not provide cabled Internet access, you need to get Internet access through an *ISP*, an *Internet Service Provider*. One of the easiest ways to get access is through the Microsoft Network, which has access programs that are available with all Windows installations. If you want Internet access through another ISP, such as a local Internet provider, your provider will tell you how to use Internet Explorer or another web browser to access the ISP's Internet system.

 An *Internet Service Provider*, or *ISP*, is a company or online service such as Microsoft Network or America Online that provides you with a phone number that you can command Internet Explorer to dial for Internet access.

 Although Internet service is relatively inexpensive, it's not free. Most ISPs charge a flat rate, such as $19.95 a month, for unlimited Internet usage.

Starting Internet Explorer

Internet Explorer is easy to start. You literally can access the Internet with one or two clicks by running Internet Explorer. After you sign up with an ISP and get the Internet phone number to access the web, you are ready to navigate the Internet.

To start Internet Explorer, double-click the Windows desktop icon labeled The Internet. If you get an Internet Connection Wizard dialog box, you must contact your service provider to learn how to hook up Internet Explorer to the Internet. Internet Explorer prompts you for the username and password that you selected when you signed up for your Internet service (see Figure 23.2).

Figure 23.2.

Log in to your Internet service to use Internet Explorer.

Assuming that you have Internet access and have been set up with a provider, Internet Explorer dials your provider and displays the page set up to be your initial browser's *start page*. Depending on the amount of information and graphics on the page, the display may take a few moments or may display right away.

New Term A *start page* is the page you've requested Internet Explorer to show first when you sign onto the Internet.

The Home button on the Internet Explorer toolbar displays your start page. You can return to the start page by clicking the Home button. You can change your start page address by entering a new start page within the View | Options dialog box's Navigation page. When you enter a new start page address, Internet Explorer returns to that page whenever you click the Home toolbar button or start Internet Explorer in a subsequent session.

Managing the Internet Explorer Screen

You can navigate Internet pages easily with Internet Explorer. If you are new to the Internet, study Figure 23.3 to learn the parts of the Internet Explorer screen. Internet Explorer displays your start page and lists the start page's address in the address area.

Figure 23.3.

Learn the Internet Explorer screen so that you can maximize the Internet Explorer browser.

Returns you to the previous web page

Web page address

Keeps track of your favorite sites

Hyperlinks to other related sites

Starts your email program

Viewing area

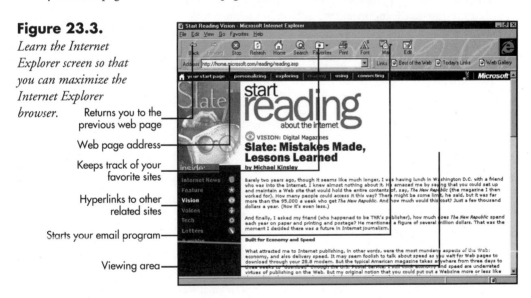

Use the following guidelines to familiarize yourself with the Internet Explorer screen:

☐ Some web site addresses are lengthy. Drag the Address text box left or right (giving more or less room to the link buttons) to adjust the address display width.

☐ Click the down arrow at the right of the address entry to open a list of recently traversed site addresses. If this is the first time you or anyone has used your computer's Internet Explorer, you may not see sites other than the current start page sites.

☐ Use the scroll bar to see more of your start page. Most web pages take more room than fit on one screen.

☐ Use the View menu to hide the toolbar and status bar so that you have more display room for the web page. The address list box can be hidden as well. You can still enter site addresses that you want to traverse from the File menu.

☐ Display the toolbar and status bar again by clicking the appropriate View menu options.

You will probably spend a lot of time on the Internet, so the better you understand Internet Explorer the more effective you will be online.

Surfing the Internet

Remember that the Internet's web is a collection of interconnected web pages. As you *surf* the Internet using Internet Explorer, you run across web pages that contain *links* to other sites. These links (often called *hot spots* or *hypertext links*) are often underlined or appear in a different color from the surrounding text. You are able to locate these links by moving your mouse cursor over the underlined description. If the mouse cursor changes to a hand, you can click the hand to move to that page. After a brief pause, your web browser displays the page.

NEW TERM To *surf* the Internet means to navigate the Internet by viewing web pages that interest you.

NEW TERM A *link*, *hyperlink*, or *hot spot*, is nothing more than a URL to another web site embedded on a web page. The link often displays a description and not a technical URL. (As you move your mouse cursor over a link, your web browser's status bar displays the actual URL to the link.) Therefore, you can traverse related web pages without worrying about addresses; just click link descriptions to move to those sites.

Suppose that you view the home page of your financial broker. The page might include links to other related pages, such as stock quotation pages, company financial informational pages, and order-entry pages in which you can enter your own stock purchase requests.

One of the most useful features of Internet Explorer and every other web browser is the browser's capability to return to sites you've visited both in the current session and in former sessions. The toolbar's Back button takes you back to a site you just visited, and you can keep clicking the Back button to return to pages you've visited in the current session. The Forward toolbar button returns you to pages from where you've backed up.

At any point, you can click the Address drop-down list box to see a list of URLs you've visited. You find addresses from the current as well as previous Internet Explorer web sessions.

If you know the address of a web site that you want to view, you can type the site's address directly in the Address textbox. When you press Enter, Internet Explorer takes you to that site and displays its web page. In addition, you can select File | Open to display an Open dialog box in which you can enter an address. When you click OK, Internet Explorer displays the page associated with that address.

If you find a location you really like, save that location in Internet Explorer's Favorites list. For example, if you run across a site that discusses your favorite television show and you want to return to that site again quickly, click the Favorites toolbar button to add the site to your Favorites list. The Address history does not keep track of a lot of recently visited addresses; you can, however, store your favorite sites in the Favorites folders so that you can quickly access them during future Internet sessions.

As you familiarize yourself with the Internet, you'll want to visit web pages that interest you. After you visit a site, you can easily return to that site. Use the following steps to become comfortable surfing web pages:

1. If you have not started Internet Explorer, start it and log on to the Internet.
2. Click the Address list box to select the URL of your start page.
3. Type the following web page address: **http://www.mcp.com**. You see Macmillan Publishing's home page appear, as shown in Figure 23.4. (Depending on the changes that have been made to the site recently, the site may not match Figure 23.4 exactly.)

> Often, you see web addresses prefaced with the text http://. This prefix indicates both for you and your browser that the address to the right of the second slash is a web page's URL. Be sure to type forward slashes and not the MS-DOS backslashes you may be used to typing for PC folder locations. The http:// is optional in Internet Explorer; you don't have to type this prefix.

4. Click any link on the page. After a brief pause, you see the linked web page.
5. Click the toolbar's Back button. Almost instantly, the first page appears.
6. After you're back at Macmillan Publishing's home page, practice building a favorite site list by clicking the Favorites toolbar button.
7. Click the Add To Favorites option. Internet Explorer displays the Add to Favorites dialog box.

Figure 23.4.

Macmillan Publishing's home page.

8. Enter a description for the page. Make the description something you can remember the page by (such as `Macmillan Computer Book Publishing`).

9. Click OK.

10. Click the Favorites toolbar button once again. You see the new entry. When you select the favorite entry, Internet Explorer looks up that entry's stored URL address and goes to that web page.

> If you add too many favorites, your favorites list might become unmanageable. As you add to your favorites list, you can create folders using the Create In button in the Add to Favorites dialog box. By setting up a series of folders named by subjects, you can group your favorite web sites by subject so that they are easier to manage and find.

Some web pages take a long time to display. Often, web pages contain a lot of text and graphics, and that data takes time to arrive on your computer. Therefore, you might click to a favorite web site but have to wait a minute or longer to see the entire site.

To speed things, Internet Explorer attempts to show as much of the page as possible, especially the text on the page, before downloading the graphic images. Internet Explorer puts placeholders where the graphic images are to appear. If you view the page for a few moments, the placeholders' images begin to appear until the final page, with all graphics, displays in its entirety.

Searching for the Information You Need

How can you expect to find any information on a vast network of networks such as the Internet? Web pages offer linked sites in an appealing format that enable you to comfortably view information and see related pages, but you must know the location of one of the site's pages before the links can help.

Fortunately, Internet Explorer offers a searching mechanism that helps you locate information on the web. By clicking the Search toolbar button, you can access a search page, such as the one shown in Figure 23.5.

23

Figure 23.5.

Select from one of several web search engines.

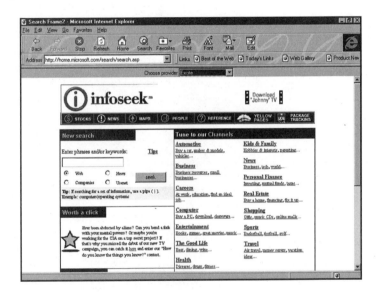

The web page you see may differ from the one in Figure 23.5 because Microsoft updates the page quite often.

The search web page offers the benefit of multiple *search engines*. The accuracy of the search depends on the words and phrases you enter, as well as the capability of the search engine. For example, some search engines you can choose from search only web pages while others search *newsgroups*.

NEW TERM

A *search engine* is a web program that enables you to enter words and phrases for which to search , and then scans the vast information on the web to locate sites that contain the words or phrase.

NEW TERM

Newsgroups are Internet discussion areas that hold files and messages related to topics. You can read messages and download files as well as post your own messages and files for others to see. Although these 24 hour lessons don't offer enough time to discuss newsgroups, you can access newsgroups with the Internet Mail and News reader that comes with Office 97 or with Outlook Express, described in this book's appendix.

> If you find that one of the search engines locates information for you better than the others, you can make that search engine the default by clicking the Set Default command button. If you do not set a default search engine, Internet Explorer selects a different one each time you visit the search site.

After the search engine locates its information, Internet Explorer displays from zero to several address links on which you can click to find information about your topic. (Figure 23.6 shows the result of one search.) By scrolling down the page (and by clicking the additional pages of links if your search turns up a lot of sites), you can read the descriptions of the pages. The descriptions often contain the first few lines of the located web page text.

Figure 23.6.

The results of a search might produce several pages of web sites.

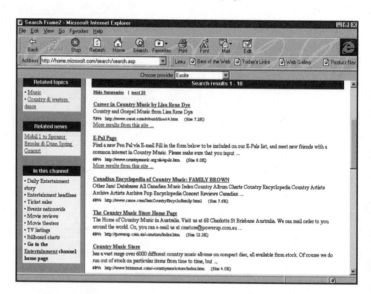

Each search engine locates information differently and each also has its own rules for the words and phrases you enter. Keep in mind that the more specific your search phrase is, the more accurately the search engine can find information that helps you.

Generally, you can use these guidelines with most search engines:

☐ Enclose a multiple word phrase in quotation marks if you want the search engine to search for those words in the order in which they're listed. For example, if you enter "West Virginia", the search engine searches for that specific name. If, however, you enter West Virginia (without the quotes), most search engines locate every site that contains the word *West* and every site that contains the word *Virginia*, most of which would have nothing to do with the state you originally wanted to locate.

☐ Place a plus sign (+) before each word for which you want to search. For example, entering +Tulsa +oil would find only those sites that contain both the word *Tulsa* and the word *oil*.

23

Remember that these search criteria rules are only guidelines that usually work well with the most popular search engines. Some of the search engines follow slightly different rules and you have to look up that search engine page's help references for specific information if the previous rules do not seem to work the way you expect.

Office 97 Products and the Web

Office 97 offers a complete set of tools that integrate the Office 97 products and the Internet. From any Office 97 product you can access files and web pages on the Internet. The following sections describe how you can access the web from Office 97.

Viewing Web Pages Within Office Products

You don't have to start Internet Explorer to view a web page from within an Office 97 product. All you need to do is display the web toolbar and type the address you want to see. For example, while creating an Excel worksheet, you may need to locate financial information from your company's web site. Follow these steps to surf the web from Excel:

1. Select View|Toolbars|Web to add a new web-browsing toolbar to Excel.

2. Click the address area of the Web toolbar.

3. Enter the web address that you want to see. (Alternatively, you can click the Favorites list on the Web toolbar to select the web page that you want to view.) If you access the Internet from a modem, Excel dials your Internet Service Provider to get Internet access.

4. Excel starts Internet Explorer for you and displays the web site that you want to view. You can switch between the web and Excel by pressing Alt+Tab. In addition, you can copy and paste information from web pages to your Excel worksheet.

You cannot type URLs directly into an Excel 97 address area. Instead, you can select File | Open and type the URL of the web page that you want to view.

Viewing Documents in Internet Explorer

In addition to starting Internet Explorer from an Office 97 product, you can view Office 97 documents directly from within Internet Explorer. Whenever you're browsing the Internet, select File | Open and type the full path (or click Browse to locate the path) and filename you want to view from within Internet Explorer.

Internet Explorer opens the file and displays the file within the browser window. Not only does Internet Explorer display the file, but all Internet Explorer menus change to enable full editing capabilities for that Office 97 document. For example, if you open a Word 97 document, Internet Explorer menus change to Word 97 menus; you can then insert a table or format the text as if you were using Word 97. If you click the Internet Explorer Tools toolbar button while viewing the Office 97 document, the Word 97 toolbars appear beneath the Internet Explorer toolbar so that you have full Word 97 toolbar capabilities from within Internet Explorer (shown in Figure 23.7).

If you click the Back button, Internet Explorer displays the previous web page, and the menus change so that you can surf the web normally.

You might wonder why the web page does not appear inside Excel 97 when you use the Web toolbar to request the web page. Excel 97 cannot access the web; for that, you need a web browser. Nevertheless, the Web toolbar that you find in all the Office 97 products does enable you to navigate between Office 97 documents without changing programs, as you learn toward the end of this hour.

Figure 23.7.

Internet Explorer offers all the Word 97 menus and toolbars if you open a Word 97 document within Internet Explorer.

Word 97 menu options

Word 97 toolbars

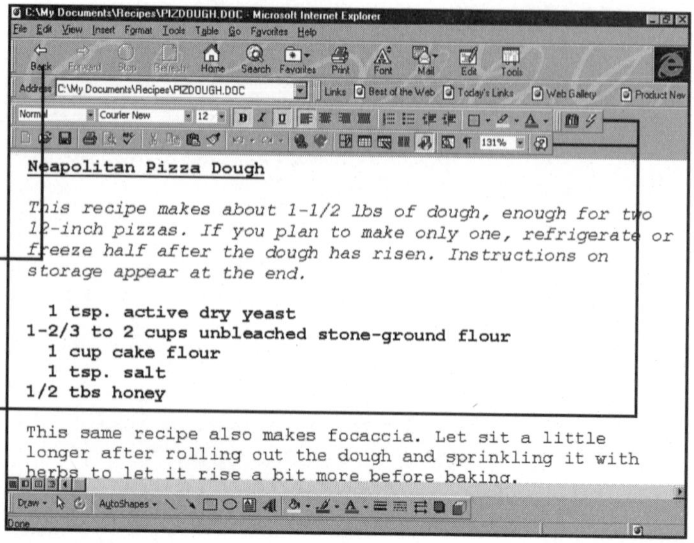

Perhaps someday, the only program you'll need is a web browser! The browser menus and toolbars can change depending on the document with which you want to work. As you see in the appendix, Internet Explorer 4 integrates with Windows itself so that the browser becomes part of your Windows environment. The Internet is so important to computing today that companies such as Microsoft are incorporating web technology into all products as well as operating systems.

23

Creating Links in Office 97

As you learned how to use Office 97 products throughout the previous hours, you learned that you can type a web address in an Office 97 document to create a link to that address. When you type a web address in a PowerPoint 97 presentation, for example, that address becomes a link to an active web site address. If you click that address, the Office 97 product starts Internet Explorer, logs you on to the Internet if needed, and displays the web page located at that address.

You don't have to use web addresses for hyperlinks in Office 97 documents. You can enter path and filenames that reside on your own PC. When you or another user clicks the link, the Office 97 product displays that link's file. Therefore, you can easily link documents together, even documents from different products within Office 97.

Summary

This hour introduced you to the Internet, the web, Internet Explorer, and how Office 97 and the Internet work together. The Internet is a vast collection of networked computers all around the world. You can access the Internet as long as you have access through an Internet Service Provider. Although Internet information appears in many forms, the most useful Internet information often appears on web pages that contain text, graphics, sound, and video.

Internet Explorer includes searching tools as well as a history system that keeps track of recent web pages. Not only can you view web pages with Internet Explorer, but you can also view other kinds of files on your computer. As the Internet becomes more organized and Internet access gets faster and cheaper, the web browser will become part of your daily computing routine. One day, you'll find that you do most of your work from web browsing software such as Internet Explorer.

The next hour wraps up the Internet discussion as well as your 24-hour tutorial by explaining how to create web pages from within the Office 97 products.

Q&A

Q I've clicked the Internet icon but I don't see web pages. What do I have to do to get on the Internet?

A Do you have Internet access from Microsoft Network or from another Internet Service Provider? Generally, unless you work for a company that offers Internet access to its employees, you have to sign up for Internet access, get the access phone number, pay a monthly fee (most Internet Service Providers offer unlimited access for a flat monthly rate), and set up a browser, such as Internet Explorer, to access that provider.

Q Does all Internet information appear on web pages?

A The Internet's information appears in many forms, sometimes in a form known as an FTP site or a newsgroup. The web page standard, however, has become one of the most popular ways to organize and view Internet information. As more people used the web page standard, more modern technology enabled that standard to evolve into a uniform container of multimedia-based information. Therefore, with a web browser, you can view all kinds of information over the web.

Hour 24

Creating Web Pages with Office 97

You don't just have to be a user of web pages. You can create them yourself with the tools available in Office 97. By utilizing the Office 97 wizards and design tools, you can quickly create web pages that equal those from the pros. With Office 97 you can hone text, graphics, and data tables and present that data to the world on the web.

Most Office 97 users use Word 97 as their primary web page development tool and import other Office 97 product data into their Word 97 web pages. All the Office 97 products are Internet-aware; they all enable you to convert their data to web pages.

The highlights of this hour include

- ☐ What you need to publish pages on the Internet
- ☐ How to save Word 97 documents as web pages
- ☐ When to use the various Office 97 wizards to generate your initial web pages
- ☐ How to export Excel 97 and Access 97 data to your Word 97-based web pages

☐ Why you should limit the amount of Access 97 information that goes into your web page

☐ How to include an animation module with a web-based PowerPoint 97 presentation so that users can watch your presentation on the web

Preparing to Publish Web Pages

Before you can publish pages on the web, you must have access to a *web server*. Perhaps your company uses a web server for its site; if so, you can store your web pages on that computer. If you have access to an online service, such as CompuServe, it may offer an area for one or more web pages that you can copy to the online site's web server.

 A *web server* is a computer dedicated to presenting web pages on the Internet.

If you want to publish a personal web page for fun, you will enjoy telling the world your stories and sharing your family photos with others. If, however, you want to start a business on the Internet, or offer timely information that you want others to visit often, you need to be aware that web page *maintenance* is costly and time-consuming. You don't just create a web page, load the page on the web, and expect to keep people's interest if you don't keep the material up to date.

 Maintenance is the process of modifying and updating web page information.

Office 97 and the Web

One of the reasons you should consider using Office 97 to create web pages is that you already have the Office 97 tools. Office 97 offers several wizards and templates that you can use to create your web pages. Nevertheless, Office 97 is not necessarily the *best* tool you can use to create web pages. Office 97 offers good tools with which you can create and maintain a web page, but if your web page generates a lot of interest, you may want to use a more specific tool for web-page creation such as Microsoft FrontPage. FrontPage is to web pages what Access 97 is to databases; FrontPage offers specific web page tools that create advanced web pages with very little effort on your part.

 All the web material in Office 97 supports both the Internet and *intranets*. Therefore, if your company maintains an intranet, you are able to save web pages to that intranet as easily (and sometimes more easily) as on the Internet.

NEW TERM An *intranet* is a local area network of computers whose users use web pages and Internet technology to communicate with each other on the network. Instead of dialing up an Internet Service Provider and accessing a web page from another location, you simply access a web page from a coworker's PC.

Each of the following sections describe how you can use Word 97, Excel 97, PowerPoint 97, and Access 97 to generate web page information. If you connect to your web server with a networked PC, you're able to offer live content on the Internet. In other words, as soon as you update your database, viewers of your web site who access that database see the updated values.

> Most of your web page creation will probably take place in Word 97. Even if you embed an Access database on a web page, you'll probably do most of that web page design in Word 97. Therefore, most of this hour focuses on Word 97's web-editing tools. The final sections describe how to integrate the other Office 97 products into your Word 97 web pages.

24

Word 97 and Web Pages

Word 97 offers two ways to create web pages: you can save Word 97 documents in a web page format, or you can create a web page using one of the Word 97 wizards. The following two sections explain each method.

Saving Word 97 Documents as Web Pages

One of the easiest ways to create a web page from a Word 97 document is to save the document in an *HTML format*. Suppose you create a company report that you want to publish on your web server. All you have to do is select File | Save as HTML, and then click OK. Word 97 then saves the file in a web-page compatible format that you then can transfer to the web server.

NEW TERM *HTML*, or *HyperText Markup Language*, is the name of the language format used by web pages. HTML pages contain formatting codes that define how the page looks from within a web browser such as Internet Explorer.

When you first save your document as an HTML document, you might see the dialog box shown in Figure 24.1. Microsoft frequently updates its web authoring tools, such as the HTML formatter. The dialog box offers to go to the Microsoft web site and download the latest web-related Office 97 tools to your computer. If you elect to update your web authoring tools, Word 97 takes care of properly installing the tools for you.

Figure 24.1.

Word 97 offers to update your web authoring tools when you save your document as an HTML file.

After Word 97 converts your document to HTML format, you can view your document from the Internet Explorer web browser by selecting File | Web Page Preview. By viewing the document from the web browser, you see how your web page will appear to other Internet users. Notice that the format differs somewhat from the format of the Word 97 document (especially italicized fonts).

When working with an HTML document in Word 97, Word 97 changes its toolbars to provide better tools for web page editing. Two of the most beneficial new toolbar buttons for web page developers that Word 97 supplies are the Increase Font Size and Decrease Font Size. When you select text on the web page and click one of these buttons, Word 97 increases or decreases the text size by one point. The toolbar buttons are easier to use than selecting from the Format | Character dialog box every time you need to adjust the font size. Although you can select a new font for your web page text, stick with the standard fonts that come with Windows, such as Courier, Times New Roman, and Arial—not all viewers of your web page have the same set of fonts that you do.

Keep in mind that web pages are often colorful. Color fonts can spruce up a web page dramatically as long as you don't overdo the colors. Use the toolbar's Font Color button to select a new font color quickly.

> If you have written HTML code before, you can embed HTML commands in your web page from within Word 97. Format your HTML code with the HTML Markup style and Word 97 embeds it as HTML code. The code does not appear on the web page but formats the page according to your instructions. All HTML markup text is hidden, but you can display the text by clicking the Show/Hide button on the Word 97 toolbar. Actually, Word 97 converts your web page elements to HTML code as soon as you add something to a web page. You can, at any time during the development of your web page, select View | HTML source to see the HTML code behind your web page. (Figure 24.2 shows HTML code for a web page being designed in Word 97.) To return to the formatted web page, click the Exit HTML Source button.

Figure 24.2.

You can view the HTML code for your web page.

Click here to see the
web page again

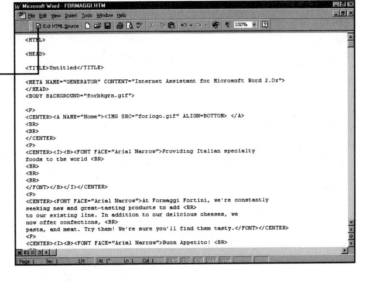

Using the Web Page Wizard

When you create a new document by selecting File | New, Word 97 offers a dialog box with a series of wizards and templates. If you click the Web Pages tab, you find the following three options:

- ☐ **Blank Web Page:** Creates a new, blank HTML document.
- ☐ **More Cool Stuff template:** Sends you to the Microsoft web site and describes several web-related programs on the Office 97 CD-ROM. The site includes several versions of bullets, separating lines, and other common web-page graphics that you can retrieve.
- ☐ **Web Page Wizard:** The step-by-step wizard that creates a web page according to your specifications.

The easiest way to create a web page according to your specifications is to start the Web Page Wizard. (Figure 24.3 shows the opening screen.)

> Microsoft's web site includes several additional web-specific Word 97 templates that you can download.

As you follow the wizard, you see the underlying Word 97 web page take shape. The wizard prompts you for the style of the web page. As you can see from the personal web page being built in Figure 24.4, the pages can be elegant.

Figure 24.3.

Word 97 builds a web page as you respond to the wizard.

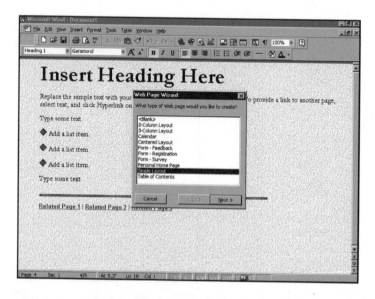

Figure 24.4.

The Web Page wizard generates many varieties of web page styles.

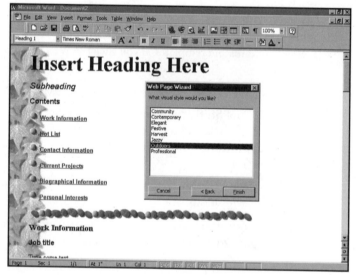

After the wizard does its job, you can edit the web page and change the general text to the specific text you want on the page. As you edit, check out the Insert menu; when working with an HTML document in Word 97, the Insert menu includes several items you can insert in your web page, including horizontal separating lines, pictures, videos, background sounds, scrolling text, and hyperlinks.

Not all web browsers support all the items that you can insert in your HTML-based web page. For example, Internet Explorer supports scrolling text, but not all web browsers do. Therefore, some users may not be able to see all the special effects on your web page.

If you want to add callout graphics to your web page, Word 97 offers all the drawing tools you learned about in Hour 22, "Office 97's Synergy," including the AutoShape tools.

24

Now that you've seen how to use Word 97 to create web pages, you already know a lot about how the other Office 97 products create web pages. Many of the web page features in the other Office 97 products work the same way as in Word 97. For example, you can save an Excel 97 worksheet as an HTML document.

The remaining sections build on your knowledge of using Word 97 and the web by showing you how Excel 97, PowerPoint 97, and Access 97 also support the web.

Excel 97 and Web Pages

Excel 97 supports most of the same web features that Word 97 does, including the capability to save worksheets in the HTML format. After you create the worksheet, select File | Save as HTML to save the worksheet in a format readable to any browser. In addition to the HTML format, Excel 97 also supports the Web toolbar that you can display by selecting View | Toolbars | Web. From that toolbar you can select other Office 97 documents to display and edit from within Excel 97 as well as enter an Internet web site address to view.

If you don't see the Save as HTML option on Excel 97 or the file menu of any other Office 97 product, you must install an extra program that comes with Office 97 called the *Internet Assistant*. Insert your Office 97 CD-ROM and select the Internet Assistant from the installation options that appear when you select Install. Don't add or remove any other options during the installation if you want to leave the rest of your Office 97 installation as is. If you don't see the setup menu when you install your Office 97 CD-ROM, select the Start menu's Run command and type **d:\setup** (where *d:* is your CD-ROM drive letter).

If your company stores worksheets on the Internet or on an intranet, the File | Open option in Excel 97 can open those worksheets. When you select File | Open, enter the URL and file name, such as `http://www.mycompany.org/accts.xls`, and Excel 97 opens that worksheet. (Excel 97 offers you the Internet Log On dialog box if you are not already logged on to the Internet.)

If you type a hyperlink web address or a hyperlink to another Office 97 document in an Excel 97 cell, Excel 97 takes you to that document and displays the Web toolbar automatically (if the toolbar is not already displayed). When you click the Web toolbar's Back button, Excel 97 takes you to the previous web page.

Step-Up

FTP sites are available to users of Excel 97 and other Office 97 products; therefore, you can store and retrieve worksheet files from an FTP site as easily as you can from your own local hard drive.

In the Open dialog box, click the Look in drop-down list and select Add/Modify FTP Locations. Excel 97 displays the Add/Modify FTP Locations dialog box in which you can enter your user account and password (see Figure 24.5). Anonymous FTP sites are also available when you click Anonymous and enter your email address as the password.

Figure 24.5.

Enter your user name and password to access the FTP site.

NEW TERM *FTP* stands for *File Transfer Protocol* and refers to the exchange of files from non-web Internet sites; these sites act like directories on your own PC. You can transfer files to and from FTP sites (some sites do not let you upload files to them but you can download files from them).

Rarely does a web page contain just an Excel 97 worksheet. Web pages contain other text and graphics; that's why you probably want to create the general web page in Word 97 using the Web Page Wizard and then import (using the Windows clipboard or Insert menu) your Excel 97 data into the web page. If you insert a link to your Excel 97 data instead of inserting a copy of the worksheet, your published web page always contains "live" worksheet data that changes as you update the worksheet.

If you use an online service to publish your web page and not a local web server networked to your PC, you have to update the web page manually each time you want to update the worksheet data.

24

Access 97 and Web Pages

Access 97 supports hyperlinks in its database forms, reports, and fields in datasheets. Access 97 supports Word 97, PowerPoint 97, Excel 97, as well as Internet or intranet hyperlinks. In addition to other documents, the hyperlink can point to other Access 97 tables, forms, and reports.

One reason you might want to store hyperlinks in a database field is to store web pages for vendors, competitors, and customers in tables. When you view forms that display the hyperlink to those tables, you can click the hyperlink to see the web site.

Obviously, a hyperlink is not active when it appears in a printed report or onscreen in preview mode. If, however, you import the report into a Word 97 document, Excel 97 worksheet, or an HTML page, the hyperlink is active.

The Hyperlink data type is one of the Access 97 data types that you can designate as you create your table (shown in Figure 24.6).

If you want to create an HTML document from an Access 97 database instead of importing data into a Word 97 document, you can select the File | Save as HTML option. Instead of converting your data to an HTML document, however, as the equivalent Word 97 and Excel 97 HTML conversion process does, Access 97 runs the Publish to the Web Wizard. (Figure 24.7 shows the first dialog box from this wizard.)

Figure 24.6.

Access 97 offers the Hyperlink data type when you design your tables.

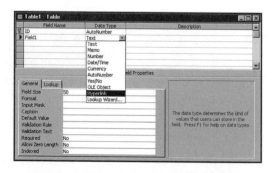

Figure 24.7.

Converting Access 97 databases to the HTML format requires that you specify exactly what data you want to convert.

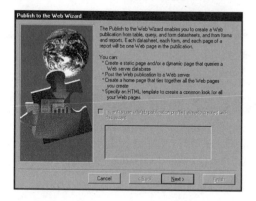

As you know, Access 97 databases contain several objects, tables, forms, reports, and queries. A simple File | Save as HTML option cannot, without more information, determine exactly how you want to export the objects to the HTML document. The wizard, therefore, walks you through the HTML document's design.

The wizard sends each object—each table, form, and datasheet—that you select to a different HTML web page. The wizard then creates a general-purpose home page that contains links to each of the other pages in the HTML document. In addition, you can select from a large assortment of web page templates to customize (such as adding a rustic or country flavor) the web page that the wizard generates. When you finish the wizard, you can send your web page to your web server or to Word 97 to make modifications.

PowerPoint 97 and Web Pages

When you save a PowerPoint 97 presentation as an HTML file, PowerPoint 97 does not immediately save the file. Instead, it presents you with the Save as HTML wizard. (The first window of the wizard is shown in Figure 24.8.)

Figure 24.8.

The Save as HTML wizard guides you through the process of saving web pages.

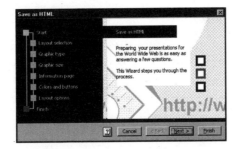

The wizard walks you through the web page design. You can control the button style, page appearance, and the default page size resolution. You also can add your email and home page addresses to the web page so that users who view the page can contact you.

If your HTML document audience uses Windows 95 (or a later operating system such as NT 4.0 or later), you can request that the Save as HTML wizard offers the *PowerPoint Animation Player*. This enables those users to view your presentation from the web as if they were using their PCs' capabilities. In other words, they see the special effect transitions that you add between slides and watch moving animated shapes if you've added such shapes to your presentation.

If you put your web presentation on the Internet for all to see, no matter which operating system people use, don't request the Animation Player. The viewers can still watch your web presentation by clicking the hyperlinks in the presentation and their browser's Back button to move from slide to slide.

NEW TERM   The *PowerPoint Animation Player* automatically downloads to Windows 95 (and later) Internet web page users, enabling them to watch your presentation's effects as if they were using PowerPoint 97. Without the player, Internet users have to traverse your presentation as they normally traverse the web using their browser.

If, before you design a presentation, you know that you'll put the presentation on the web, select an online presentation template when you start a new presentation. When you select File | New Presentation and click the Presentations tab, each template, such as the *Corporate Financial Overview* template, includes two versions: a *standard* version and an *online* version. The online version adds a web feel to the presentations and ensures that your presentations function well in a web environment.

24

Summary

This hour showed you how to use Office 97 products to create web pages. Word 97 certainly offers the advantage in your initial web page design, unless, of course, you want to put a PowerPoint 97 presentation on the web; in which case, the PowerPoint 97 templates offer the best place to start your web page design.

You can use Word 97 as your primary web page development tool and import other Office 97 products as needed to add their elements to the web page that you save from Word 97. PowerPoint 97 offers a unique web page design wizard that designs web-based presentations with the same look and feel as other web pages.

Now that you've concluded your 24-hour Office 97 tutorial, you are ready to use that knowledge to design the most effective, eye-catching documents and databases you've ever created.

Q&A

Q Can I use my Windows 95 PC as a web server?

A You *can,* but you probably don't want to tie up your PC by using it as a web server. Windows NT computers are better equipped to be web servers. If you want to try, however, your Office 97 CD-ROM contains a special folder called *ValuPack.* ValuPack contains a web server program named PwebSrv.exe, which you can copy to your disk with Windows Explorer and run to set up a web server. If you use a slow PC and if you use a dial-up Internet connection, your PC offers slow web page viewing. Therefore, no matter how effective your web page content is and no matter how well you used the Office 97 tools to develop an attention-getting web page display, your web server is probably too slow to keep your viewers' interest.

Q Can I include Excel 97 graphs on my web pages?

A Certainly. You can copy the graph to your Windows clipboard and then paste the graph directly into your Word 97 or PowerPoint 97-based web page. An Excel 97 graph is no different from any other kind of data that you can copy and paste into a web page from any of the Office 97 products.

Windows supports *OLE (Object Linking and Embedding)* technology that enables you to insert virtually any object inside any other kind of document. If you want to insert an Excel 97 graph or a video file with sound into a web page, you can do so by using the Insert menu from the Office 97 product's menu bar.

Appendix

Internet Explorer 4 and Outlook Express

Microsoft has updated Internet Explorer to version 4. If you still use Internet Explorer 3, you are not alone. Version 4, however, does offer new features and integrates better into the Windows desktop. Therefore, you should consider upgrading to Internet Explorer 4.

Upgrading to Internet Explorer 4

Like most Office 97 users, you probably have Internet Explorer 3, which came with your copy of Office 97. If you want to upgrade to version 4, you have these options

- [ ] Download Internet Explorer 4 free of charge from Microsoft's web site at `http://www.microsoft.com/ie/ie40/download/win95.htm`.
- [ ] Purchase Internet Explorer 4 from a mail-order or local PC store.
- [ ] Wait for the next version of Windows, which should include Internet Explorer 4.

The Internet Explorer Browser

Internet Explorer offers numerous features with which to browse the web easily. Internet Explorer offers extra viewing windows, setup options, and ease-of-use features that enable you to concentrate more on your web pages and less on the browser that you're using to access those web pages.

The Internet Explorer 4 Desktop Connection

When you install Internet Explorer, your Windows desktop takes on an entirely new look. The goal is for your Windows desktop to actually look and feel like a web page browser. Your Windows toolbar changes to display web-related icons. You can add one-click access to your desktop icons (you'll no longer have to double-click a program icon to start that program). Figure A.1 shows a Windows desktop with Internet Explorer 4 installed. As you can see, the icon labels now have underlined titles (indicating one-click access) and the toolbar includes Internet-related buttons and an address field in which you can enter a web address to view directly from your Windows desktop.

Figure A.1.

Your desktop changes styles as soon as you install Internet Explorer 4.

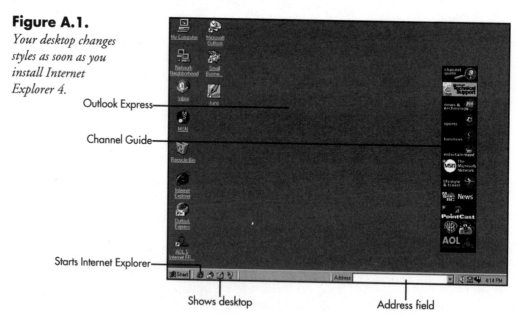

Outlook Express

Channel Guide

Starts Internet Explorer

Shows desktop

Address field

The desktop is more important than ever before because Internet Explorer enables you to store *active content* on your desktop. If, when viewing your favorite web page, you want to drag the page or a portion of the page to your desktop, that web content is attached to your desktop and actually becomes part of your Windows wallpaper background. The web content creates Internet Explorer 4's *active desktop*.

Although the active desktop is an optional part of the Internet Explorer 4 installation, if you install the active desktop, you get the benefits of using active content from the web, one-click selection of desktop icons, an improved interface for managing desktop windows, and new Start menu features.

 Active content is web information that you place directly on your Windows desktop. When you access the Internet, your active desktop content updates as well. Therefore, you can pull information such as news and stock market tickers down from the web to your desktop so that you can view that information whenever you view your desktop.

 Active desktop is the name applied to a Windows environment with Internet Explorer 4 installed.

 The Show Desktop icon offers you a fast way to view your desktop no matter how many program windows you open. When you click the Show Desktop icon on the toolbar, all open windows minimize immediately, giving you access to the Windows desktop.

Subsequent sections explain the Outlook Express and Channel Guide features.

Why should the desktop be distinct from the online world? You access files on your disk drives, perhaps on networked drives, and also on the Internet. Shouldn't you use the same browser to access all of them? Shouldn't your interface for any file be the same, no matter where that file resides, so that you don't have to learn two separate programs to manage your data?

Microsoft is certainly pushing the desktop/web combination, and for good reason. The Internet is part of today's computing environment. Although millions of PC users don't use the Internet, the Internet's growth has outpaced all expectations; the sheer number of current users, plus the expected number of users in the next five years, makes the Internet the most important component in the computing world.

 If you use a modem to access the Internet, you face two real obstacles: *speed* and *connection*. You must fight busy signals, log in, and use a fairly slow connection (as you have to do even with the fastest of today's modems). Even though the Windows desktop provides access to a seamless Internet connection, the reality is that you always must make an effort to get onto the Internet.

A

> Perhaps you can be reassured that such Internet connections are probably not going to last forever. Wireless (satellite-based) Internet connections are here and getting less costly every day. The industry is working on the Internet's slow modem speeds. The seamless desktop is worth the trouble even if you still use a modem for Internet access. Although you still face the modem connection woes that often arise, your Windows desktop is prepared for the day when that fast Internet connection arrives.

The Improved Start Menu

Internet Explorer 4 also improves the way your Start menu works. Suppose that you want to move a Start menu option, rename an option, or delete an option. Before Internet Explorer 4, you had to access the Start menu's Settings | Taskbar dialog box and mess with commands. Now, if you want to move any item on any Start menu's submenus, you only need to click and drag that item to another location on its submenu or to another menu altogether. If you want to rename or delete a Start menu item, you only need to right-click over that item and select Rename or Delete from the pop-up menu.

Your Start menu itself changes so that your Favorites list, the same Favorites list that Internet Explorer 4 keeps track of, appears on your Start menu. If you want to view one of your favorite web sites, you don't have to start Internet Explorer 4; select the site from the Favorites option and enable Windows to start Internet Explorer 4 and load that page for you. Do you have a web address that you want to see but that you did not store in your Favorites list? Type the URL in the Address field on your new taskbar, and let Windows start Internet Explorer 4 and load that web page for you.

The New Look of Windows

As Figure A.2 shows, Internet Explorer 4's active desktop also improves the look (and functionality) of all your windows. All windows now have a toolbar and a new look because all windows now conform to an HTML format that *you can change*. In other words, if you want to add your own graphics to the My Computer window, you can. You probably go to and from windows as you work with your PC from day to day. Therefore, the Back and Forward buttons found in every window's toolbar now enable you to traverse the typical data tree you've traveled during your work sessions.

Other New and Improved Internet Explorer Features

Internet Explorer 4 offers new browsing features. For example, instead of displaying a Favorites list only when you click the toolbar Favorites button, Internet Explorer 4 keeps your favorites list on the screen (shown in Figure A.3).

Figure A.2.

*All windows take on
added features, including
a toolbar and HTML
formatting that you can
change.*

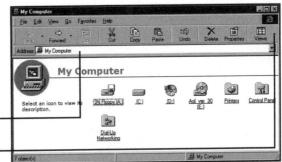

Enter a web or PC location ⎯

This toolbar appears on
every window

Figure A.3.

*Your favorites are always
only a click away when
you select from your
Favorites list.*

Favorites list ⎯

If you click the X in the Favorites list area, the Favorites list goes away,
giving you more room to view the web page content.

Internet Explorer 4 keeps track of your recently visited web sites. If you click the History
button on your toolbar, Internet Explorer 4 adds a History list in the left pane (where the
Favorites list resided) so that you can traverse sites you've visited in the past few days.

Internet Explorer 4 helps improve the way that you view web pages with graphics. Some web
pages take several seconds, and possibly longer, to display. Although the text appears right
away, the graphics take some time to load. Internet Explorer 4 puts a status bar at the bottom
of the browser so that you know how much (by percentage) of the current page is loaded and
how much is left. If you don't want to wait on a long load, you can load another page.

Push Content

The Internet is a vast collection of data, much of it random. When you want something, you have to locate it. Even when you know the location of a web site or information, you must traverse the web to get to the information. All that is changing. Instead of going after Internet data, you can now have data sent to you.

Internet Explorer 4 offers new *push technology* to get Internet data to your desktop. Push technology is much more than getting regular email (although some push technology-based sites incorporate email).

NEW TERM   *Push technology* refers to information that comes to your desktop from the Internet without your having to first locate the data.

When you receive push technology, information comes from the web to your desktop or web browser. Several forms of push technology exist. In its simplest form, you can elect to receive regular email (such as the morning news) so that when you get to your PC the information is waiting. All the channels you see when you activate the Internet Explorer 4 Active Desktop are some of the more popular channels that you can access from your Windows desktop.

NEW TERM   A *channel* is a web site that offers push content; when you point your browser toward a channel, your browser automatically downloads the content of the channel to your computer.

As you learned earlier, Internet Explorer 4 enables you to place web components right on your desktop. You can get web pages and specific content on your desktop or in your Internet Explorer web browser automatically. In addition, you can view only information that has changed since the last time you visited a web site. The push information might appear on your taskbar (such as a scrolling stock ticker with your personalized stock quotes) or in a screen saver during your PC's lull times. Internet Explorer contains special window panes in which you can view push technology information.

Some channel content can be made into screen savers. When you subscribe to the content's channel guide, you learn whether a screen saver is available. You can request that push technology appear only when your screen saver activates. Not all channel sites are available as screen savers, so you have to check with the specific channel content provider to see if a screen saver option exists.

Outlook Express

Internet Explorer 4 includes a new program called *Outlook Express* that manages both email and newsgroup information. Outlook Express replaces older Windows messaging programs called *Windows Messaging* and *Windows Exchange*. By combining a newsgroup reader with email capabilities, you can manage more information easier than before.

Outlook Express works on a general and detailed double-pane view just as Outlook 97 does. Outlook Express shows your folders on the left pane and the details on the right.

> Outlook Express is not the same program as *Outlook 97*, which comes with Office 97. Outlook 97 is much more powerful than Outlook Express. Subsequent versions of Outlook 97, however, may take on the look and feel of Outlook Express. You may prefer the email interface of Outlook Express over Outlook 97, but you'll want to keep using Outlook 97 for the other functions that it offers, such as scheduling.

A

Sending Web Pages over Email

One of the biggest benefits of Outlook Express over Outlook 97 is Outlook Express's capability to send web pages as an email message. Outlook Express works with Internet Explorer 4 so that, when you click the Send Page toolbar button, Internet Explorer starts Outlook Express, opens an email page with the web page embedded on the email message body, and enables you to assign a receiver's email address to which to send the page (see Figure A.4).

Figure A.4.

The recipient sees the web page when viewing this email.

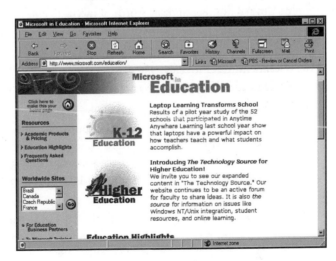

Your recipient, too, must use an email program, such as Outlook Express, that can display HTML code; otherwise, he gets a lot of garbage in the message. Your recipient is still able to read the mail's text, but the email is messed up because of all the HTML formatting codes he sees that are normally hidden. You can convert HTML pages to straight text from the Tools | Options | Send dialog box.

Using Newsgroups

In a way, a newsgroup acts like a combination of a slow email program and a community bulletin board. Newsgroups have little or nothing to do with the daily news. *Newsgroups* are thousands of lists, arranged by subject, that hold messages and files that you and others can post and read. Outlook Express, a program that Internet Explorer 4 offers, provides newsgroup access. Even Outlook 97 with all its features cannot display newsgroups. With Outlook Express, you can manage both your email and newsgroup access from the same program.

NEW TERM A *newsgroup* is an Internet-based messaging center from which you can leave and read messages on hundreds of topics as well as upload and download files.

Suppose that you are interested in rollerblading and want to trade information you have with others who are interested in the sport. You can find one of the several newsgroups related to rollerblading and read the hundreds of messages and files posted to that newsgroup. Depending on the Internet service you use and the newsgroup filing rules, you may find messages months old or only from the past few days. Often, the larger newsgroups can keep only a limited number of days' worth of messages and files.

This is how newsgroups act like slow email services: If someone has posted a question to which you know the answer, you can post a reply. Your reply is seen by everyone in the newsgroup who wants to read the reply. The person who submitted the question may never read the answer, but the postings are for everyone who is interested.

Each Internet ISP provides access to a different number of the thousands and thousands of newsgroups in existence. To see newsgroups available to your service, click Internet Explorer's Mail button and select Read News. Although your ISP may give you access to thousands of newsgroups, you want to subscribe only to those that interest you. Click Outlook Express' Newsgroups button to display the Newsgroups listing dialog box (shown in Figure A.5).

You may see one or more news servers in the left column. Each news server contains a different set of newsgroups. Your ISP determines the number of servers that appear in the news server column. When you click a server, the list of newsgroups that reside on that server appears in the center of the window.

Figure A.5.

Select the newsgroups to which you want to subscribe.

Selected newsgroup message

News servers

Selected server's list of newsgroups

Selected message's details

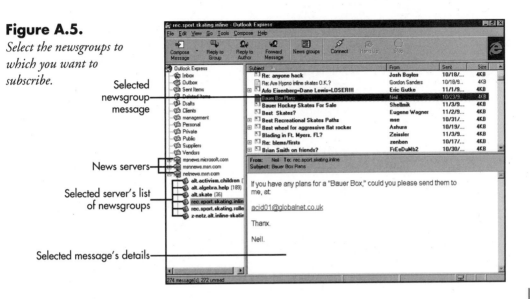

 Bear in mind that some servers contain thousands of newsgroups. The first time you connect to a news server, the Outlook Express newsreader downloads a list of that server's newsgroups. This download process may take a few minutes, as indicated by the dialog box that appears during the download.

The newsgroups have strange names such as `rec.pets.dogs` and `alt.algebra.help`. Table A.1 describes what the more common newsgroup prefixes, the first part of the name, stand for. Somewhere else in the newsgroup name you can often glean more information about the newsgroup's primary topic; for example, a newsgroup named `rec.sport.skating.roller` would probably contain skating news and `alt.autos.italian` would contain files and messages pertaining to Italian cars.

Table A.1. Common newsgroup prefixes.

Prefix	Description
alt	Groups that allow for informal content and are not necessarily as widely distributed as the other newsgroups
biz	Business-related newsgroups
comp	Computer-related newsgroups

continues

Table A.1. continued

Prefix	Description
edu	Education-related newsgroups
misc	Random newsgroups
rec	Recreational and sporting newsgroups
rel	Religious-related newsgroups
sci	Scientific newsgroups
soc	Social issue-related newsgroups
talk	Debate newsgroups

Probably the biggest problem with newsgroups is the time you waste in them! You may hop over to a newsgroup to see whether the group contains an answer you need, and two hours later you're still reading the postings. Newsgroups can provide a wealth of information on thousands and thousands of topics. Although the web is great for organizing information into collections of pages, newsgroups are useful for the straight messages and files that people want to share with each other.

Should You Upgrade to Internet Explorer 4?

In summary, Internet Explorer 4 not only adds Internet-browsing features, but Internet Explorer changes the way you work in Windows. From the active desktop to an integrated email and newsgroup reader, Microsoft has packaged a lot of power into Internet Explorer 4. Before long, some web content may not be viewable by a pre-Internet Explorer 4 browser because of the active push technology. Therefore, as soon as you get a chance to upgrade your Office 97 Internet Explorer 3 to version 4, do so. You'll appreciate the extra power you get.

INDEX

E

Edit menu commands
Excel
  Clear, 167-168
  Delete, 168, 179
  Fill, 169
  Fill, Series, 173
  Replace, 165
Office 97, Links, 354
Word
  Copy, 79
  Cut, 79
  Find, 80
  Paste, 79
  Redo, 88
  Replace, 82
  Undo, 88
editing
Access
  forms, 313
  query-extraction fields
    (Access), 329
  table AutoNumber fields,
    315
  table data, 307
  table records through
    query results, 324
cutting/copying/pasting
  Excel data, 165-167
  Word text, 79-80
dragging/dropping between
  applications, 351-352
Outlook contacts, 271
WordArt text, 362
email
Outlook, 275-279
  checking for messages,
    277
  converting HTML to
    plain text, 400
  creating, 275-277
  deleting (Deleted Items
    folder), 275
  Inbox, 275
  inserting (attaching) files,
    277
  Outbox, 275

previewing messages,
  278-280
reading messages, 278-279
replying, 279-281
sending messages, 276,
  281
Sent Items folder, 275
Outlook Express, sending
  web pages, 399
embedding, *see* **linking files**
erasing, *see* **deleting**
events
Outlook, scheduling, 261
PowerPoint, mouse event
  actions, 230-231
Excel 97, 4, 8
calculations, 188
  see also formulas; functions
closing (exiting), 158
comments, 174
  deleting, 168
date/time
  worksheet data, entering,
    156-159
  Today( ) function, 192
deleting
  cells, 179
  comments, 168
  data, 167-168
  formatting, 168, 175
  rows/columns, 179-180
  undoing deletions, 168
editing
  AutoCorrect, 163
  correcting cell data,
    163-164
  cutting/copying/pasting,
    165-167
  deleting cells, 179
  deleting data, 167-168
  deleting rows/columns,
    179-180
  finding/replacing,
    164-165
  insert mode, 164
  overtype mode, 164
  selecting cells, 162
  spell checking, 162

filling cells, *see* filling
  worksheet cells
formatting, 193-196
  alignment, 203-204
  AutoFormat, 200-201
  categories, 195-196
  cell borders, 204-205
  cell patterns, 205
  fonts, 194-195
  justification, 193-194
  locking/hiding cells, 206,
    211
  row/column height/width,
    194
  styles, 200-202
  troubleshooting, 175, 197
inserting
  cells, 178
  rows/columns, 178-179
formulas, *see* formulas
functions, *see* functions
graphs, 206-210
  adding to web pages, 392
  chart types, 207-208
  customizing properties,
    210
  data series, 208-209
  data tables, 209
  legends, 209
  titles, 209
navigating, 157-158
security, locking/hiding cells,
  206
sharing data, *see* sharing, data
  between applications
Small Business Financial
  Manager add-on, 157
starting, 148
tracking revisions, 157
web pages, 387-389
  saving worksheets as
    HTML, 387
  updating page data, 389
wizards, *see* Chart Wizard
see also workbooks;
  worksheets
exiting, *see* **closing**
**exponentiation, Excel
formulas, 183**

previewing
Access
  print jobs, 313-314,
    341-342
  reports, 334-335, 341-342
Bookshelf Basics Preview of
  the Day screen, 43-44
Outlook email
  AutoPreview, 278
  preview pane, 279-280
PowerPoint slides, 227
print jobs, 28-29
  Access, 313-314, 334-335
  Word, 107-108, 112
Word
  print jobs, 107-108, 112
  web pages, 384
**primary key fields (Access
  tables), 290**
duplicates, 301
setting, 296
printing, 27-29
Access
  forms, 313-314
  reports, 334-335
  tables, 308-309
PowerPoint, 233-235
previewing, 28-29
  Access, 313-314, 334-335
  Word, 107-108, 112
Print dialog box, 28
Word, 107-108, 112
**Product( ) function
  (worksheets), 192**
Professional Edition, 6
programming, Visual Basic 5, 6
promoting outline items, *see*
  outlines
**proofreading Word documents,
  115-123, 127**
grammar, 119-121
hyphenation, 121-122
spelling, 116-119
thesaurus, 122-123
protecting worksheet cells, 206
editing cells, 211

**publishing web pages,
  383-391**
Access, 389-390
creating pages, 382-383
Excel, 387-389
  saving worksheets as
    HTML, 387
  updating page data, 389
Internet Assistant, 387
maintaining web sites, 382
PowerPoint, 390-391
  PowerPoint Animation
    Player, 391
  Save as HTML wizard,
    390-391
Publish to the Web Wizard,
  389-390
Web server access, 382
  Windows 95 as server,
    392
Word, 383-386
  Web Page Wizard,
    385-386
  see also Word 97, web
    pages
**push technology, Internet
  Explorer 4, 398**

Q

queries (Access), 321-330
complex queries, 327
  Between keyword, 329
  entering criteria, 327-328
  relational operators, 329
creating
  Query Design view,
    324-327
  Query Wizard, 322-324
criteria, 327-328
  specifying multiple
    criteria, 329
dynasets, 322
exporting data to Word, 355
naming, 330
reports, *see* reports

results, 324
  customizing, 331
  displaying with forms,
    324
  editing, 324
saving, 330
  saving filters as queries,
    321, 331
synchronizing multiple-table
  queries, 324
versus filters, 321, 331
see also filters
**Query menu commands, Show
  Table (Access), 328**
quitting
Access, 300-301
Excel 97, 158
Outlook, 265
PowerPoint, 223
Word, 90
**quotations, Bookshelf Basics,
  47**

R

ranges (worksheets), 180-182
anchor points, 180
naming, 180-182
  range names in formulas,
    184-185
versus selections, 197
**reading email, Outlook,
  278-279**
records, Access tables, 288
adding in Form view, 313
deleting, 307
hiding, 307
record selector, 308
  New Record button, 313
size, adjusting, 307
sorting, 307, 314
**Records menu commands
  (Access), Filter Excluding
  Selection, 319**
**recurring appointments
  (Outlook), 258-259**